AF575475

PEN & INK DRAWING

Pen & Ink Drawing

Frank J. Lohan

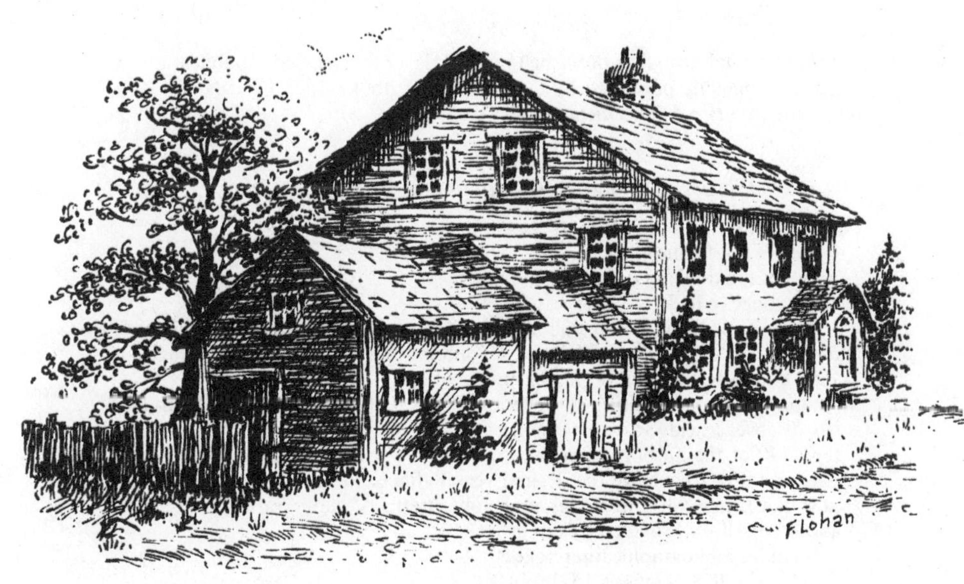

Dover Publications, Inc.
Mineola, New York

Bibliographical Note

This Dover edition, first published in 2013, is an unabridged republication of the work originally published by Contemporary Books, Inc., Chicago, in 1981 under the title *Pen & Ink Themes*.

Library of Congress Cataloging-in-Publication Data

Lohan, Frank.
[Pen & ink themes]
Pen & ink drawing / Frank J. Lohan.
pages cm.
This Dover edition, first published in 2013, is an unabridged republication of the work originally published by Contemporary Books, Inc., Chicago, in 1981 under the title Pen & Ink Themes.
Summary: "An inspiring sourcebook for all skill levels, this guide helps artists discover a wide variety of subjects and ideas for their next sketch. More than 140 of the author's own drawings include partially finished details that illustrate how to achieve the desired visual effects. Stimulating topics include nostalgic scenes, old engravings, atmospheric effects, photographs, landscapes, and life itself."—Provided by publisher.
Includes bibliographical references.
ISBN-13: 978-0-486-49715-0 (pbk.)
ISBN-10: 0-486-49715-1 (pbk.)
1. Pen drawing—Themes, motives. 2. Pen drawing—Technique. I. Title. II. Title: Pen and ink drawing.

NC905.L63 2013
741.2'6—dc23

2012045736

Printed in Canada
49715106 2025
www.doverpublications.com

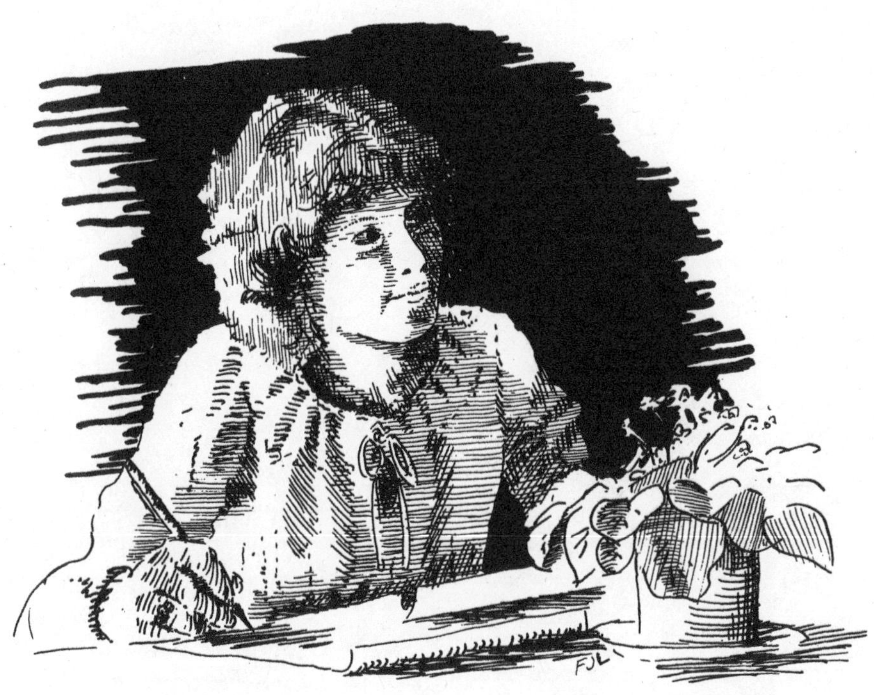

This book is dedicated to all those who work to acquire skills they admire and want for their own.

Contents

Foreword

Visual artistic expression is one of the oldest and most enduring forms of communication. Constant changes in social customs and cultures have coincided with—and, in some cases, followed—the trends of innovative artists. From the beginning, the artist has played an unique and indispensable role in our lifestyles. It is very clear that illustrative material and written copy are extensively employed in advertising to produce sales and use of products and services. Not so readily apparent, however, is the fact that each automobile, appliance, fabric, carpet, and wall-covering design, as well as virtually every product we use—even down to the plain little button on a piece of clothing—first saw the light of day on an artist's drawing board.

Those are the commercial aspects of art. But we also have a vast array of drawing, painting, and sculpture reflecting the personal artistic views of countless individuals who immerse themselves in this universal form of expression. Obviously, not everyone desires to enter the art field on a professional or occupational level, but anyone can learn to draw or paint with proper instruction that includes fundamentally sound groundwork in drawing and techniques.

Fortunately, the knowledge of many recognized artists has been preserved through instructional books designed to help the novice, as well as the more experienced artist, further develop his or her talents. It does not hold true, however, that all artists are good teachers. Furthermore, not all teachers can or do write books.

Frank Lohan is not only technically proficient with pen and ink, but also is a metal sculptor, painter, engineer, and, very importantly, a fine art teacher. It is fortunate, indeed, that he has found time within his most active schedule to call upon his varied experience and disciplines to become an author. His earlier book, *Pen and Ink Techniques*, has become a valuable addition to the art library as a source of reference and inspiration.

Convinced that sharing his ideas in such a manner could benefit others, he has been induced to write this current volume, *Pen and Ink Themes*. In it, Frank Lohan again uses his expertise to guide the reader visually and methodically through yet another phase of that most useful and effective line medium, pen and ink. He also provides a wealth of information on his own approach to linear expression, proving that art is a personal entity that provides many avenues to a common goal.

Enriched by informative, concise text and more than one hundred forty of his illustrations, the book reflects the author's philosophy that drawing can and should be a most pleasant activity.

From the standpoint of instructional value, *Pen and Ink Themes* explains with clarity the various ways to handle simple as well as more complex subjects. Some of this instruction stems from material the author has compiled as lessons, demonstrations, and teaching aids for his students; the remainder was prepared specifically for this book.

Underlying each instructional chapter are the basics of composition and the relationships of values, shapes, and that all-important white space. The reader learns what to look for and how to choose subject matter from the environment for interesting textures and pictorial effects. The value of sketch notes and the use of photographs as supplemental reference are discussed from several points of view.

The techniques described in this book were tested in actual classroom situations and surely will be helpful to student, experienced artist, and art instructor alike.

On page after page of this volume, Frank Lohan's work will capture your imagination so completely that you will just have to reach for the pen—and you will find it difficult to put your pen and paper aside.

Truly, *Pen and Ink Themes* is not a book you will want to read and place on a shelf. Rather, it will become a frequently used source of learning that will help you improve your artistic skills through practice with subjects it shows you how to see.

Frank Lohan uses a clear, concise, educational presentation. His enthusiasm and love for the creative visual arts clearly show through.

Arthur F. Chargois
Boynton Beach, Florida
1980

Professor Chargois formerly was head of the Commercial Art Department, DuCret School of Art

Introduction

"What shall I sketch?"

This is a question my students often ask after they have completed a semester or two in one of my classes, once they have learned the fundamentals of working in pen and ink and become familiar with the variety of implements and materials available.

Sources of inspiration for any individual artist are unlimited. In this book I have tried to point to just a few of my own general sources of inspiration—nostalgia, old engravings, photographs, and, of course, that best of all sources, life itself. Within these loosely defined categories I exhibit some of my pen work; in many cases some partially finished details are also drawn so you can see how I proceeded with the sketch.

This is a true how-to book, since I show exactly how *I* did it, thereby offering the reader *one* way to sketch. How I did it is, of course, only one of the many ways the same thing can be done successfully. As I stated in the introduction to *Pen and Ink Techniques*:

> Your technique, your style, that distinctive way *you* have of making and arranging the lines, dots, and dark areas on the paper will evolve if you really have the desire and if you persevere.

Someone once said that nature produces, that it is only man that categorizes. The categories around which I have organized this book are quite arbitrary and, if any thought is given to them, rather meaningless. This does not matter as long as they serve as a catalyst by planting some seeds, some ideas on where you might find inspiration for subject matter. These categories are meant simply as a framework on which to hang my ideas for your consideration.

What shall you sketch? I don't know. But in this book are a few ideas that may help you answer that question.

Many tools and materials are available to the pen and ink artist. They vary widely in price and convenience. If you are serious about the medium, you will eventually try most of them. Many of the sketches in this book were done with several different pens—an inexpensive crowquill nib in an equally inexpensive holder, a moderately expensive artist's fountain pen, and a slightly more expensive technical pen. For some of the sketches I used just one of these pens.

The salespeople in any well-stocked art supply store (not your corner drugstore) will be able to show you the various pens, inks, and paper and advise you on what you need to begin. Remember, if you really become interested in this medium, you will be back for additional material—so they are as interested in your success as you are. Do not be afraid to ask for advice and recommendations from salespeople.

Pens

Replaceable nibs come in many types and degrees of stiffness. The good old crowquill by Hunt or Gillott or other manufacturers is an excellent compromise between stiffness and flexibility. It is quite inexpensive and you should have several different ones, from very small and sharp to those that will draw a wider line. Use them to practice and work. These points will work with any india ink. Wipe them frequently as you use them so the ink does not dry and cake on them.

Several brands of *artists' fountain pens* are on the market. These pens spare you the hassle of constantly dipping the point in ink and, generally, they have replaceable points. They are more expensive than the crowquill, but the convenience more than makes up for the extra cost. Artists' fountain pens usually require an ink made specially for these pens. It costs just a few cents more than the other inks but will not dry up and clog your pen.

Draftsmen use *technical pens,* tubular-point pens that have no flexibility at all as to line thickness. These are fountains pens and are very well suited for sketching once you learn to hold them more perpendicular to the paper than you would a fountain pen. They also require special ink that is made for them. My favorite point is a "000," or triple zero. Many of the sketches in this book were done using only this point.

Fine-point felt-tip or nylon-tip pens can also be used, as well as fine watercolor brushes such as double or triple zero size.

Inks

There is a wide variety of inks, some strictly for fountain pens and others just for nib pens. There are waterproof and nonwaterproof inks, as well as inks of every imaginable color. It is fun just to look through a display of colorful Winsor and Newton inks.

Ninety-five percent of my work is done with black ink. The remaining five percent is done with a dark brown ink (I like Winsor and Newton's peat brown) on rough off-white watercolor paper such as 140-pound Morilla board.

Note that some inks are made for "film," that is, for sketching on clear acetate or mylar film.

Paper

Bristol board is the customary paper for ink. It is available in pads or sheets and in a variety of finishes. I like two-ply kid finish. Watercolor paper also takes ink well. I like the interest that a rough watercolor paper adds to certain subjects.

You can sketch on *vellum,* a rag tracing paper that is great for placing directly over your pencil sketch and going directly to work with the ink. You can also do this with clear *acetate,* but be sure to use an ink that is made for working on film. Since the acetate is not porous, the ink needs additives that prevent it from easily rubbing off the surface.

Scratchboard is a special paper with a clay coating on one side. You do your ink work on this side, drawing the usual black lines on a white surface. Then, however, you can use a scratchboard tool that fits into a nib-penholder to scratch through some of the black ink marks and produce white lines or marks on the black. Several of the sketches in this book were done on scratchboard.

Pen Strokes

Hatching indicates parallel ink lines that are used to create a dark tone on the paper. *Crosshatching* is the tone created by hatching an area, then doing the same thing on top of that but in a different direction. *Stipple* or *stippling* refers to toning an area by using dots rather than lines.

Basics

For more details on the basics—enlarging or reducing a sketch by the grid system; matting and framing your work; hatching, crosshatching, and graded tone practice exercises; stippling; and so on—see Part I in my earlier book, *Pen and Ink Techniques.*

1: Nostalgic Subjects

Things and places of the past are the ingredients of many a favorite painting, sketch, poem, and story. A wistful oversimplification almost always goes hand in hand with a nostalgic piece in any art form. One temporarily sets aside all unpleasant aspects of reality and focuses on the remembered—or imagined—beauty and peacefulness of long past moments. One basically provides an emotional glance at something that was, or that might have been if . . .

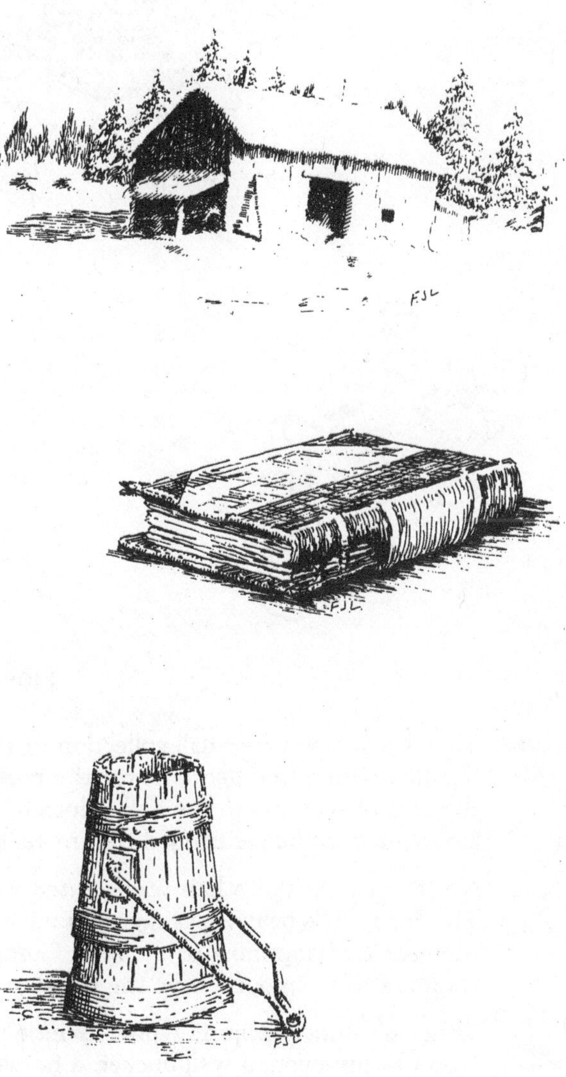

Nostalgia implies pleasant memories of or fantasies about things that will never again be; for instance, the security and warmth of a happy childhood remembered only as a hazy overall feeling when toys of that era are seen, or the imagined comforts of a far less hurried life when old-time photographs are rediscovered, or the rosy image of a place still loved but unlikely to be visited again.

If you travel—either near or far—you have a wealth of sketching material stored in your memory. Places that are imposing, modest, or downright dingy but still hold a special place in *your* life's experience are great subjects. They are good choices because they have spoken to you, touched you, so that your rendition of them can truly be your statement about something of value to you. The way you capture such scenes becomes your personal nostalgia. It may well touch someone else in a similar manner. This is what all art should be. Interpretations by critics are relatively meaningless; the important element is what the artist felt as he or she executed the work and how well he or she feels the statement was made. If seeing the work touches a viewer's heart, then the work is even more successful. This added success should be considered only a bonus, however, since the basic success is determined solely by the artist.

Nostalgia can encompass a variety of subjects as wide as your own imagination when tapped as a source for sketch ideas. So, once upon a time . . .

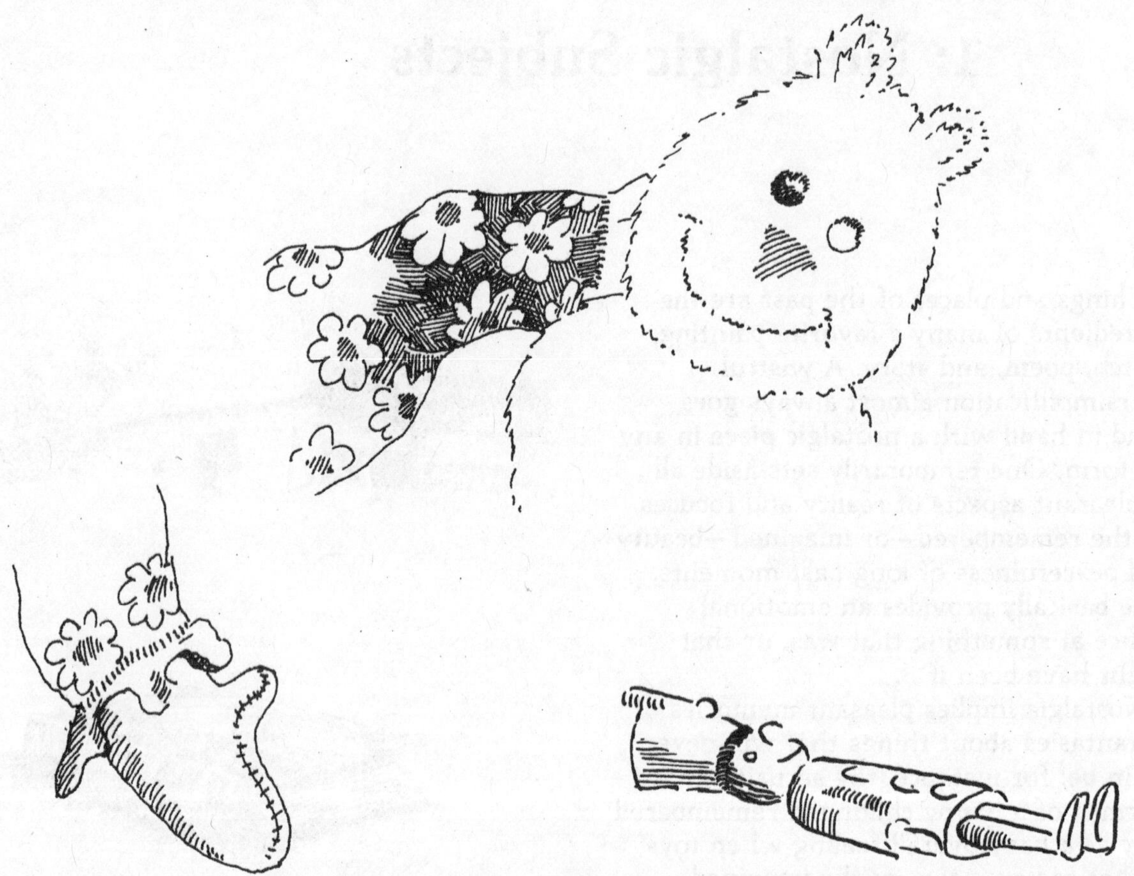

The Old-Timers

This is a sketch of a small collection of toys that probably predates most of us. It was handled with a fine pen and, for the most part, delicate line work in order to carry out the idea of softness in the doll's clothing and the bear's fur. Bold pen work would have created a valid but entirely different feeling.

Notice that the doll's hair was created with relatively few strands actually being drawn. The fur on the bear was suggested with a very few fur indications, the fuzzy outline of the bear carrying most of the idea. Compare the bear with the doll's feet, which are comparatively smooth, as is the wooden toy soldier.

Other old-timer subjects would include some old books, an old Tiffany lamp, a steamer trunk laying open, a well bucket, a horse collar and other tack, and so on.

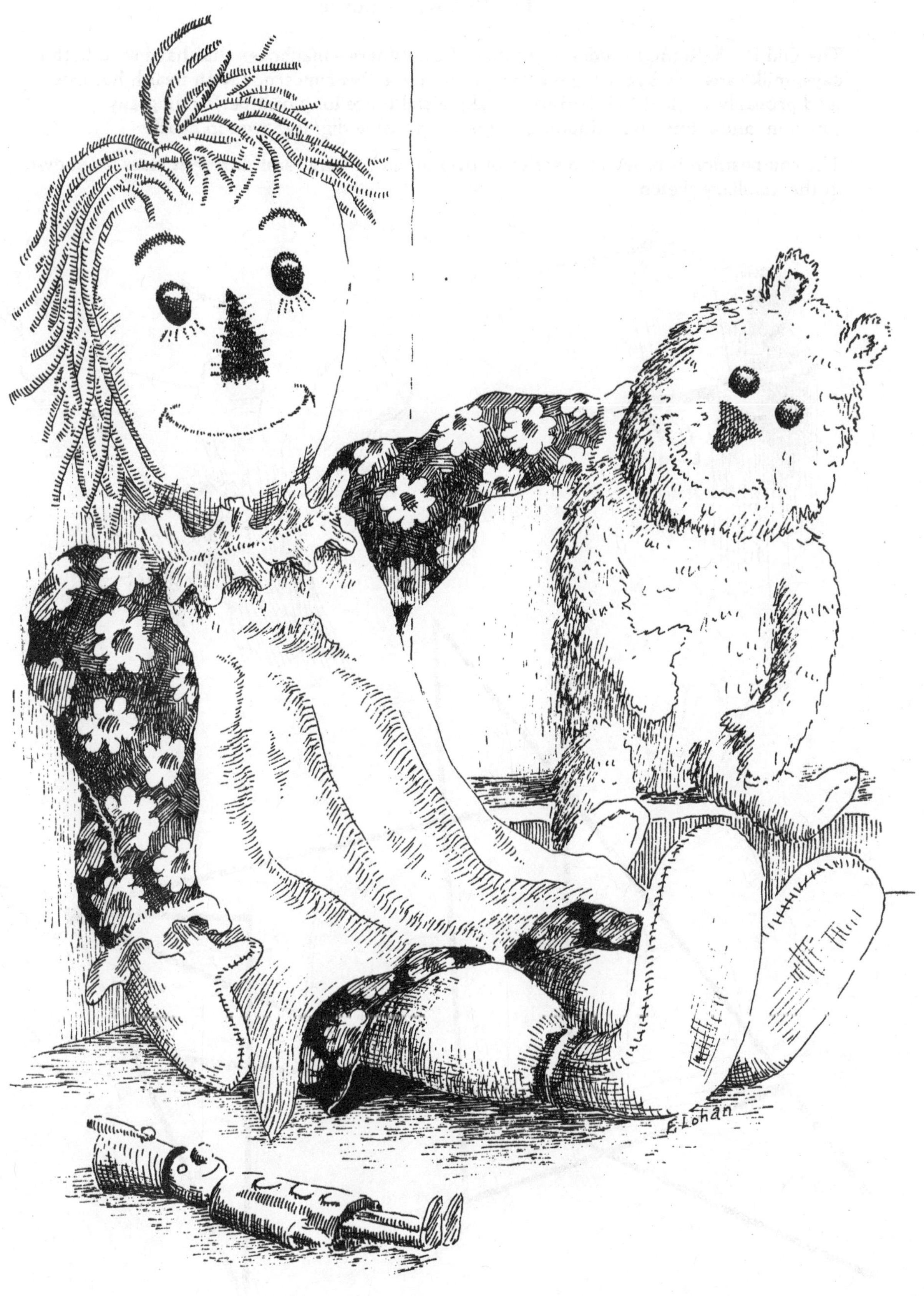
E. Lohan

The Old Rural Route

The Old Rural Route includes a number of old-timers—mailboxes that have seen better days, milk cans of a bygone age when people were less concerned with health hazards (and probably worked too hard to be sick), a rail fence long past performing any function, and a tree still exhibiting a rugged, massive dignity, even in death.

The composition is based on a series of overlapping triangles of different sizes, as shown in the auxiliary sketch.

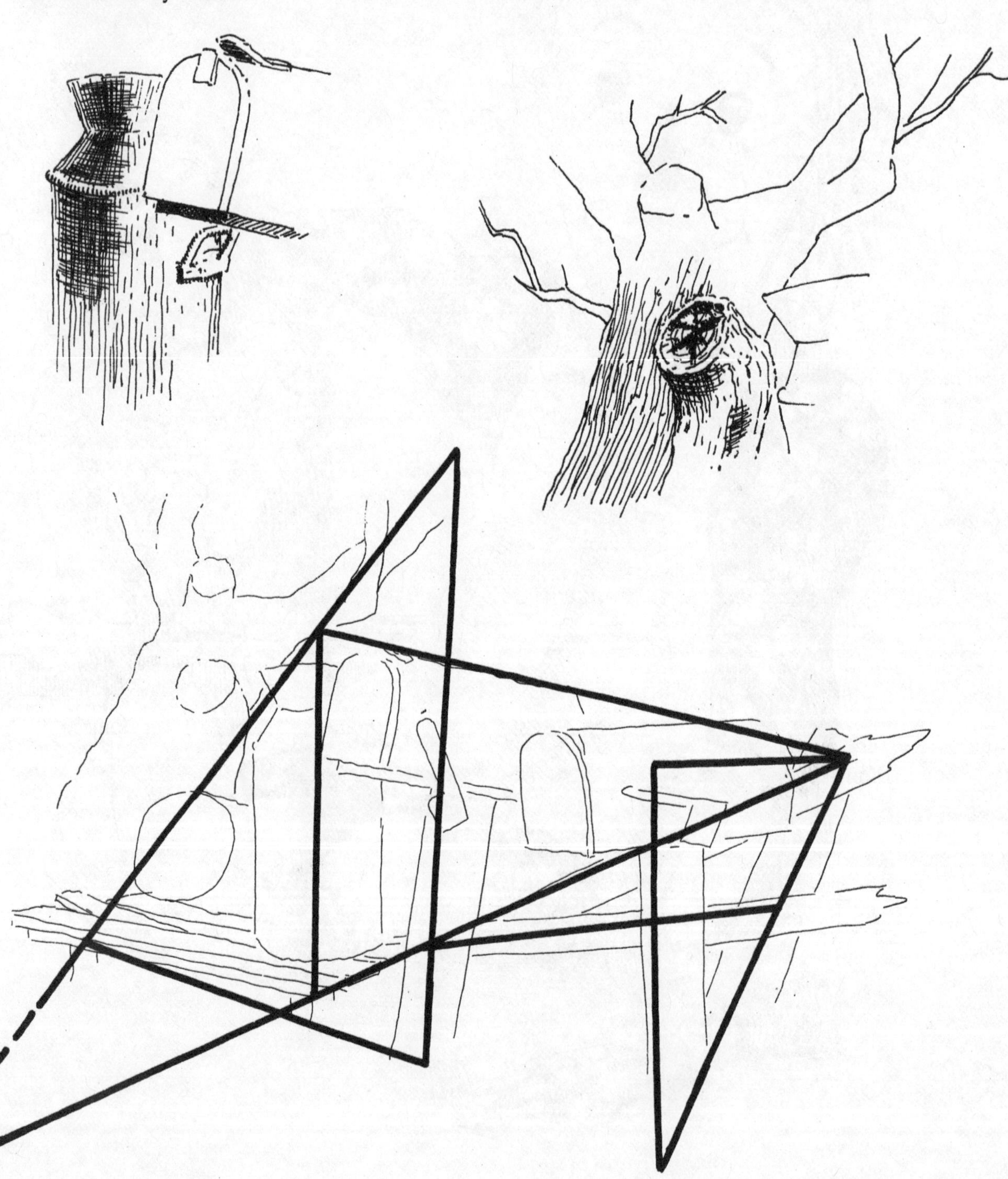

The predominance of old weathered wood in the composition dictated a bold, rough approach to both the outlining and the texturing lines. A heavier pen was used here than that in the preceding collection of toys.

When I sketch a jumble of weeds and grasses, as around the mailboxes and the milk stand, I indicate just enough to carry the idea of mixed vegetation. Too many strokes make it look dark and shadowed in what should be the sunlit areas.

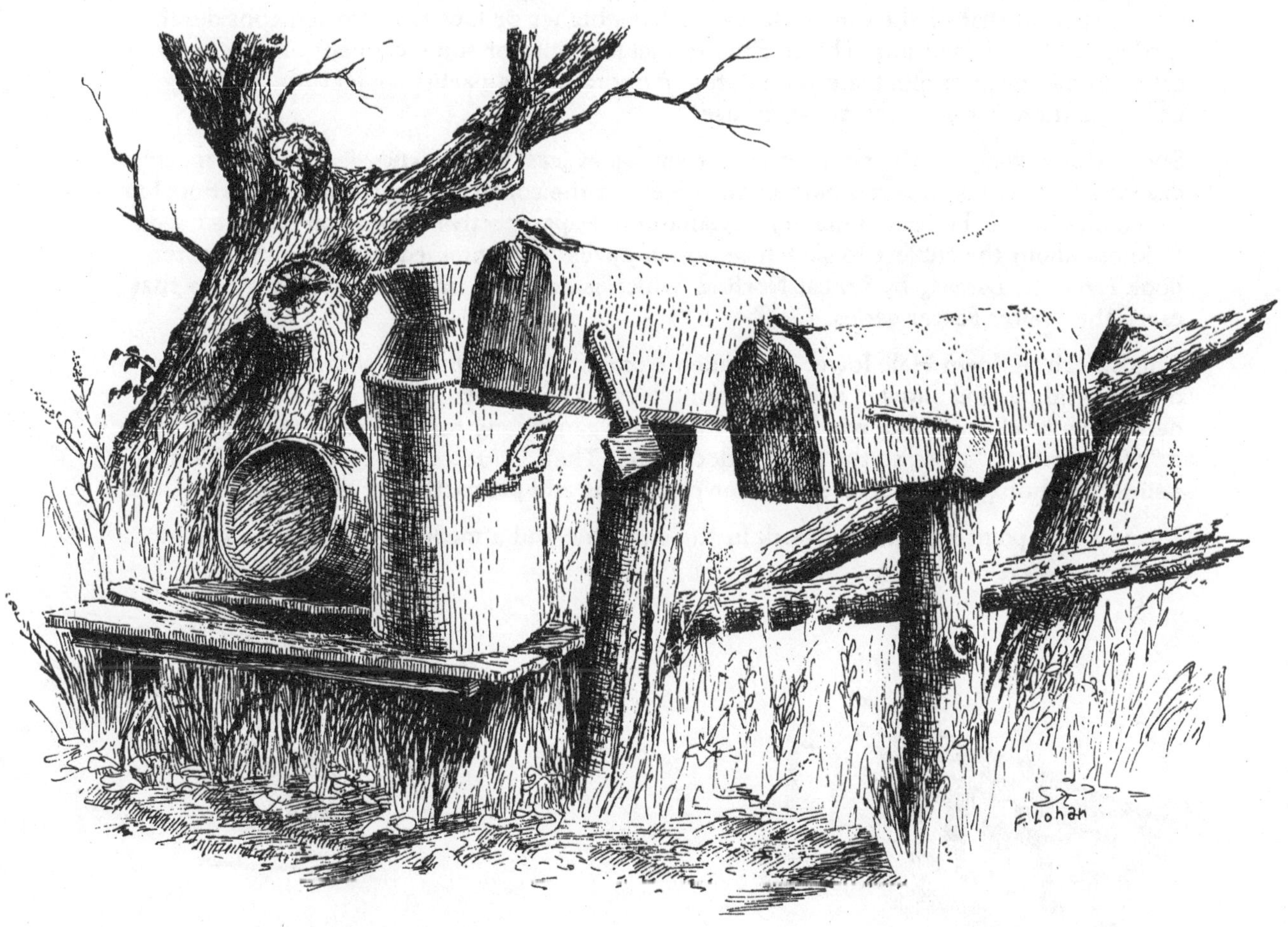

The four sketches on the following pages are based on old photographs taken about 1900 in Farmington, Michigan, now a Detroit suburb.

The Old Home Town

Correct perspective is vital to successful rendering of structures. Whatever method you use, be certain that you eliminate all perspective problems in your pencil sketch prior to starting with the ink. The best way I have found to catch mistakes in perspective is to look at the working pencil drawing in a mirror. This seems to magnify such problems and lets you spot them more easily.

If you are like me, you are never quite satisfied with the exact view presented by a photograph. Almost without exception I change the angle, move the "eye" to a position different from that of the camera lens—perhaps higher or lower, and often considerably farther to the left or right. This is done to include more of some element or another and often to minimize or eliminate the relative monotony of a particular feature. Artistic license is there for you, the artist, to use.

Successfully changing the point of view requires at least a little knowledge of perspective drawing so that you can reconstruct the object in the correct proportion and relationship of detail. One of the best summary explanations of perspective basics—all anyone needs to know about the subject to sketch reasonably well—is contained in the Walter Foster book *Perspective Drawing* by Ernest Norling, which is available in artist's supply stores that carry the Walter Foster series.

This sketch of Town Hall Tower was taken from a photograph that showed much more of the building, and showed it from ground level. The pattern of the Mansard roof, decorative brickwork, and windows of the tower caught my fancy. I imagined I was up in a "cherry picker," close to the second floor level. Then I created my own composition, using the photograph as a reference for placement and proportion of details.

I used a fine point for the line work in the sunshine and a medium one for the shaded work.

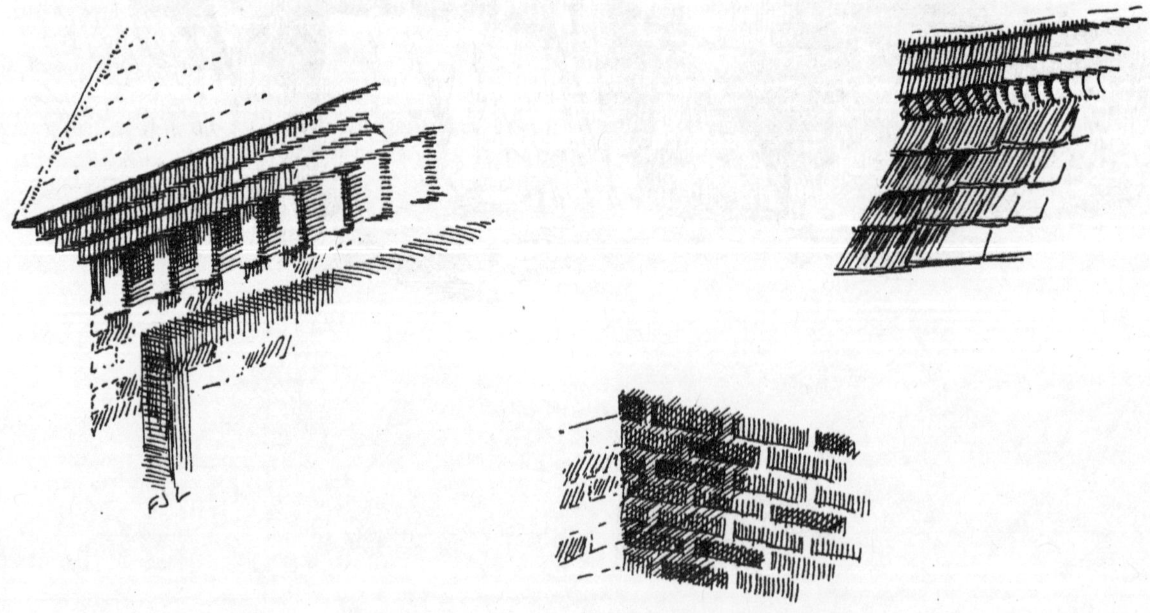

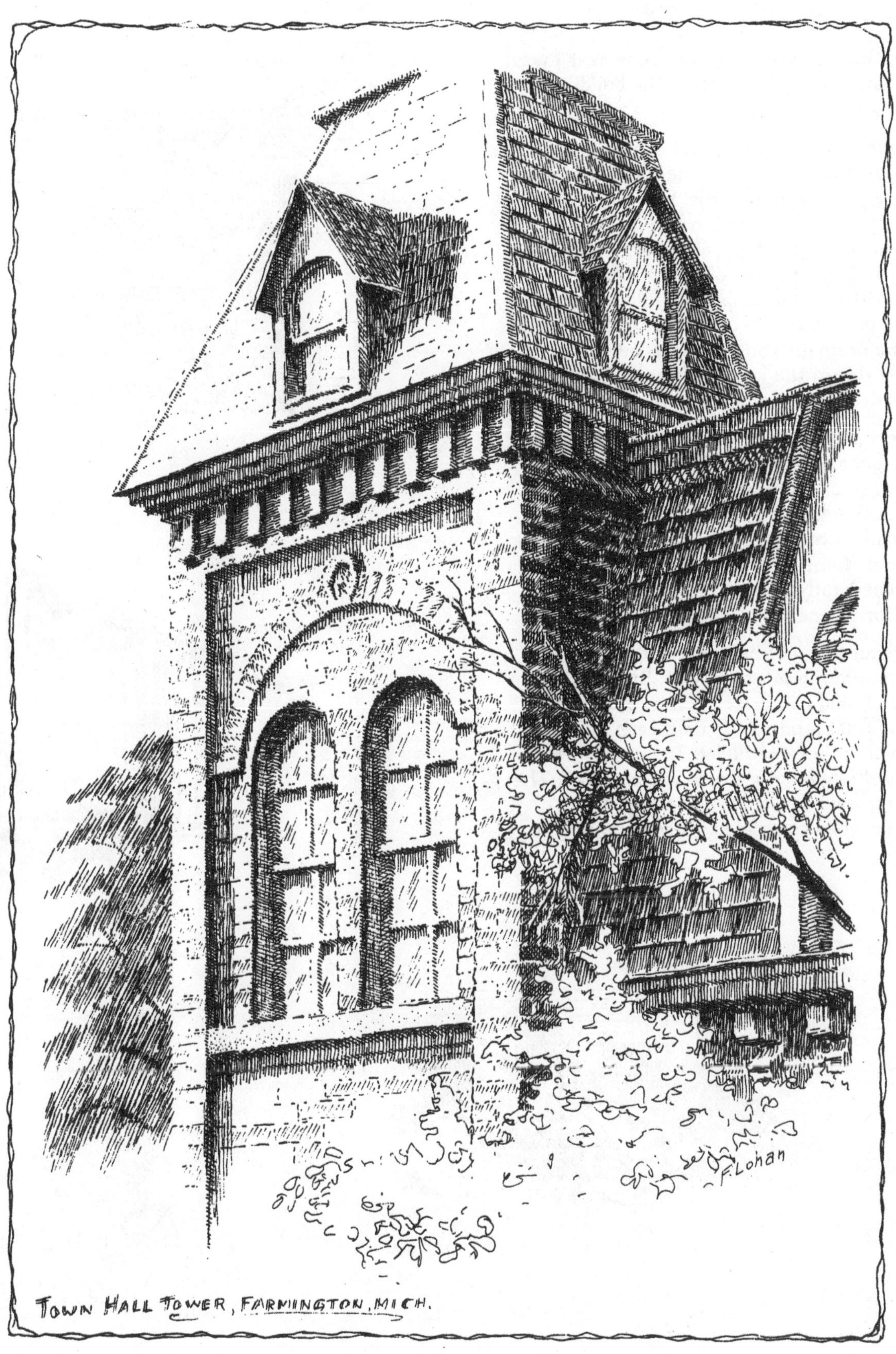

TOWN HALL TOWER, FARMINGTON, MICH.

The Steele Mill

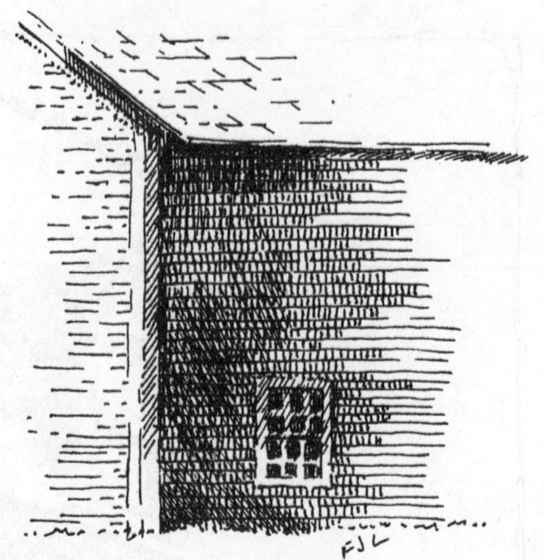

The Steele Mill sketch was done as if I was looking across the creek at the building on a bright, hot summer day.

I have learned that when I sketch grassy, weedy patches, less is generally better than more. I try to put a little variety into the indications of vegetation and let the viewer's imagination supply the rest. When showing the bright foliage of a bush or grass that is catching full sunlight I try to juxtapose it with a cool dark tone to work some dramatic contrasts into my sketch. I tried this in the lower left-hand corner of this drawing.

The shaded side of the building has just one door and two windows. This broad expanse of clapboard is relatively monotonous, so when the sketch was finished I broke up the shade by going over it with some irregularly shaped dark patches, rather than creating a fairly uniform tone.

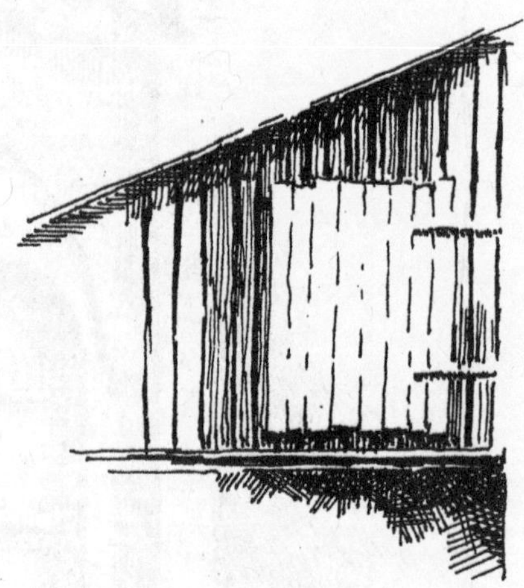

I frequently mention that outlines should be minimized in your work. By this I mean you should eliminate outlines in ink on your final product. By no means skimp on pencil outlines of *all* detail work, which are erased when your sketch is completed. The better your initial sketch in pencil, the better your completed ink version will be.

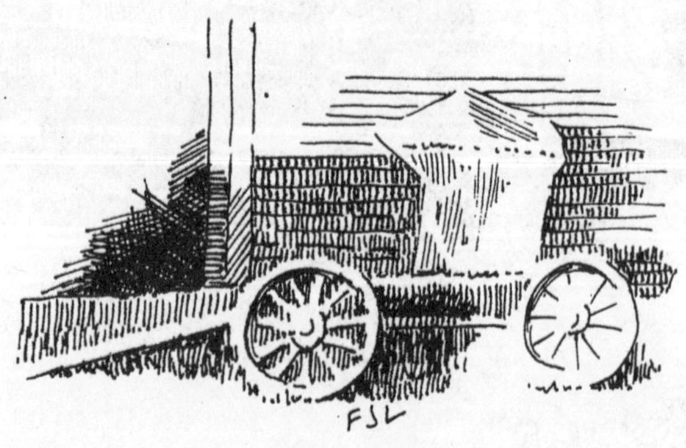

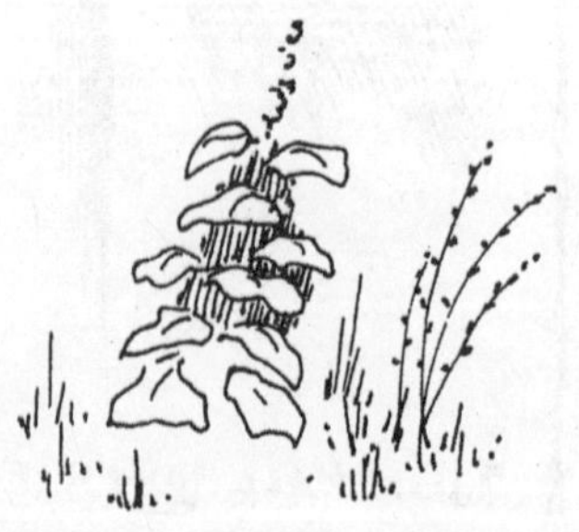

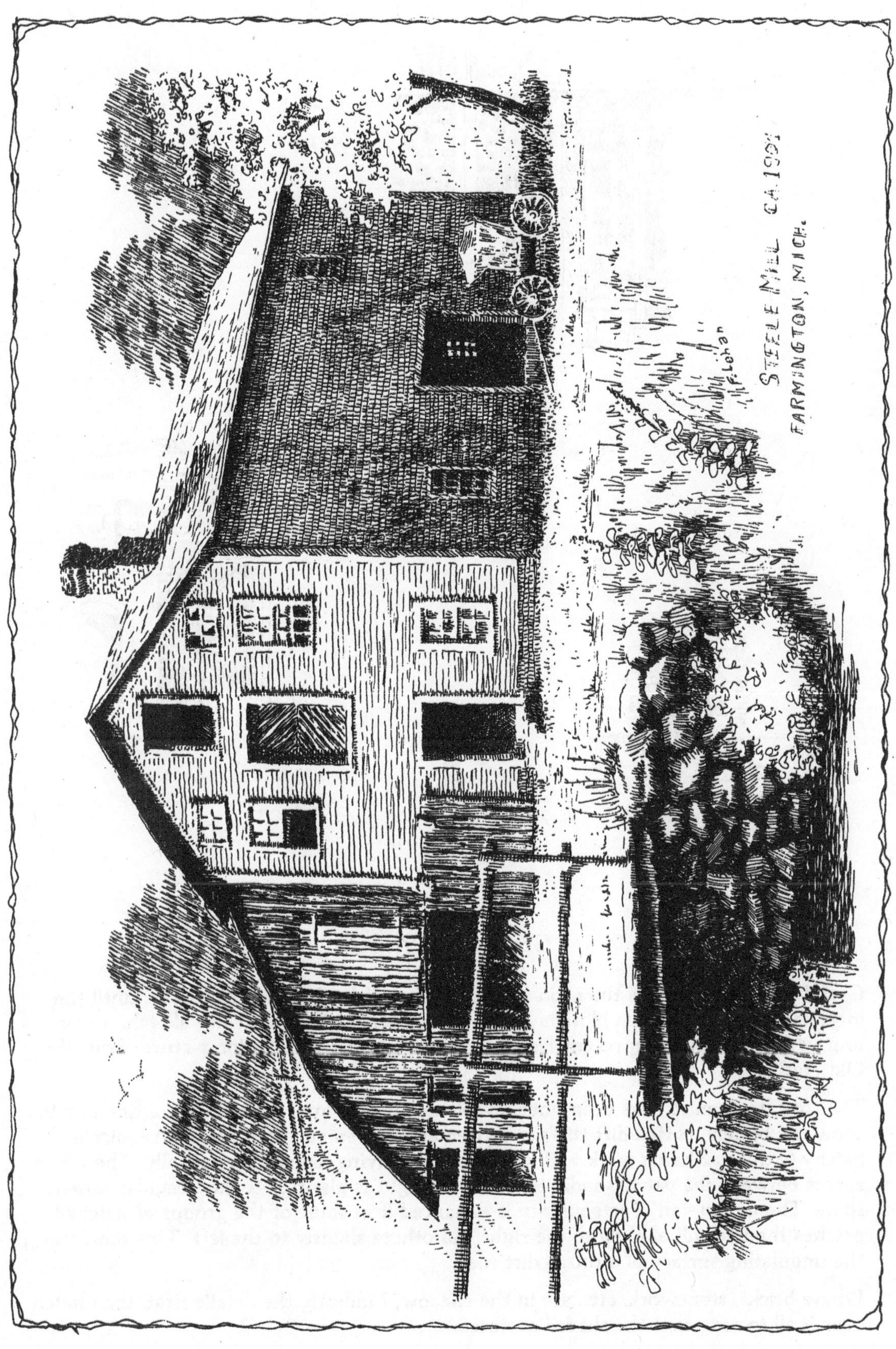
STEELE MILL
FARMINGTON, MICH.
F. Lohan

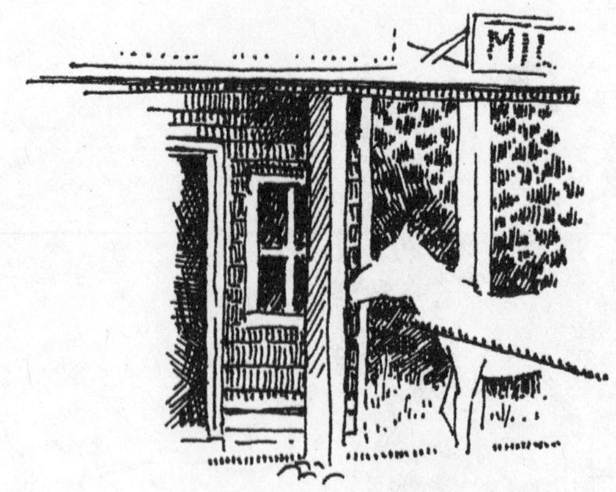

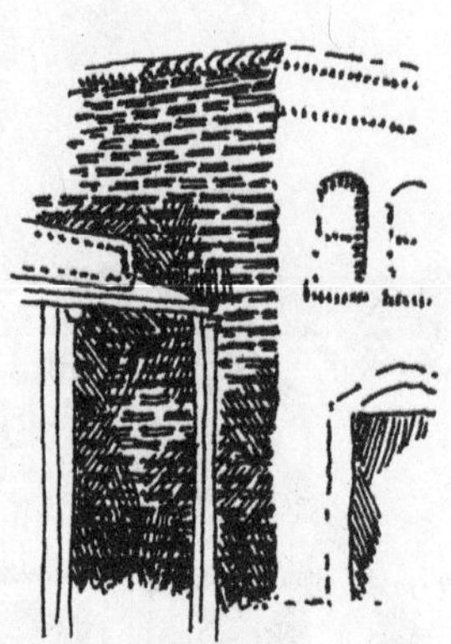

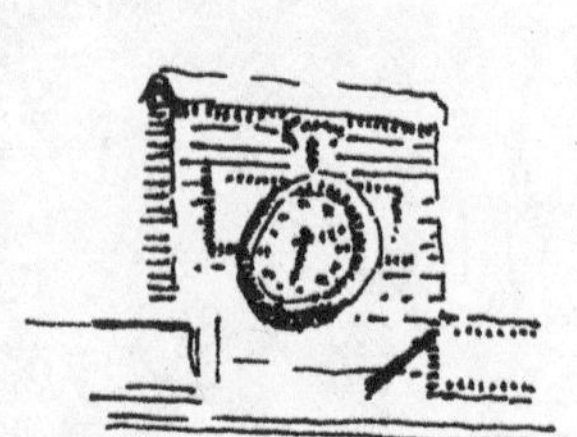

Grand River Avenue

Grand River Avenue was the main road from Detroit to Lansing, Michigan, until the interstate highway system blossomed. In the 1870s, as pictured in this sketch, it was unpaved and Farmington resembled a town from almost any motion picture about the Old West.

The road itself must have been unbelievable during a rainy spring. I used a fine pen to show the bumpy, rutted dirt surface. Extremely uneven surfaces like this require a patchy texture of hatch work with the hatch lines lying almost horizontally. The white spaces between the patches indicate where sunlight is glaring off the irregular raised spots. The impression of irregularity is enhanced if in some of the groups of hatched patches the lines tilt slightly to the right and others slightly to the left. This simulates the undulating surface of a rough dirt road.

Where bricks, stonework, etc., are in the shadow, I indicate the details first, then hatch over it all to represent the shaded surface.

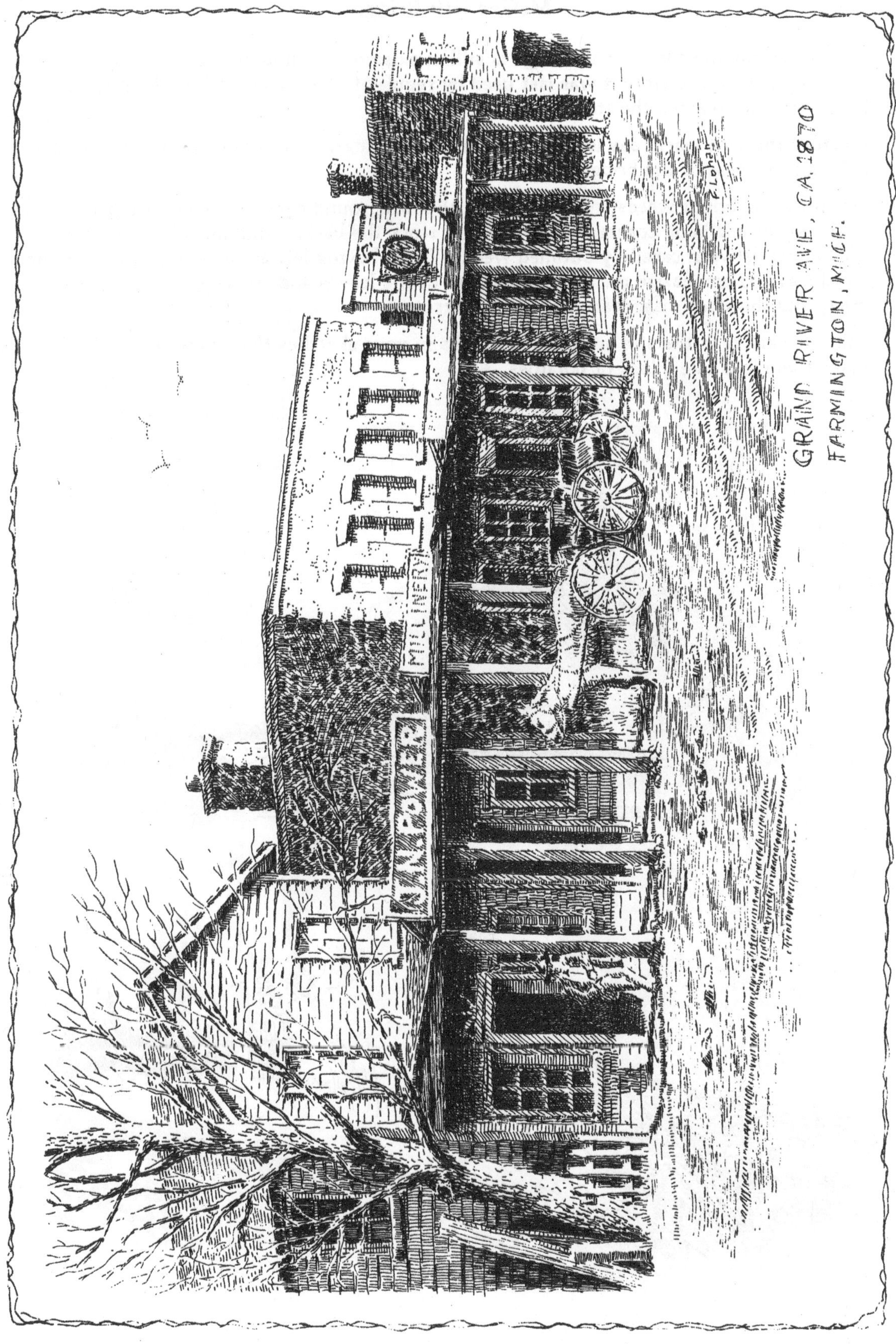
GRAND RIVER AVE, CA. 1870
FARMINGTON, MICH.
MILLINERY

The Old Smithy

This is an imaginary nostalgic scene. I like barns, old wood, and some of the clutter I associate with abandoned old rural structures. This was a rainy day exercise in which I used the same basic composition as that on page 73 of my earlier book, *Pen and Ink Techniques.* In this sketch, however, I rearranged some of the trees and redesigned parts of the barn, but I retained the same general layout. I don't know just what I'm looking for when I do this, but there are several basic settings involving old buildings that I sketch from time to time with some variations in the details—just for my own pleasure and relaxation.

This is another example of rough, undulating ground that calls for patchy, horizontal hatch work. The barn wood in this case was rendered with bold, deliberate lines using a medium pen. The same applies to all of the foliage, which is indicated here primarily in outline or silhouette with a style that is more decorative than realistic.

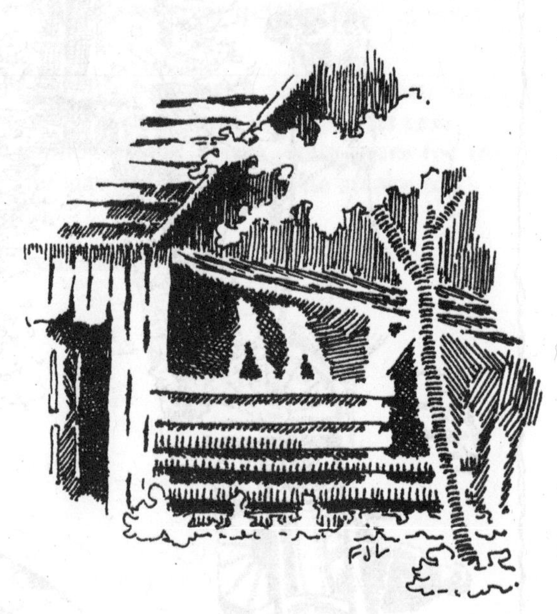

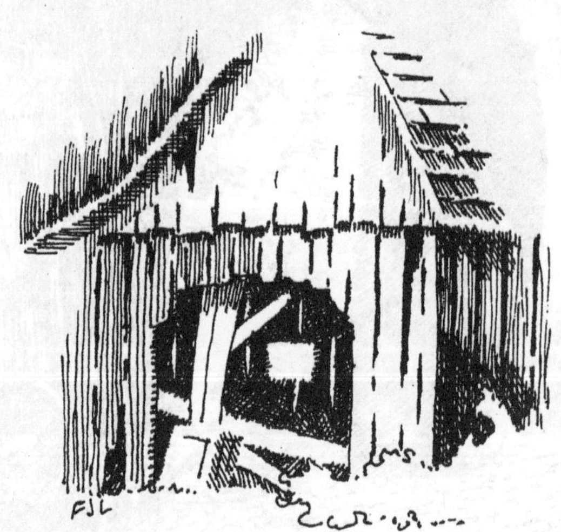

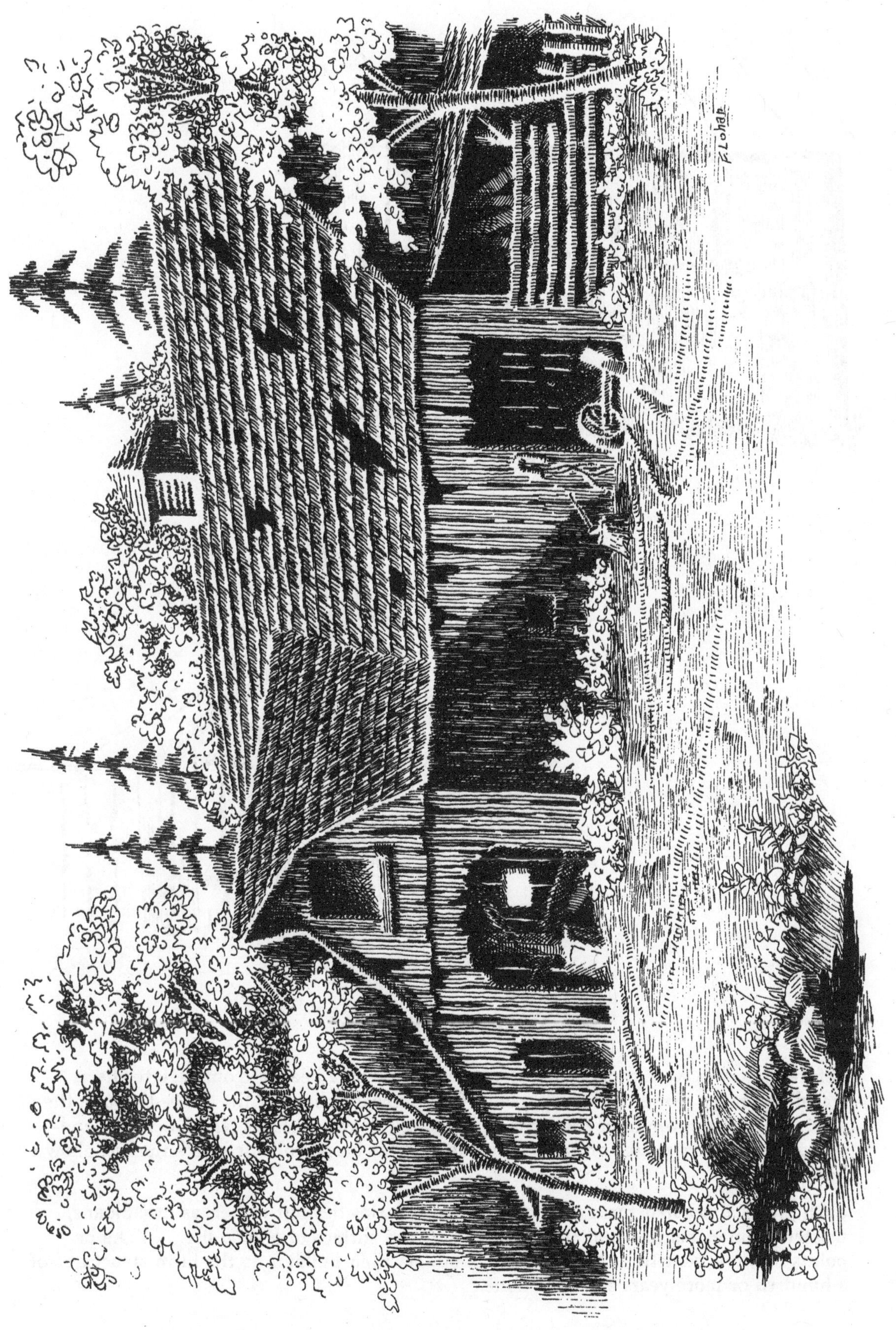

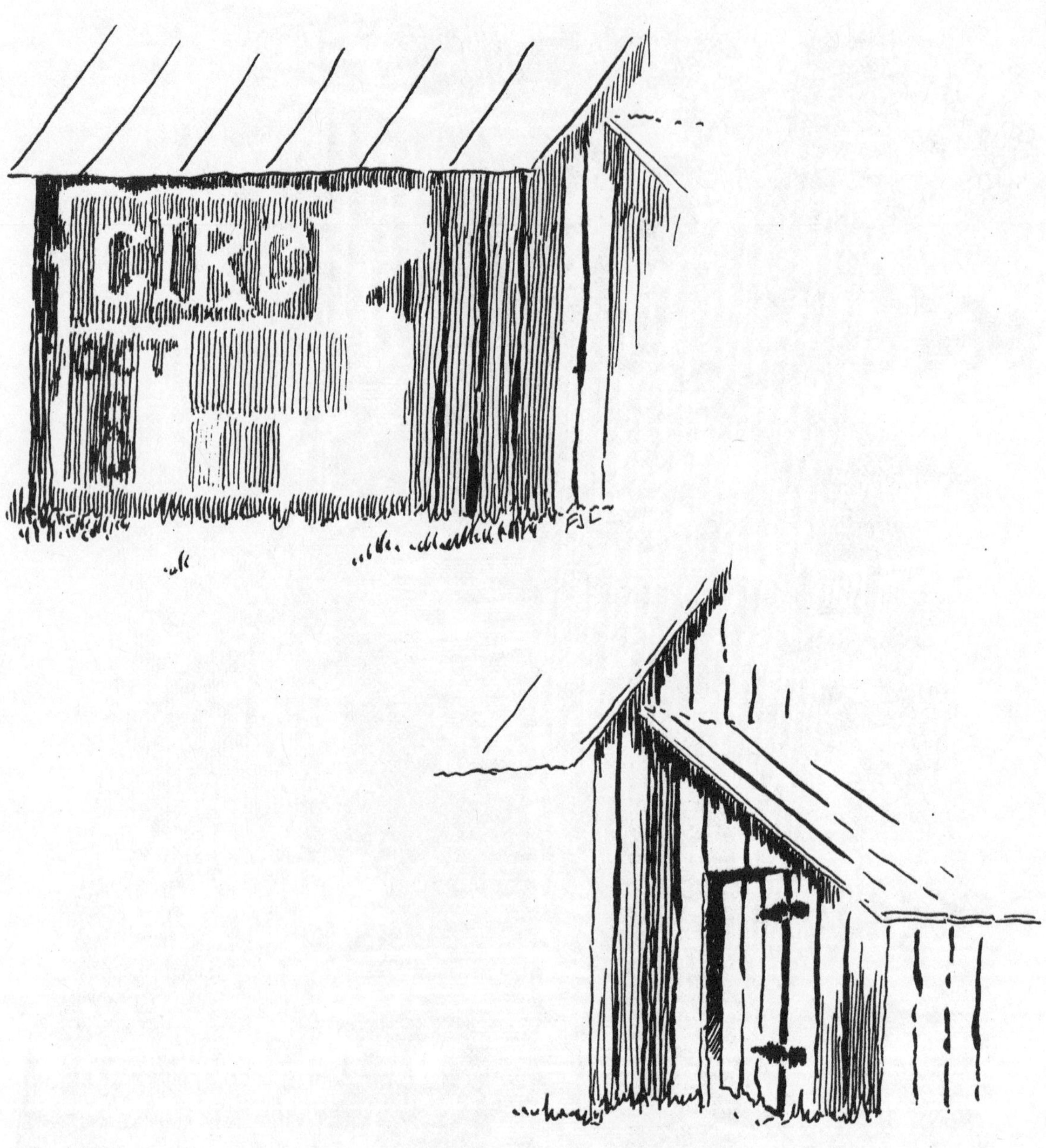

An Original Billboard

Before highways were constructed to convey traffic on a beeline from here to there, travel was much slower and more scenic. Our billboard blight of the 1940s through the 1960s was an outgrowth of the signs advertising tobacco, circuses, and Doctor so-and-so's pills that were pasted or painted on old roadside barns and sheds like the one shown here.

Such practical old structures are not mere rural curiosities but rather, as Eric Sloane, master penman, painter, and author, said, ". . . the shrines of a good life. . . ." As he points out, few structures built today will outlast their builders as the farm structures of a hundred or more years ago have done.

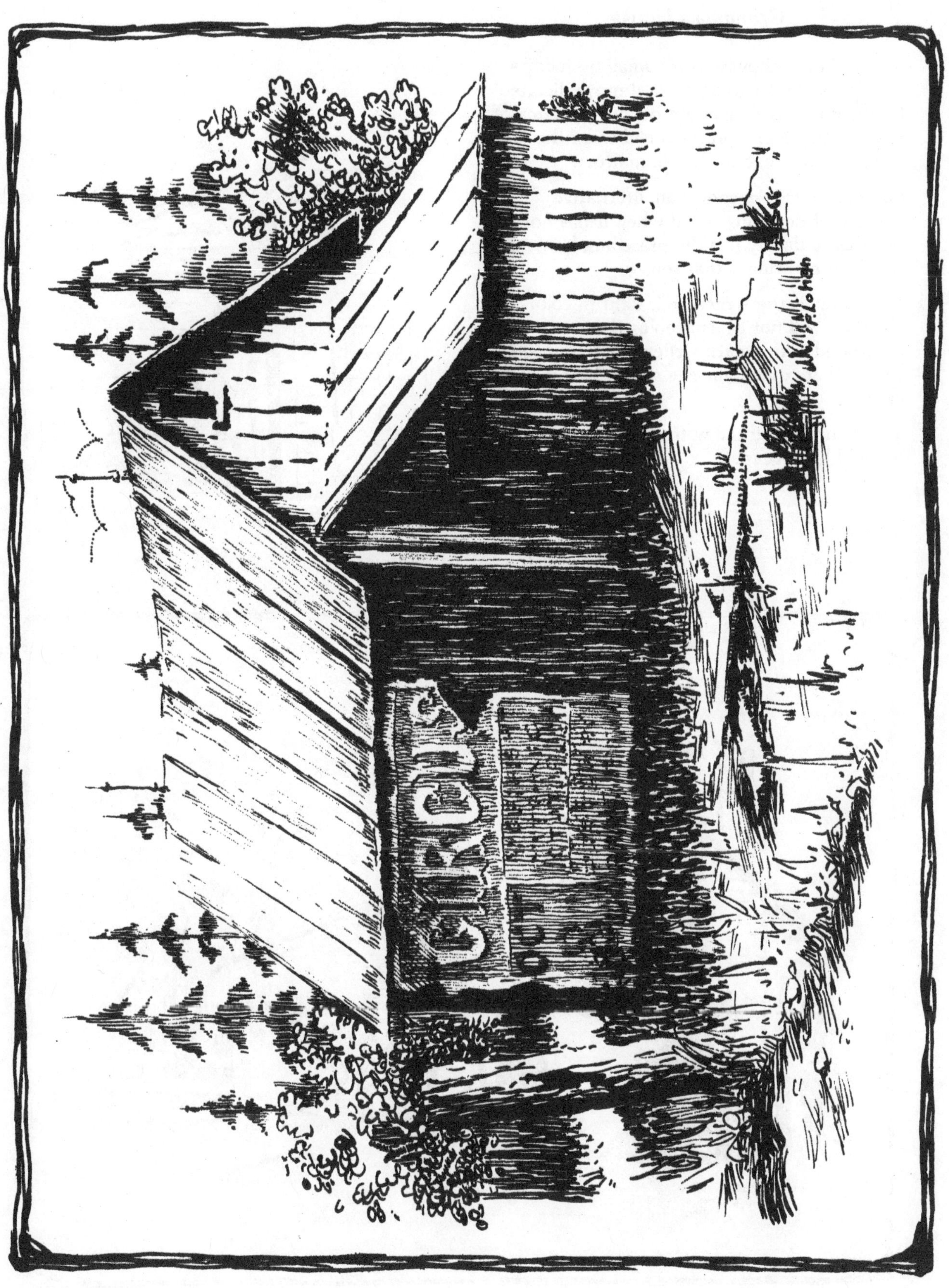
CIRCUS

Grandma's House

Many old farmhouses were small by today's standards. This was a practical move dictated by the poor insulation and heating systems of the era. Small and practical had to be the thing to minimize winter discomfort.

Grandma's House shows an alternative method of depicting wood when it has not weathered deeply like the preceding barns or the covered bridges that follow.

Generally, if the structure is light in color, the shadows will not be as deep as those associated with a dark structure. A fine pen rather than a medium one serves best in this case.

This is not my grandmother's house; however, it could have been.

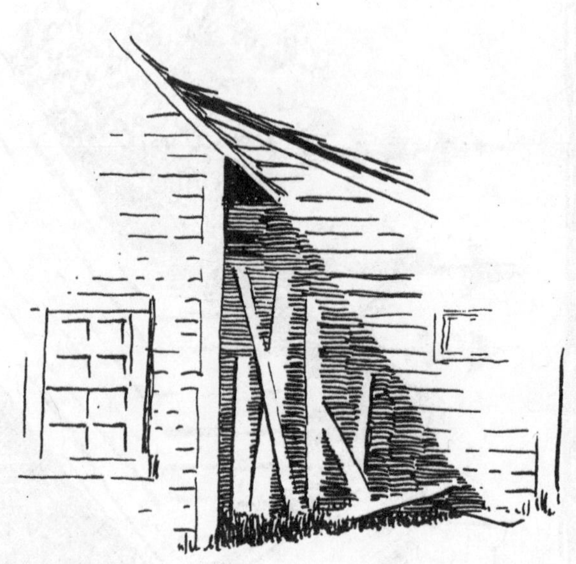

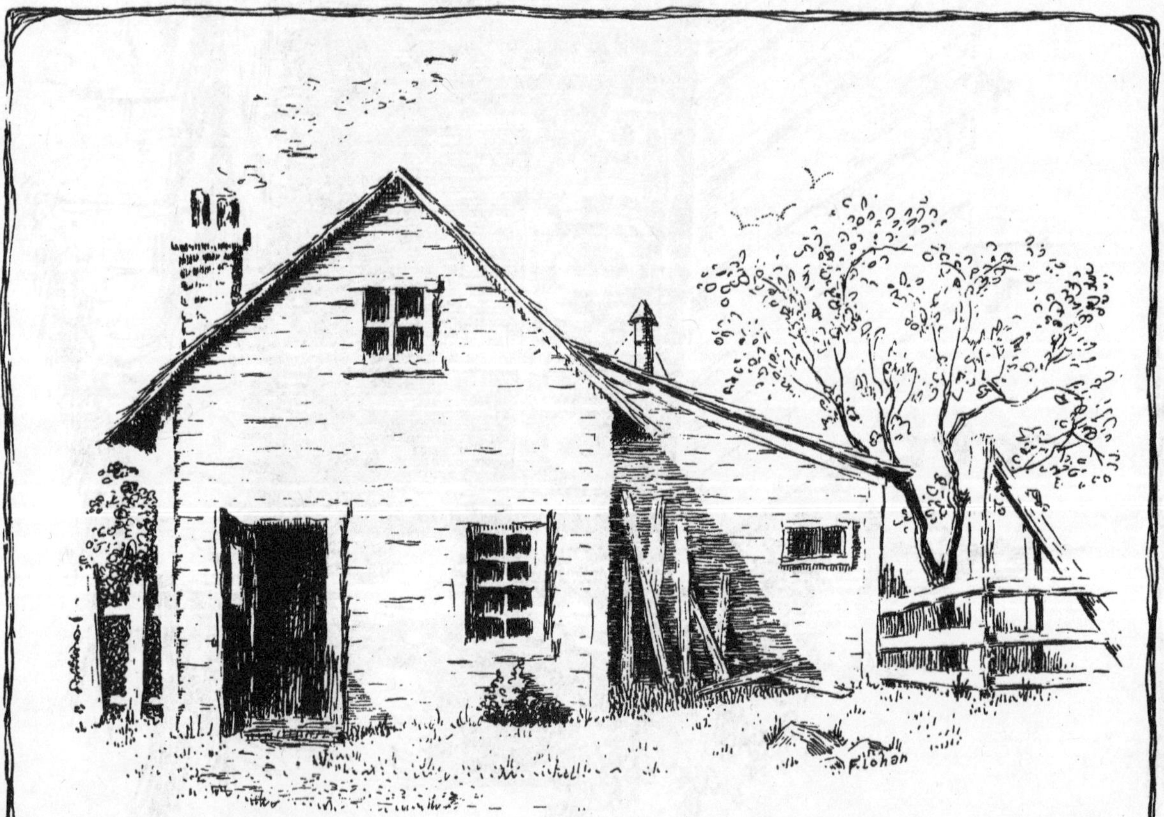

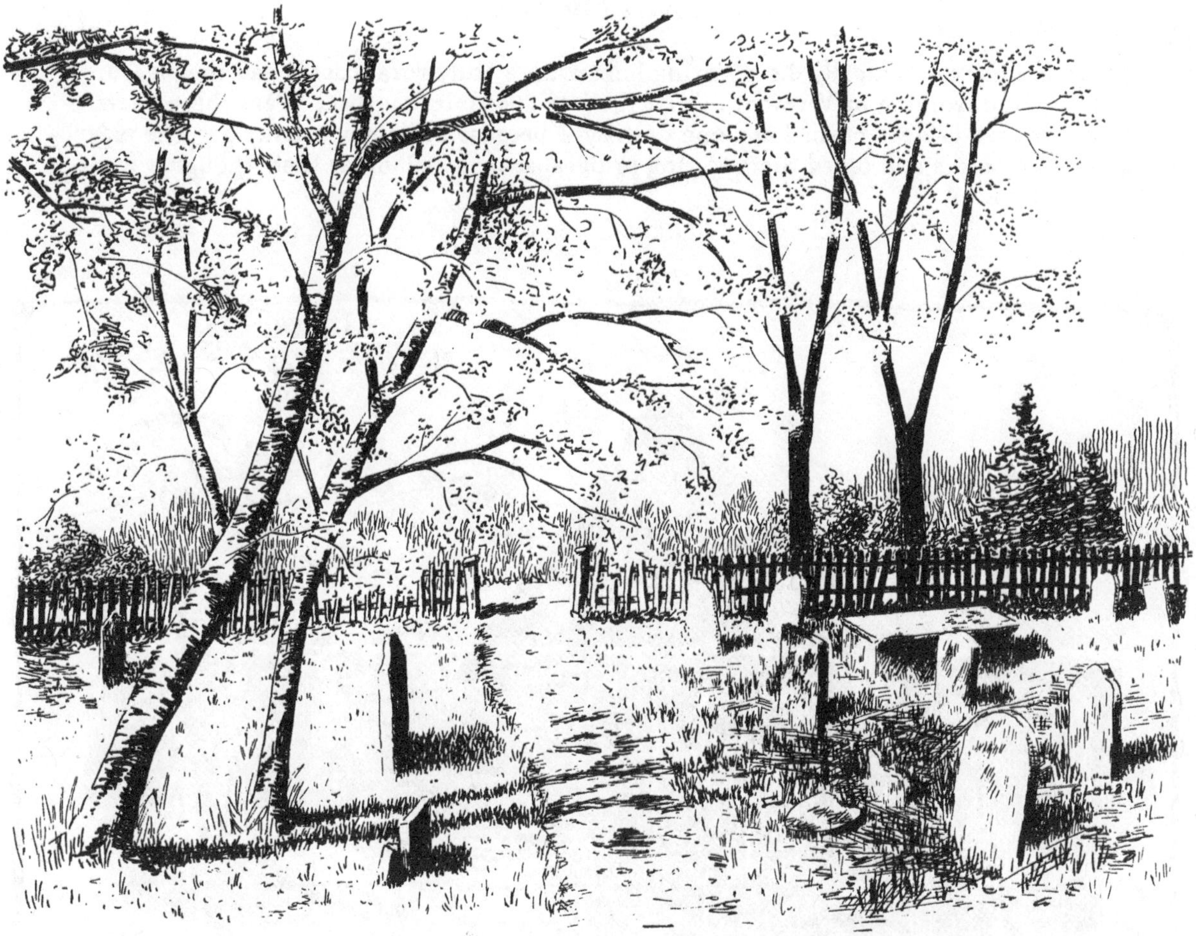

Forgotten

This cemetery scene—with its rickety picket fence, tombstones broken and worn by the weather, gravel path, and birch trees—could be typical of any of thousands of such rural burial grounds.

It is interesting to walk through such a cemetery on a pleasant spring or summer day. Many tombstone inscriptions are still legible after a hundred or more years. They bring to mind sad stories of Civil War casualties and, even sadder, they point to the terribly high infant mortality rate of that era. In many ways the "good old days" are better in our imagination than they ever were in fact.

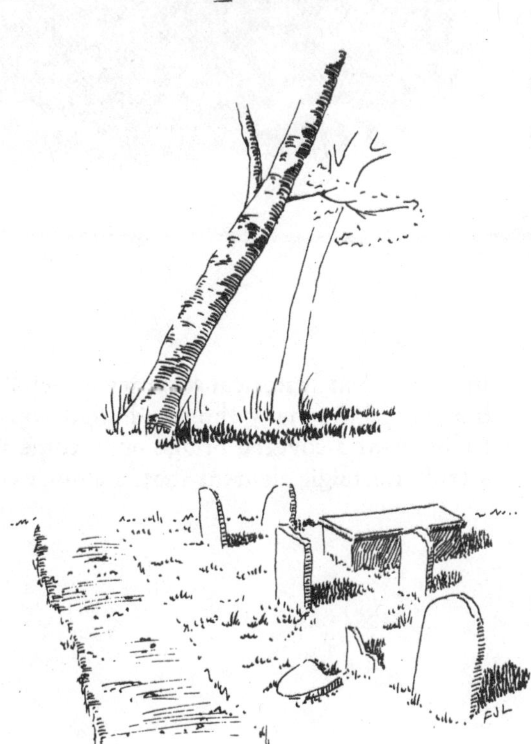

Covered Bridges

These are our most rapidly disappearing links with a truly rural past. I had the pleasure of living and working in Vermont during the late 1960s. In my three years there I saw three covered bridges burned and one destroyed because of dam construction. The older local Vermonters still called them kissing bridges, always smiling as their thoughts went back in time.

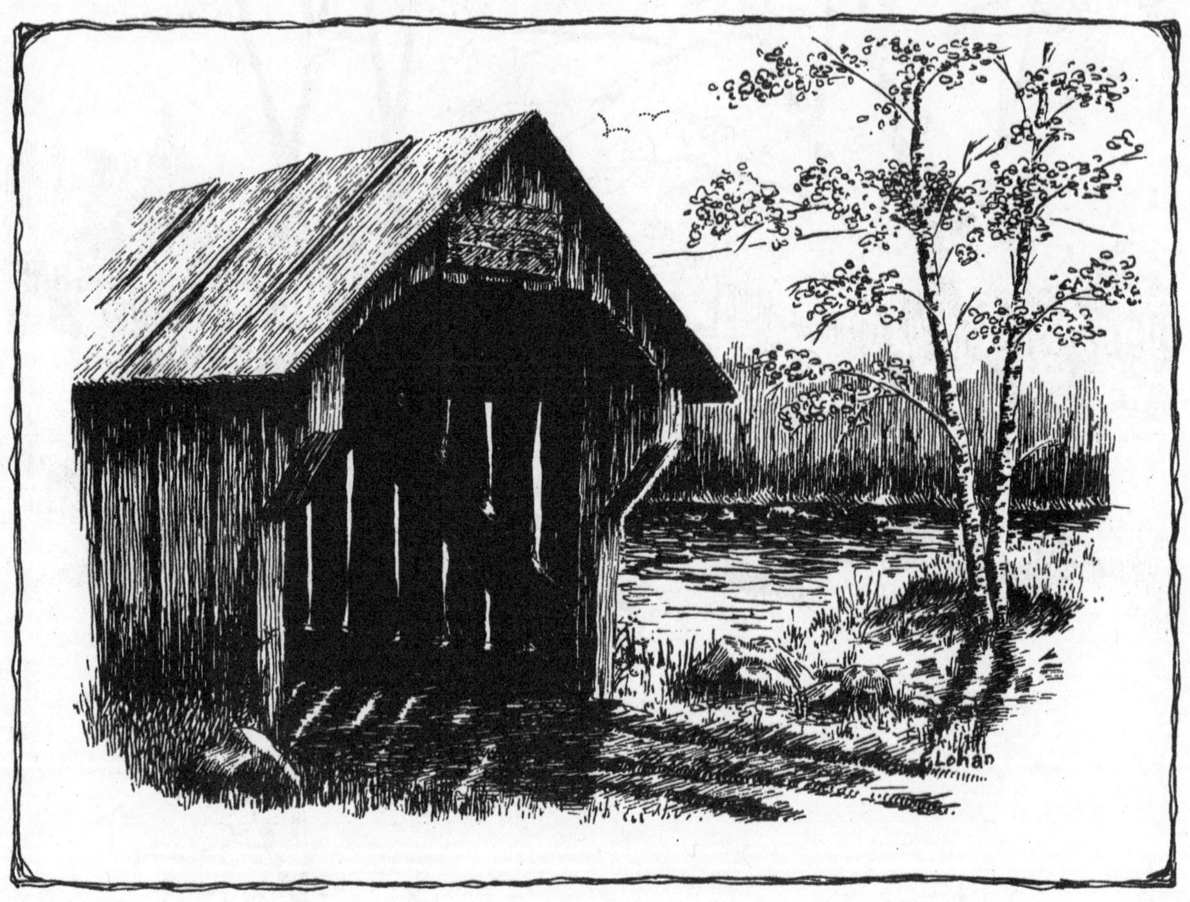

In some areas historical societies do what they can to preserve or restore these bridges, but few of the many thousands that were built still exist. So if you are fortunate enough to live near a covered bridge or to come upon one when traveling, take a second look at a truly nostalgic element that is almost certain to be lost forever in the near future.

Such structures make marvelous subjects for any artist, but somehow they are ideally suited to pen and ink.

The dark interior in the largest subject here was done using a small watercolor brush, blending the ink into the textured dark areas done with pen.

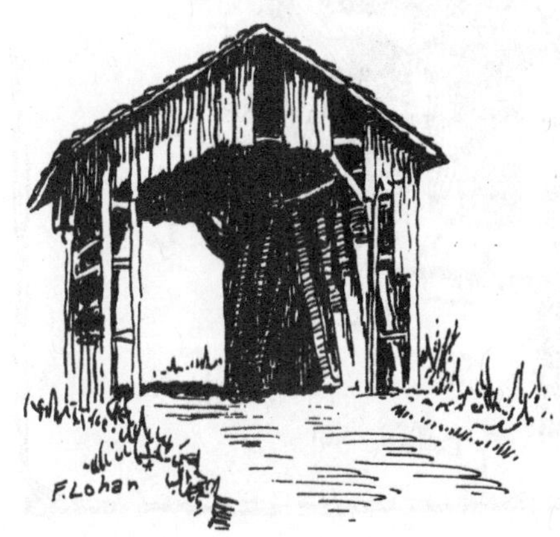

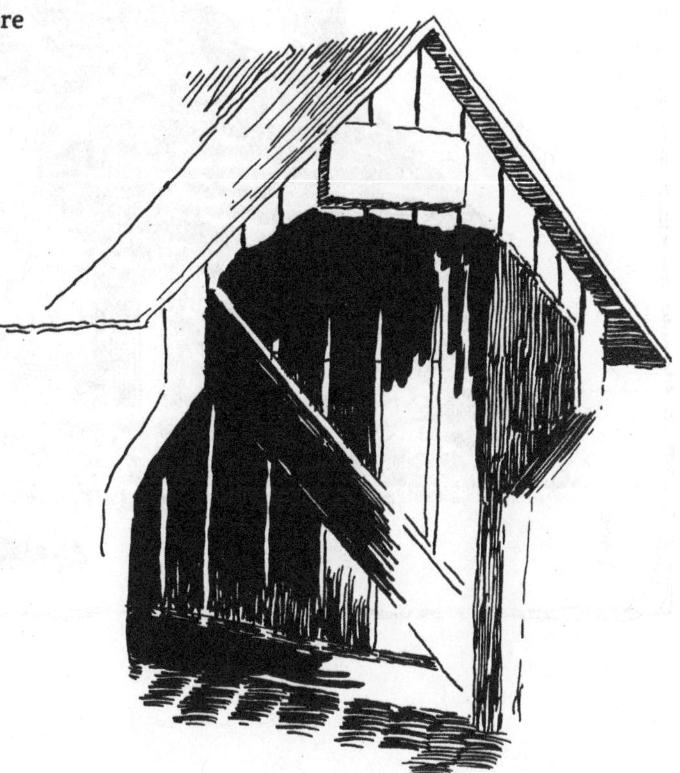

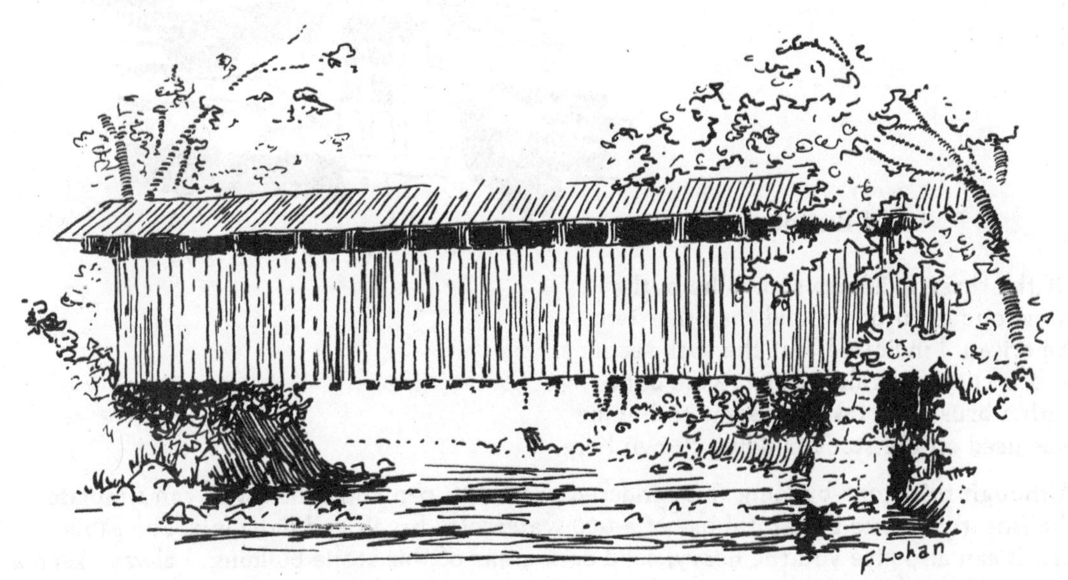

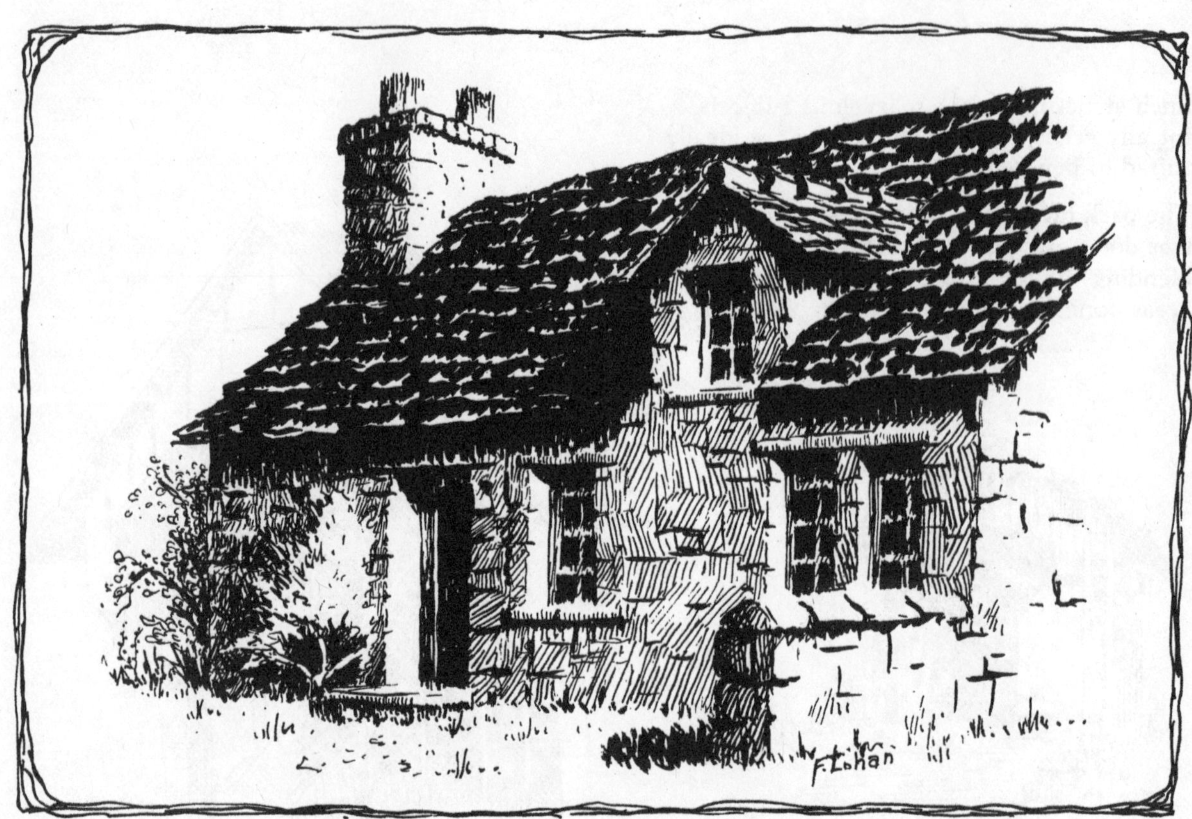

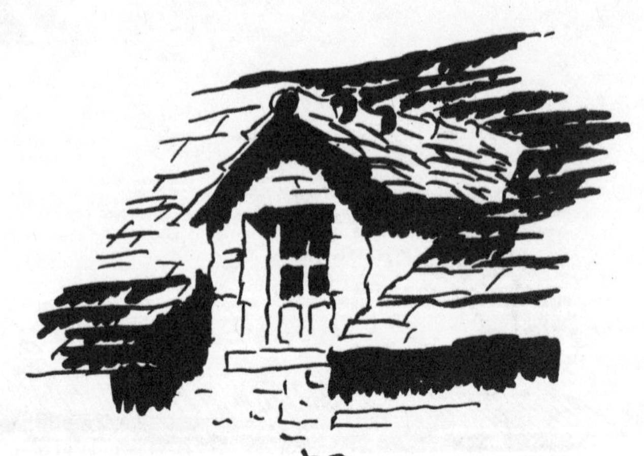

Old Buildings

Of the three buildings shown here, the stone one is European and the other two American. I indicated that the dark sections of one covered bridge sketch were done with a brush and ink. The same technique was used on the stone building shown here.

Although this stone building was rendered with both pen and brush, you can simulate the finest pen lines by careful use of a 000 watercolor brush and india ink. The same brush can also give you the heavy, solid dark areas of this stone building. I always keep a couple of small watercolor brushes handy with my pens.

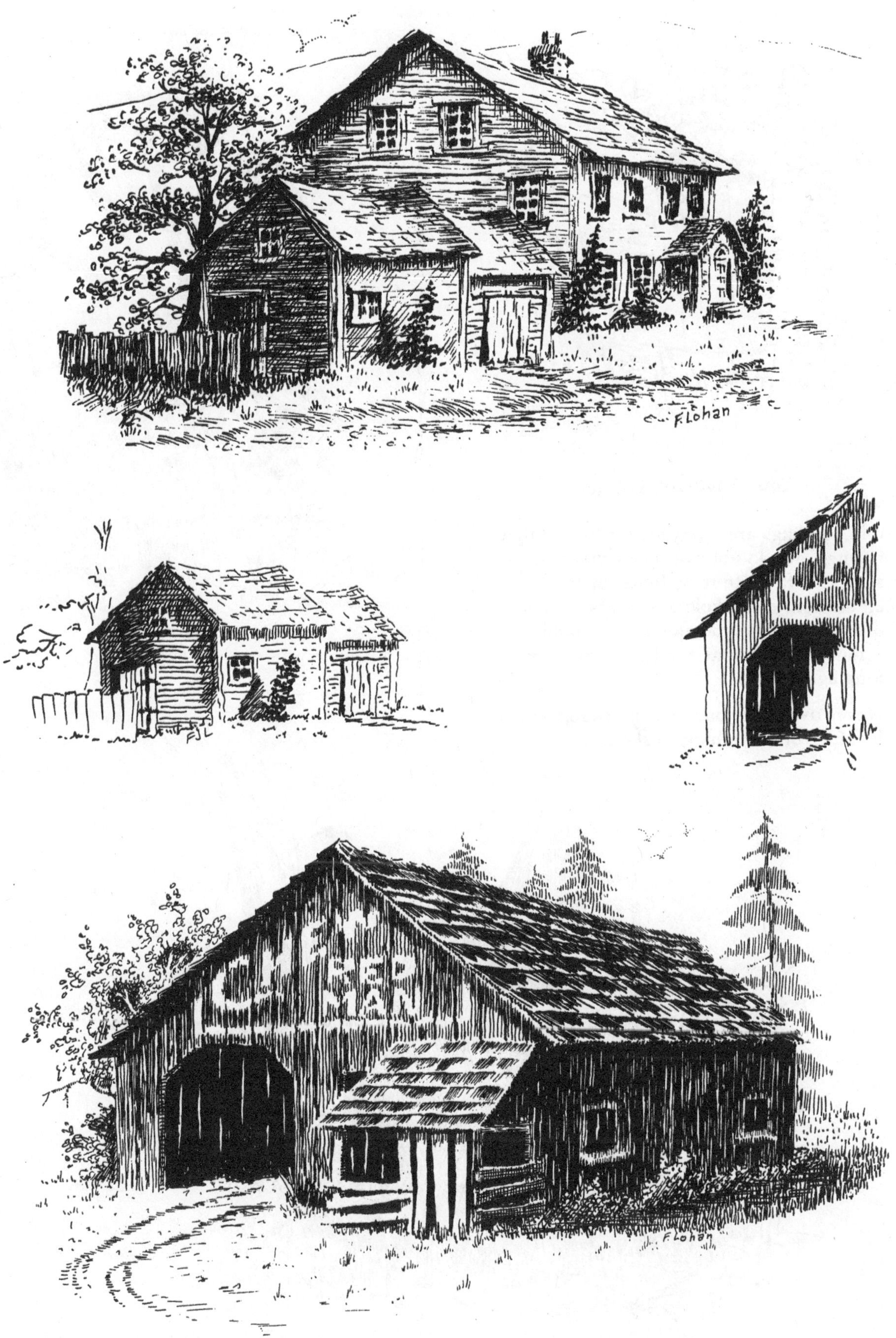
F.Lohan
FJL
RED
MAN
F.Lohan

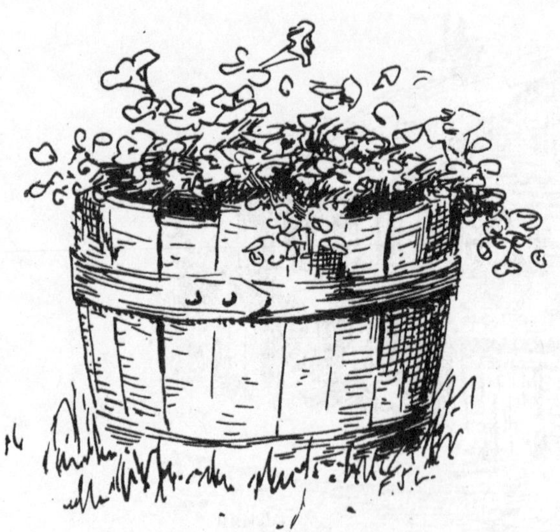

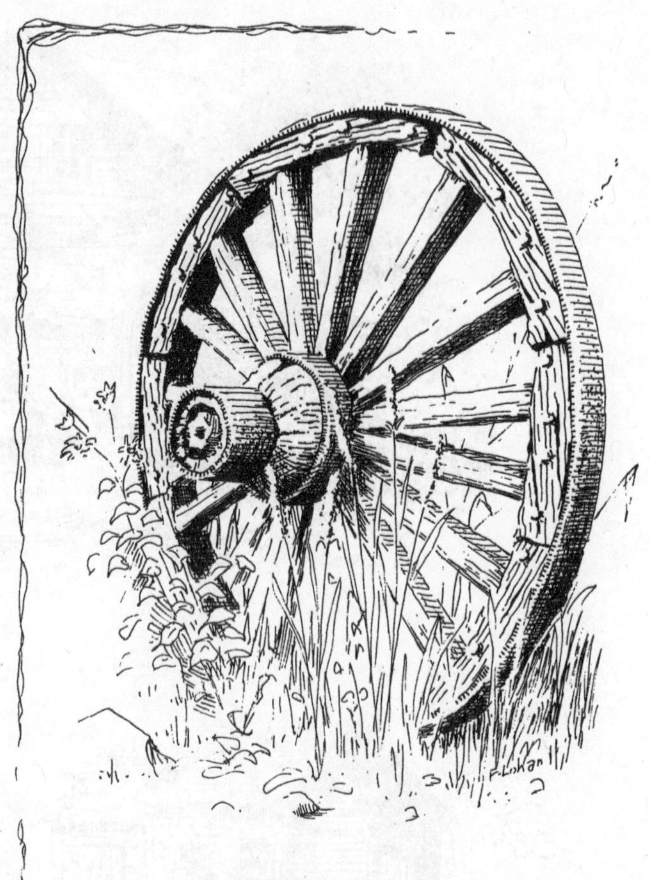

Your Favorite Things

Old buildings are always favorite nostalgic themes, but do not overlook other things, such as a favorite rock, fence, or tree. Such an element could hold a memory that is dear to you and you alone, or it could remind you of some fond incident from long ago.

Never overlook your favorite things when looking for something to sketch.

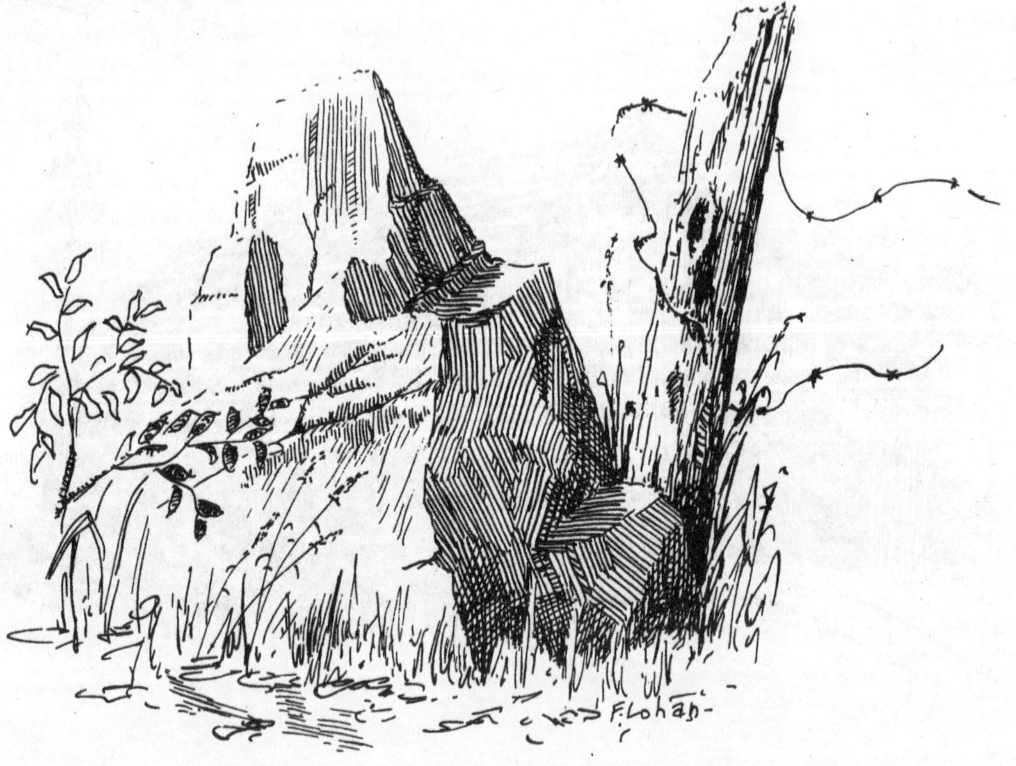

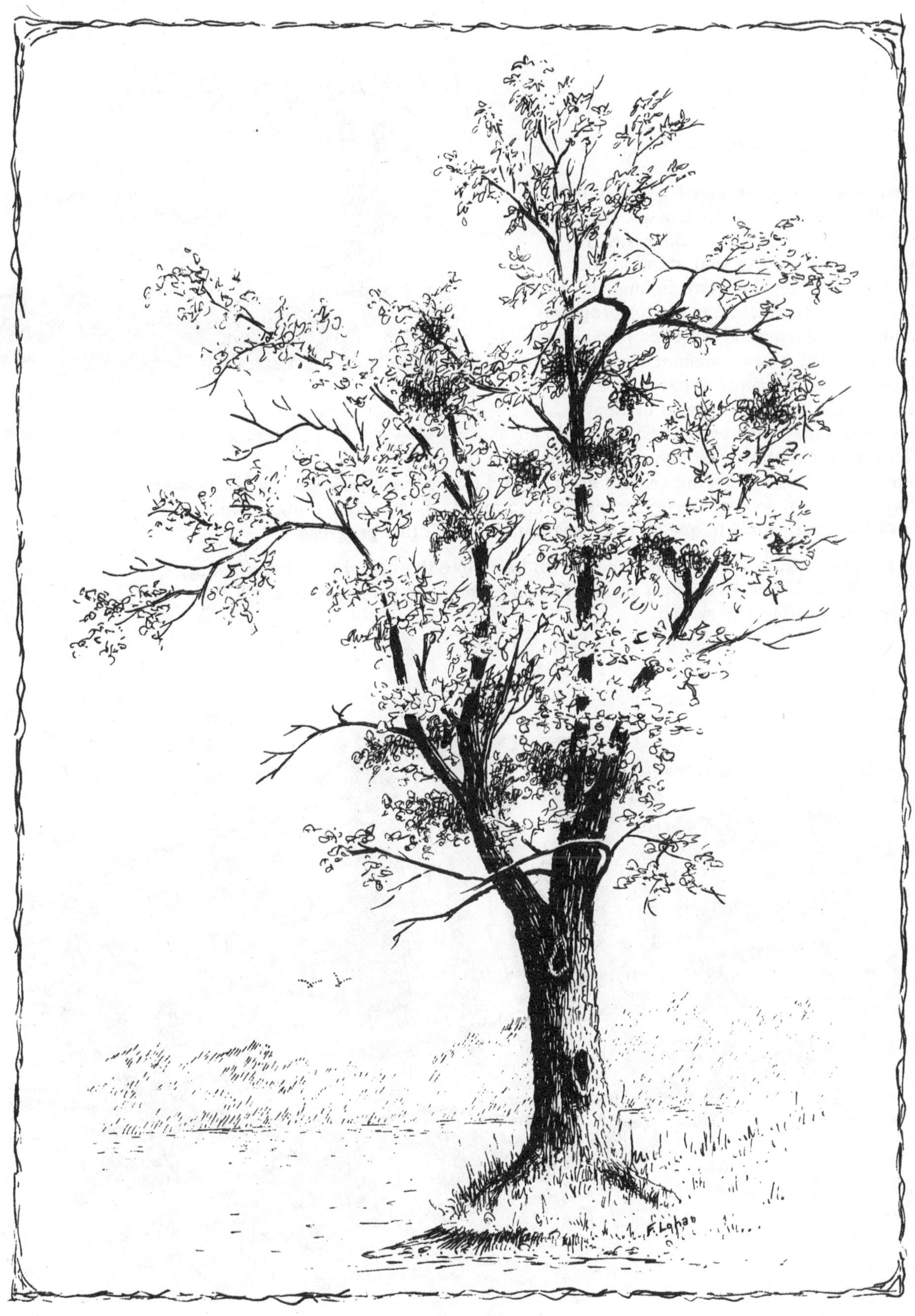
F. Lohan

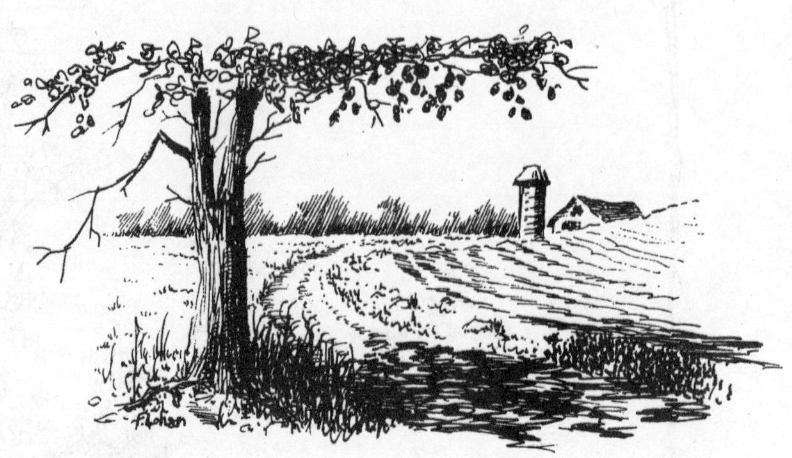

Progress

An ancient Chinese Taoist poem states "... all things alike do their work and then we see them subside...." So it is with the rural structures that stand in the way of land development. Sooner or later the way must be made for progress and the enduring old removed to make room for the often transient new. Nowhere is this more apparent than in the rural suburbs of twenty or thirty years ago that have become "developed." This means that streets have been paved, homes built, and shopping centers erected; and that service stations and traffic signals have appeared on every prime corner. It also means many other things, which can only lead thinking people to question the real quality of all this progress.

It is sad to watch a once proud and useful barn, like the one shown here, being demolished. If you happen on such a dismemberment in progress, you will have an interesting subject to sketch.

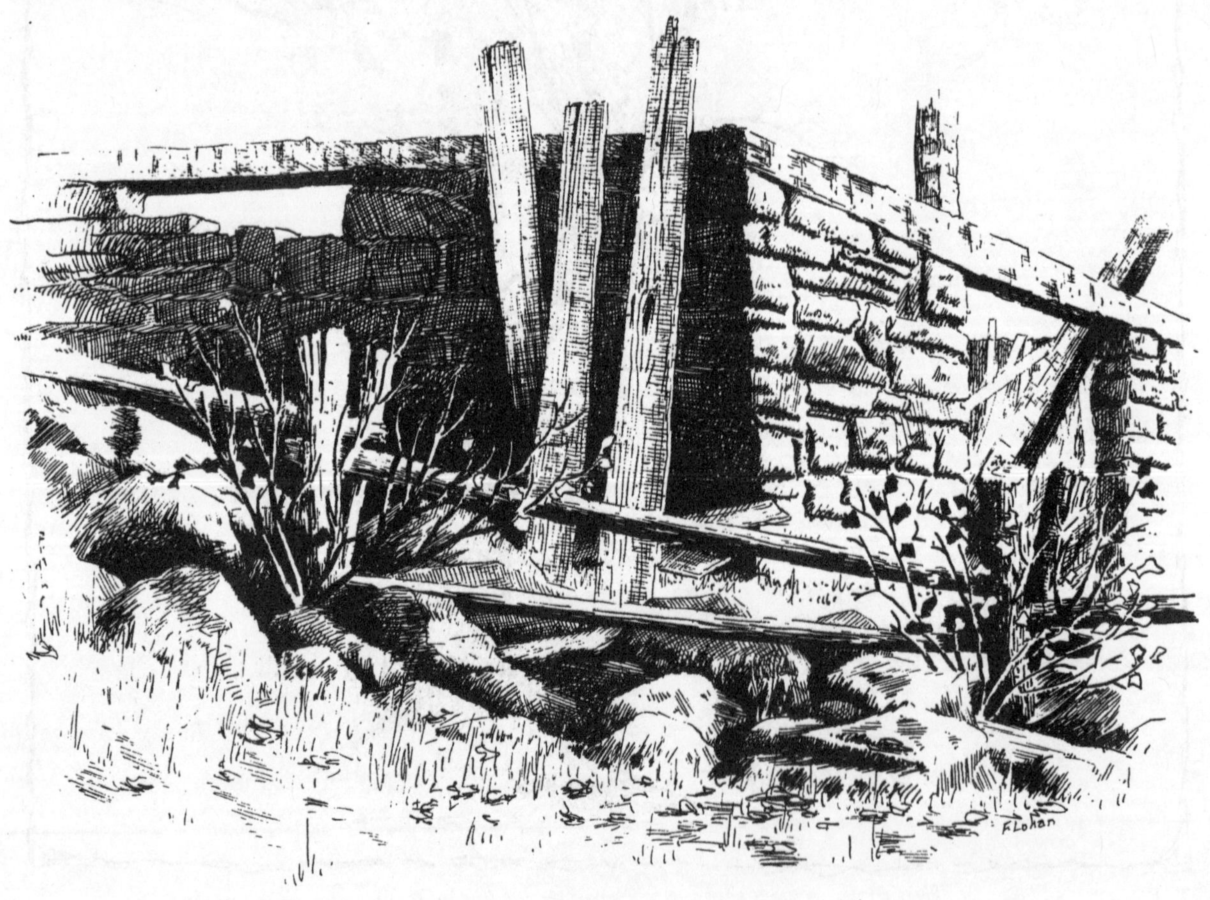

2: Subjects from Old Engravings

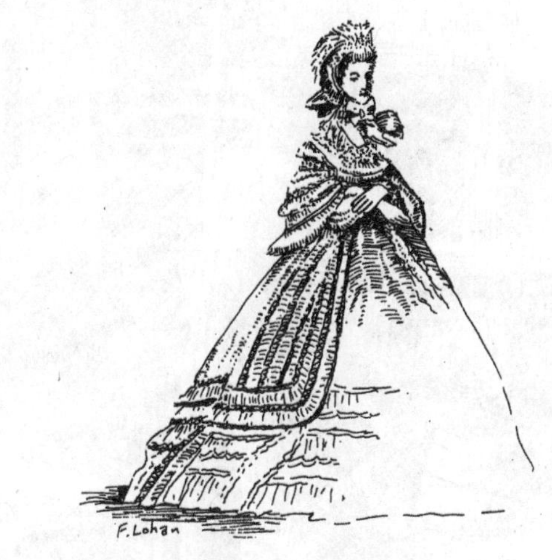

Most pre-1900 magazines liberally used engraved illustrations. Many of these are superb little drawings that represent some of the best examples of engraving craftsmanship.

Such fine examples of line work can provide you with endless themes for practice if you take a small detail in an engraving that attracts your eye and enlarge on it. Additionally, engravings can be very useful as studies of how talented professionals handled juxtaposition of light and dark, how they led the eye into their drawing, and—a most important thing to learn—how they "got out of" their drawing. This latter point is learned only after a great deal of trial and error. Just how and where to stop after you have surrounded your center of interest with enough detail to establish the setting is as important a consideration as the basic composition.

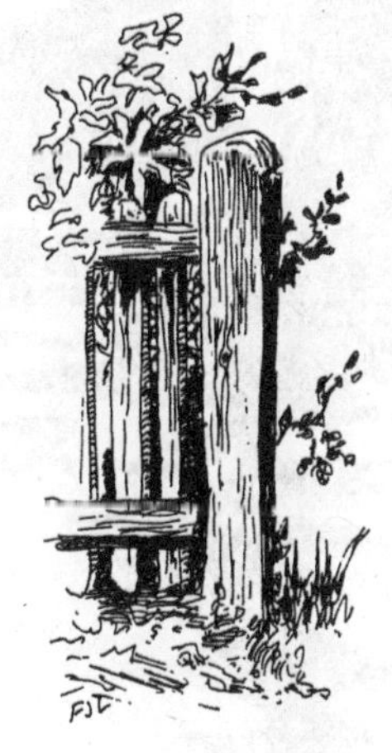

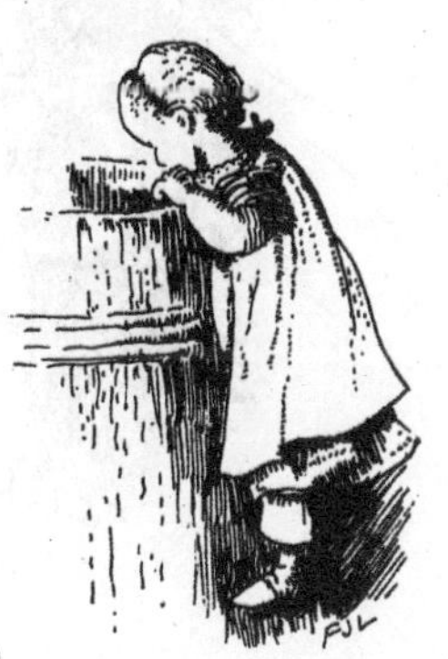

Some of the studies in this section were based on some pre-1890 engravings I happened upon. As usual, I took liberties with composition and content after something in the engravings caught my eye and got me going on the sketch.

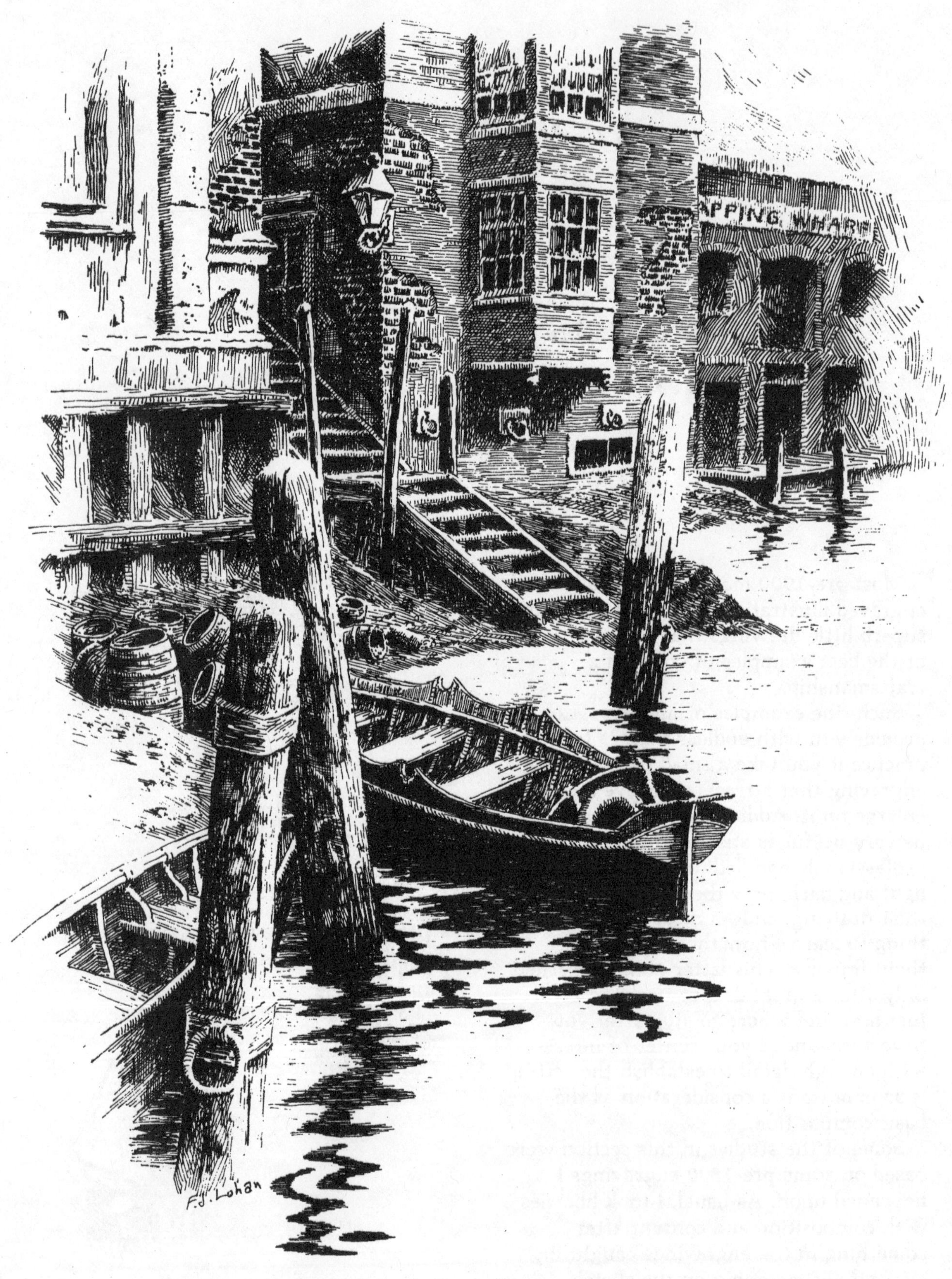
APPING WHARF
F.J. Lohan

London Riverside

The reproduction of the engraving I used as inspiration for this sketch was many times smaller than my interpretation. I eliminated numerous other boats and a number of figures when I made my sketch. I was attracted by the many different textures contained in the scene—stucco, brick, smooth stone in the buildings, mud, water, rough wooden pilings and herring barrels, as well as the painted boats.

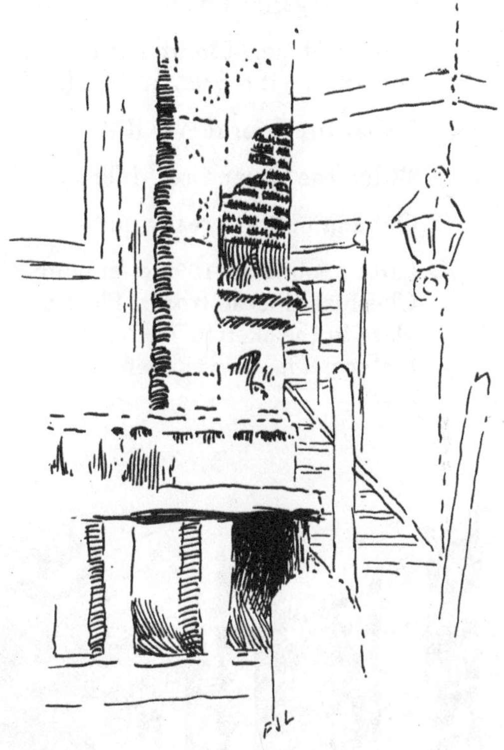

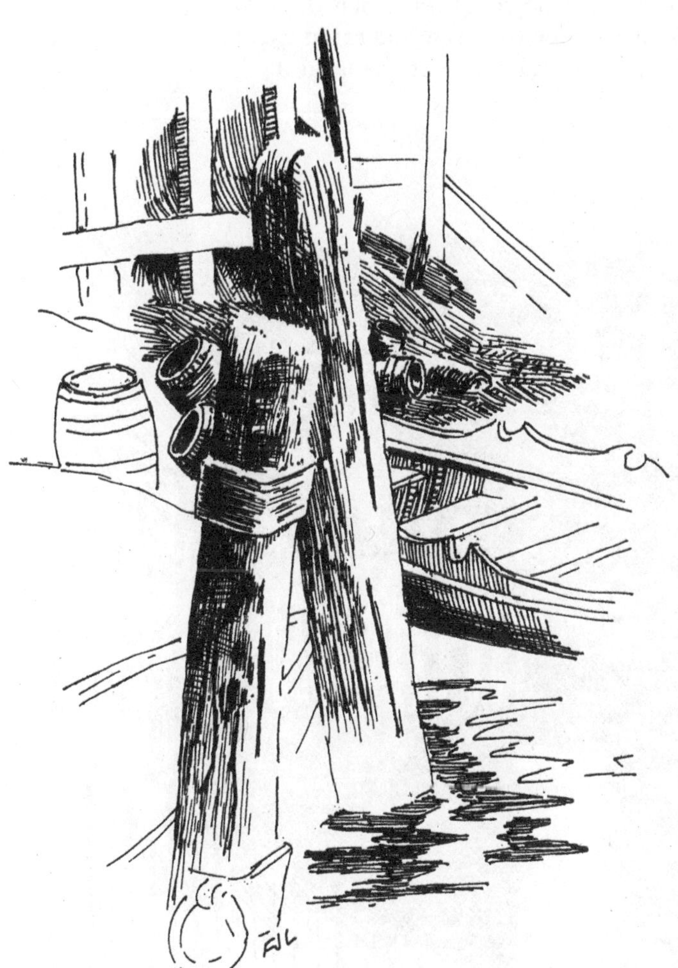

When browsing for inspiration, do not feel obligated to copy the source material faithfully. That is not the objective. Rather, the primary function of such source material is to provide you with practice subjects. Its second purpose is to point out surface treatments that you might profitably work into your own subjects.

The full tonal range—from solid black to stark white paper—is used here. The dark portions were built up carefully after the underlying detail was established in ink.

The Old Cheshire Cheese

This famous London pub and restaurant is just a few yards off Fleet Street. Until the mid-1970s it had been open to men only and was frequented by newspaper writers. One evening in the 1960s David Ward, a noted opera singer, returned from an extended stay in Rome and burst boisterously into the pub to greet some of his many friends. I was there at the time and had the pleasure of sharing a pint of bitters and some light conversation with this huge, gregarious man in the unimposing, historic men's pub.

Ward told me, "Oh, this is the *new* Old Cheshire Cheese—original burned, you know—the fire . . . rebuilt immediately after."

"What fire, World War II?"

"Why, the Great Fire—1666, you know—destroyed most of London . . ."

Old and new are really quite relative.

Later I found an 1890 engraving of the dingy little court on which the Old Cheshire Cheese fronts. Fleet Street is just under the arch, indicated by the glare in the sketch. The entrance to the pub is under one of the largest lanterns I have ever seen.

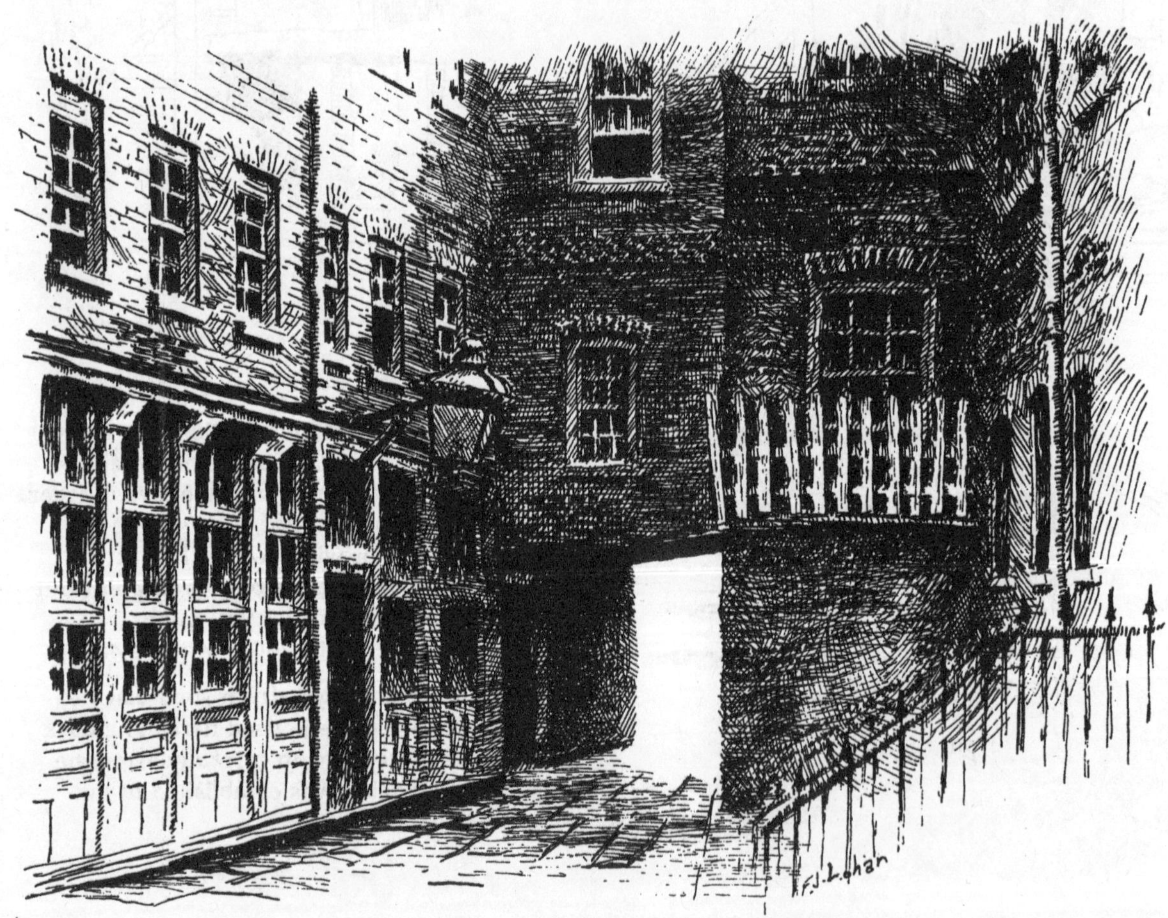

Redrawn
From 1890 Engraving of Ye Olde Cheshire Cheese, London

The location had not changed in the seventy-odd years between the time of the engraving and my visit. Neither had the ancient tradition barring women from the tiny pub changed. The publican told me that even the queen herself would be denied entrance. Since my visit, however, this tradition has crumbled along with many cherished relics of the past.

In spite of my frequent admonition to avoid outlining, this sketch utilizes quite a bit of it, as you can see in the partly completed details. However, note how the effect of the glare from Fleet Street is enhanced by omitting a hard edge on the walls that frame this white area. A hard-line edge would be totally inappropriate here. Outline was also avoided on the bright parts of the two vertical rain pipes.

A sketch like this calls for establishment of details first, followed by a careful buildup of the dark shades over these details. Also note how relatively few individual bricks require delineation to get across the idea of a brick wall.

The matter of "getting out of a sketch" frequently arises—just where and how to stop after your center of interest is surrounded with adequate detail. The top and right side of this sketch show how architectural details such as windows can just sort of fade out without looking at all incomplete. The viewer's eye will fill in details that are obvious by implication, such as the steps that must exist at the lower right. There is no need to show them in this case.

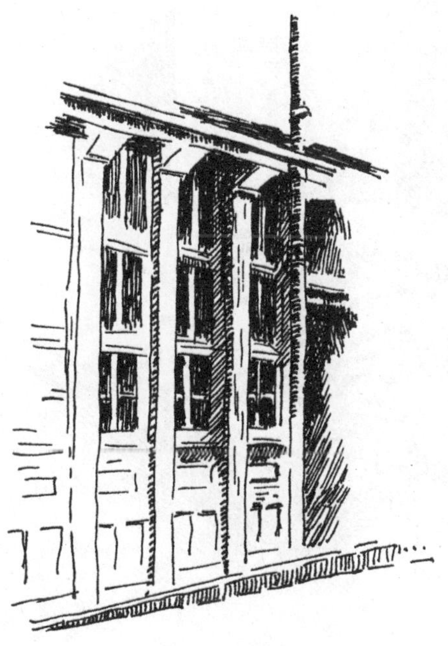

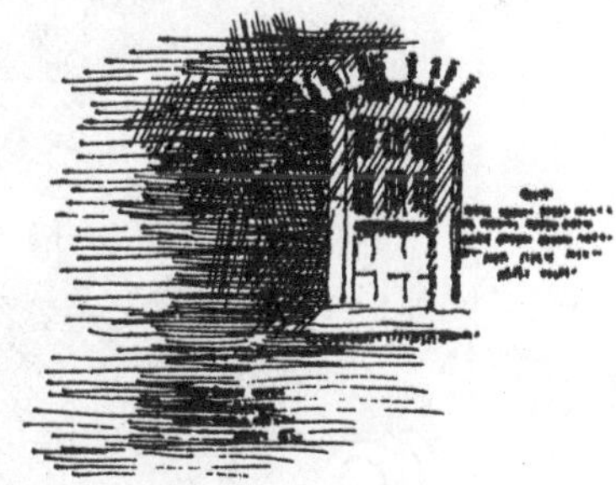

From Albrecht Durer

Albrecht Durer was born about twenty years prior to Columbus's discovery of America and was acknowledged in his own time as a supreme technician of woodcut and engraving. Anyone interested in fine line art must study his works and carefully examine his techniques.

Browse through a volume of Durer's works and you will find countless details that can act as inspiration for small studies. Again, anything that prompts you to sketch is legitimate practice material. In a case like this, first try to duplicate the line technique. Then try the same detail but treat it differently—your way. Study how Durer created the forms of various surfaces, how he treated lights and darks, how he frequently stylized his trees to fit into and enhance his basic composition.

The three sketches here are based on details from three different works by Durer—*Saint Jerome, Saint Eustace,* and the *Nativity.* They are not exact copies of his work; rather, they represent pen technique based on his treatment of the surfaces and textures involved. His treatment of tree trunks was applied to some of my own compositions in Chapter 6: Landscape Subjects. Examine those landscapes, each of which illustrates a different treatment of trees, and compare the effects produced by each treatment.

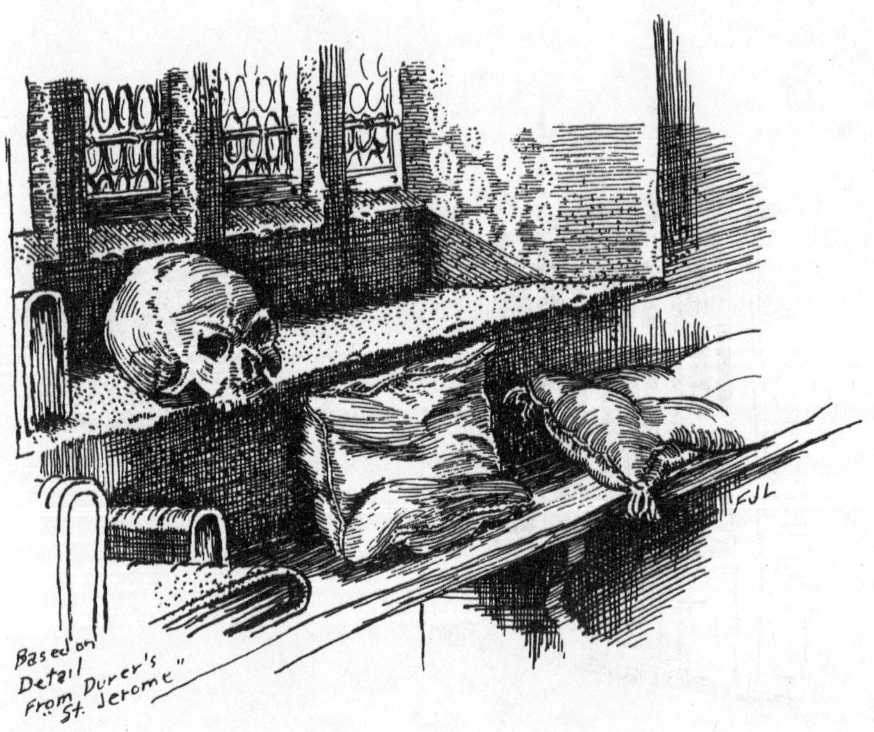

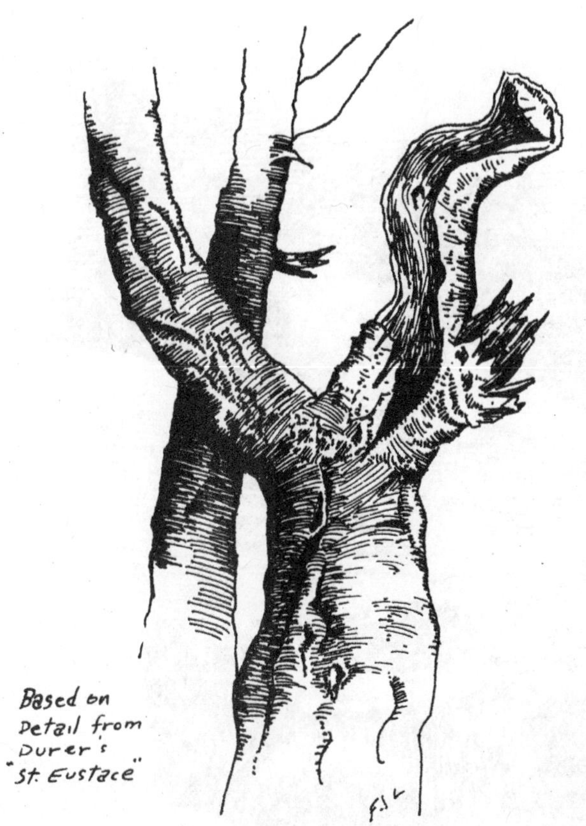

In his *Nativity* Durer's rendering of the thatched roof post-and-beam building is also very useful. Note that the artist did not overdo the thatch and that he gave interest to the building by indicating cracked and eroded stucco with brick work showing through. These techniques can also be applied to suitable subjects in your own sketches.

Take a simple, small pillow, toss it into a chair, and use it as a sketch subject. You can get some ideas on how to depict such a surface from the two pillows in the *Saint Jerome* detail. Also note how Durer treated the worn and chipped edge of the window sill in the same subject.

I strongly recommend careful and thoughtful study of master works such as Durer's. It doesn't matter that his work is seldom seen except in museums. Look at the myriad details, both foreground and background, and you will be certain to find many instructive treatments that you can apply to your own work. As I said in my previous book, this sort of thing "becomes your inventory of ingredients from which you select those you need to create your own original works."

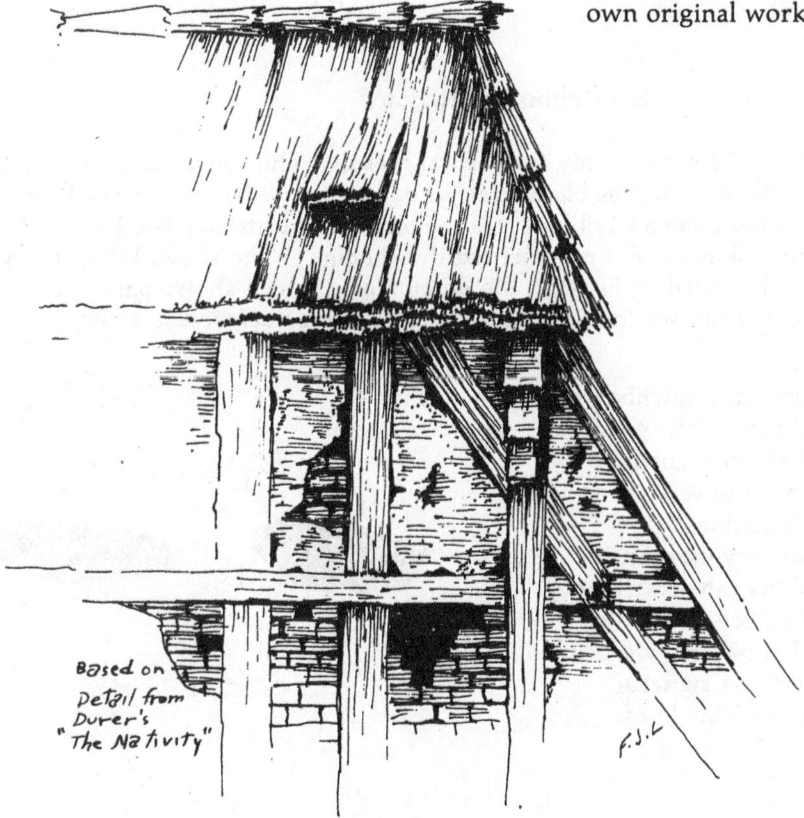

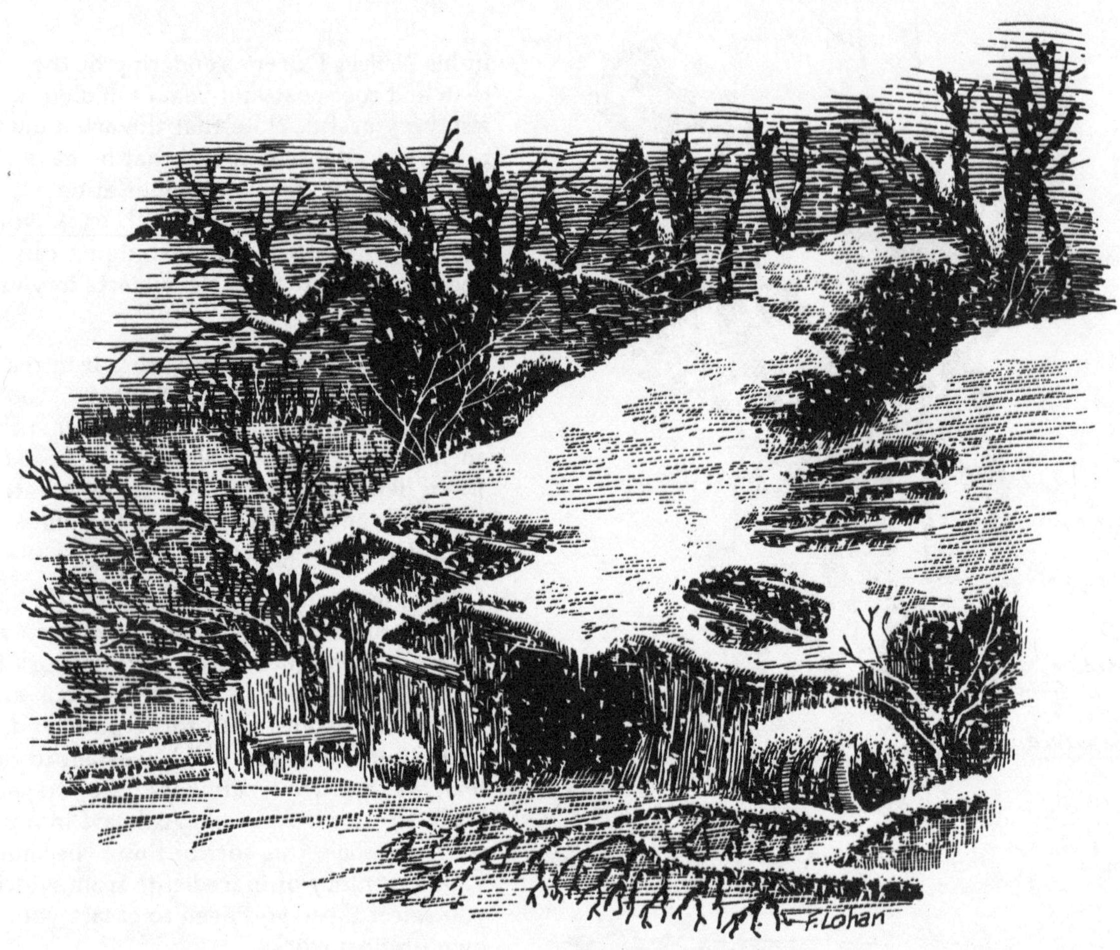

A Scratchboard Blizzard

Scratchboard was a natural for this study for several reasons. The convenience of being able to put white over black as well as black over white was just what was needed for this snow-covered building from a Civil War–era magazine illustration. Also, I wanted the ability to soften the ink lines that represented the shading in the snow. I did this by scratching across the inked shading lines. In the detail study, which shows part of the sketch in early stages, you can see lines in the snow on the roof before and after scratching.

For those not familiar with scratchboard, it is a heavy clay-coated paper. You paint or draw the ink lines on the clay coating. When the ink is dry you can scratch through it to make white lines. Scratchboard tools are very inexpensive (about a dime apiece) and can scratch very fine details in the black. See the small illustration in which I show the two painted areas, one of them with my signature scratched through in very fine lines.

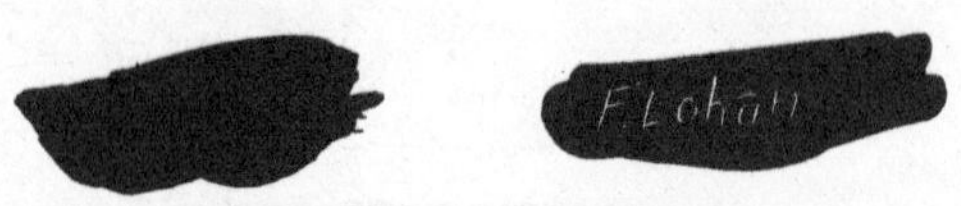

The smaller studies show partially completed details to give you a better idea of how I proceeded on this sketch. As usual, I painted in the solid black areas after doing a tight pencil drawing, but I made the pencil lines as faint as possible on the scratchboard. Then I put the line work in with a pen. A word of caution: *Do not* use your technical or rapidograph-type pen on scratchboard—the coating can cause the point to clog since the moist ink softens it. Also, it is not a good idea to do much erasing on the scratchboard after the ink has been applied. This can easily remove or lighten the ink in areas you do not want affected.

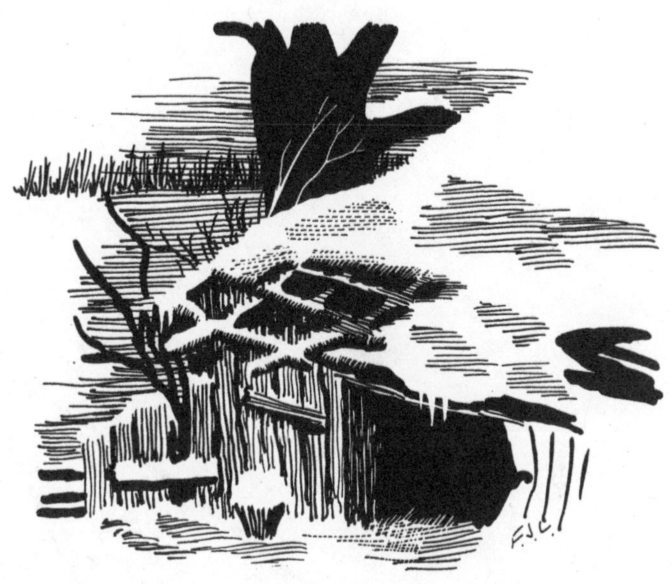

After your ink work is done, you can lend emphasis to some elements with the scratchboard tool, as I did to the branches in the detail study by scratching a white line on one side of the black lines. This works well for rigging on ships as well as for branches when you use a dark-lined sky.

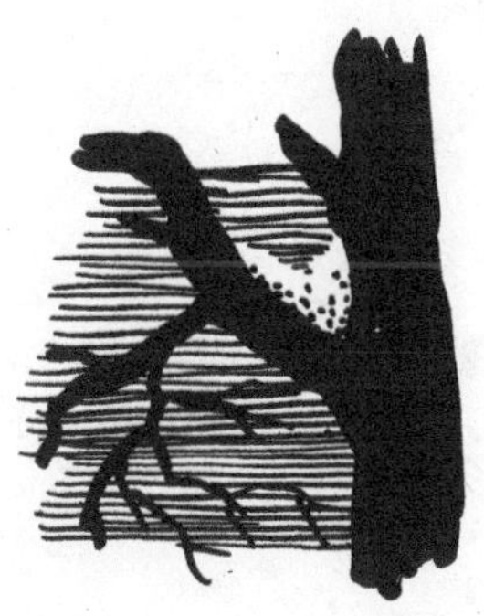

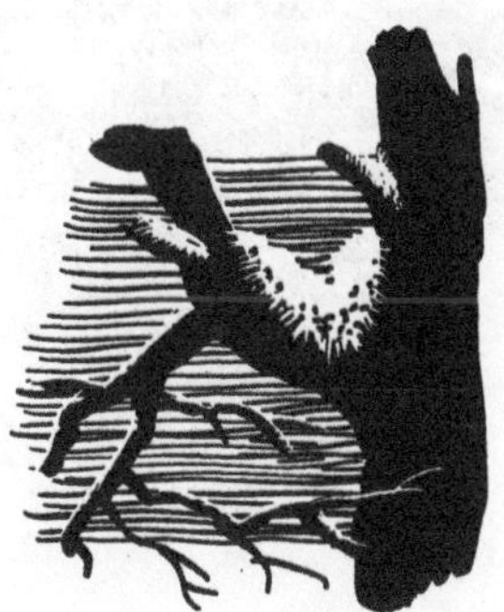

The last thing I did in this sketch was to scratch in the snowflakes. On this exercise I found that I had overdone the snowflakes, so I went back in with a brush and painted some of them out. Scratchboard makes it fun to go from white to black to white again, bringing out the precise effect you want.

This sketch was based on an illustration from a Civil War–era engraving or woodcut. It showed cannon and men in a blizzard with this wreck of a barn off to the side. I liked the barn in the snow with the dark tree trunks behind it, so I eliminated the men, armaments, and other elements of the original.

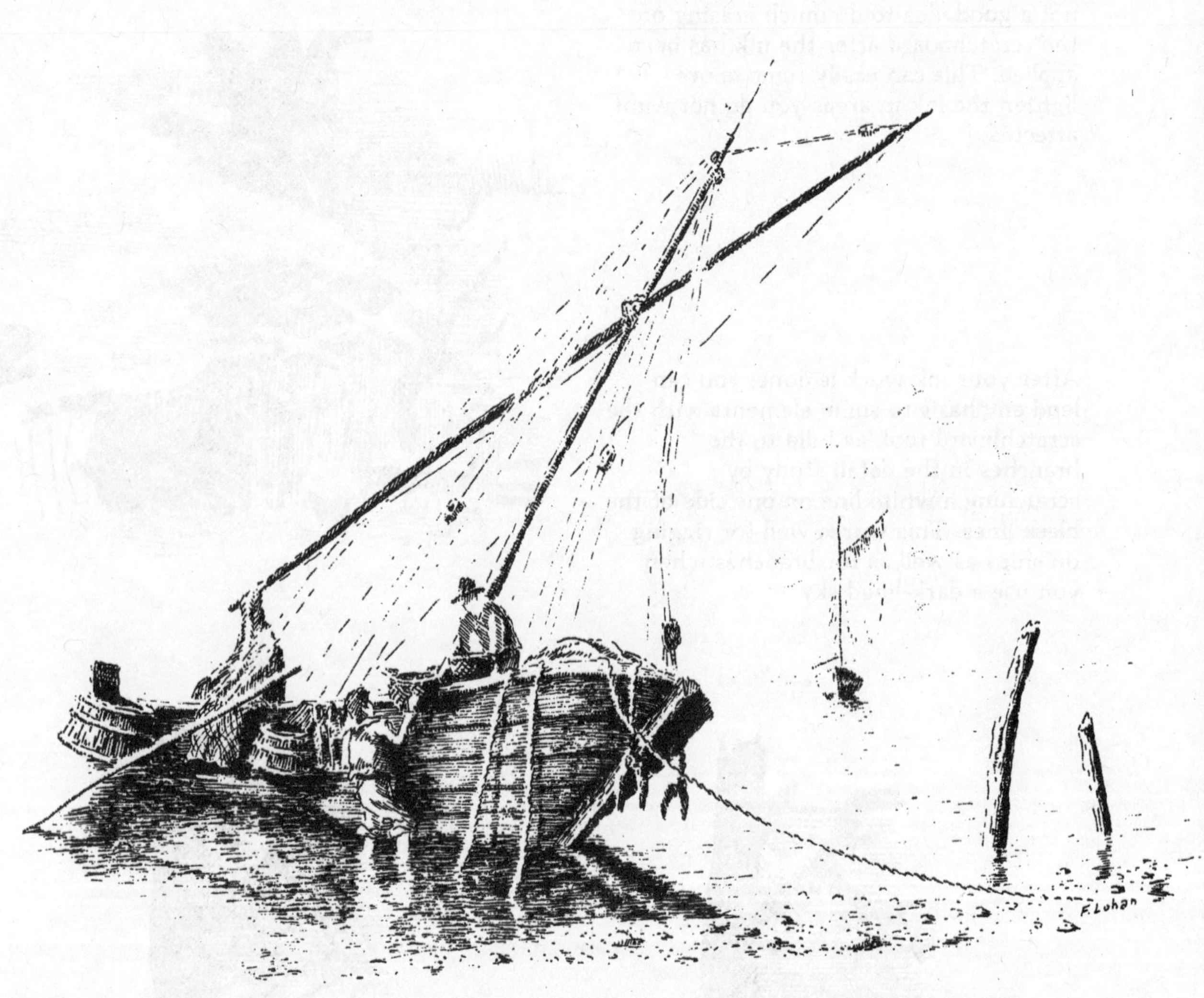

Portuguese Fisherman

3: Atmospheric Effects as Subjects

"How do I show the sky?" is a question my students sometimes ask. My answer is always, "Unless the sky is your subject, your principal focus, I recommend you don't sketch it."

Most of my students are not professional artists. They have a creative drive, which attracts them to art for a variety of personal reasons. They are frequently working people. They are looking for an avocation—an outlet through which they can achieve whatever level of proficiency their time and dedication will allow. Some, of course, have ambitions far beyond their capability. Others have an inherent talent for the medium. "Why," I ask them, "take on something that at best is rather difficult to carry off, even for professionals?" I tell them, "In most cases, the addition of sky and cloud effects, unless you do them very delicately, will tend to clutter your sketch. Achieving the required delicacy of touch takes practice—lots of practice—and lots of mistakes."

This is quite a challenge to toss at a group of students. Some of them react with, "Well, I guess you are right," and they apply themselves to other things. A

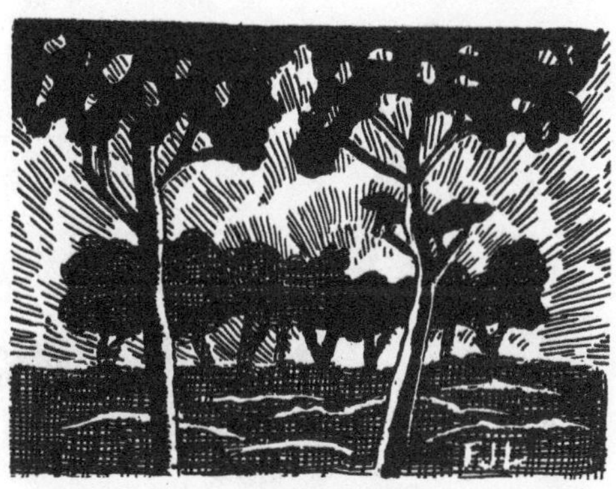

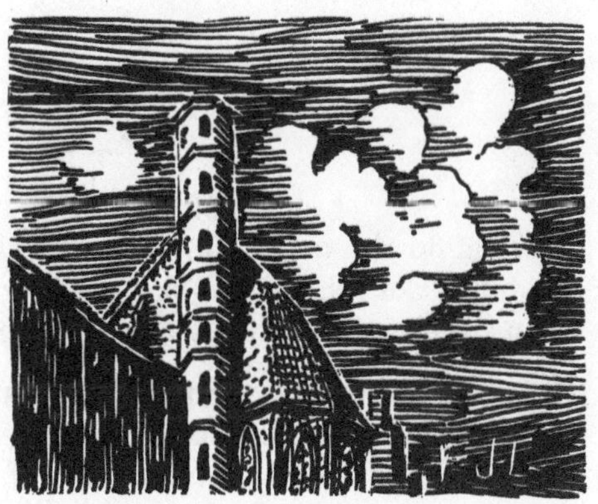

few, however, react in a positive manner to my challenge. They think, "What does he mean, *I* can't do it!" Whenever I toss this challenge out I know that later in the course I will be shown a sketch or two incorporating sky and cloud texture. This permits a good discussion of the subject with the students themselves telling the class how many times they had to try different things before they achieved an effect that satisfied them.

Working with atmospheric effects can be fun but requires a lot of practice, trial, and error.

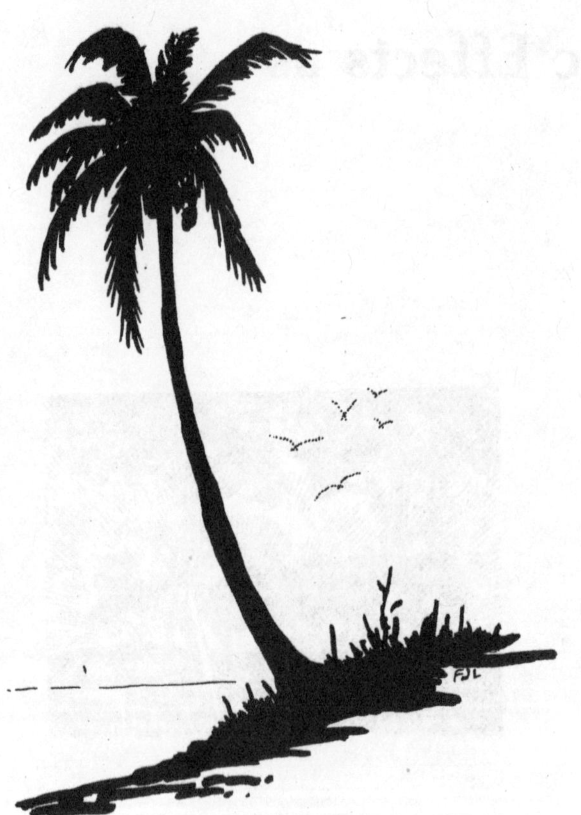

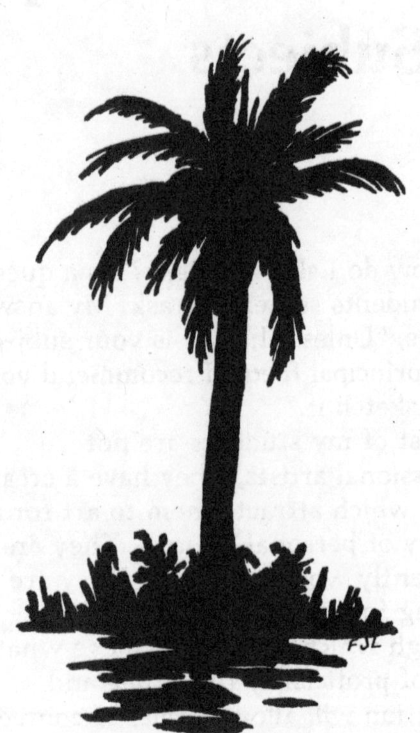

Sundown

There is no sky texture in these sketches. The dazzling, bright, colorful sky is there only by implication, the bright sky and bright water surface implying dusk because of the strong silhouettes. This is one form of atmospheric effect.

This approach—dark silhouette against bright sky—can be particularly effective with palm trees in a tropical scene. Windmills also make unusually attractive silhouettes when properly handled. How about some of your own subjects?

The sketch with the house was done using only a pen; the palm trees were drawn using only a brush. For the windmill I used pen, brush, and the edge of a man-made kitchen sponge. The sponge is the only tool that will create such lacy foliage silhouettes.

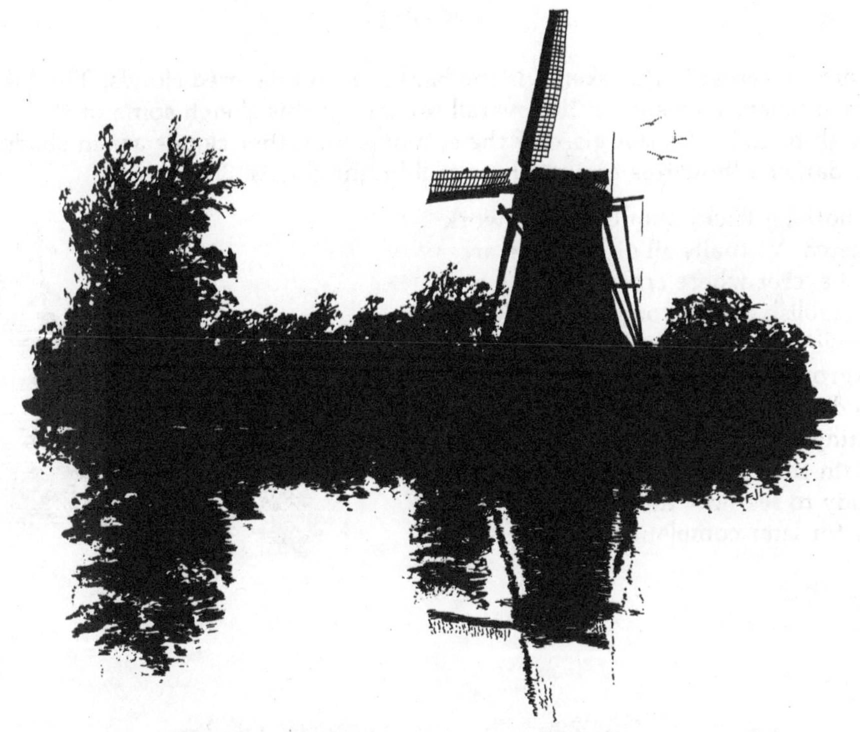

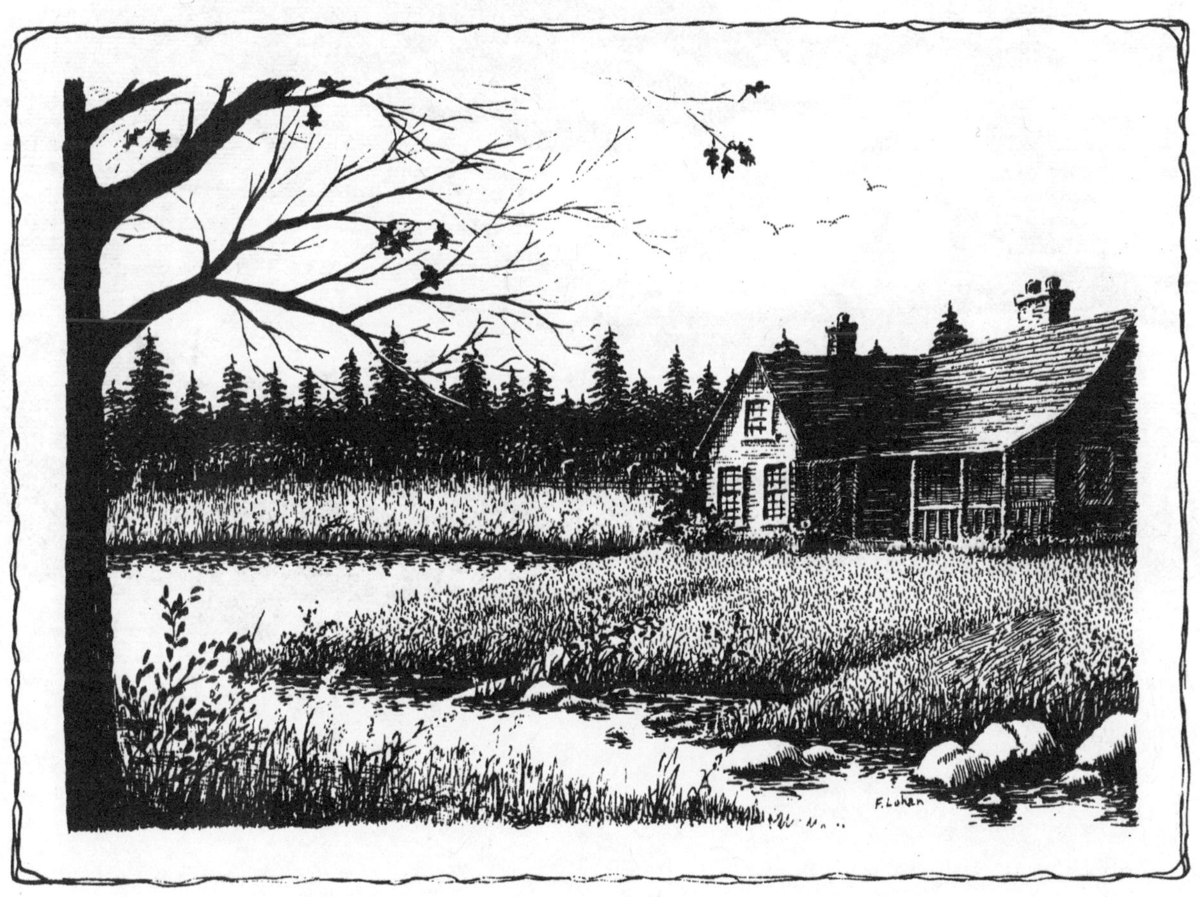
F. Lohan

Evening

The center of interest in this sketch is the banks of multilayered clouds. The hills and trees are subsidiary elements in the overall setting. In this sketch some of the clouds are high enough to catch the last glare of the setting sun. Other clouds are in shadow and appear as darker silhouettes against these still bright clouds.

There is nothing tricky about the pen work in this sketch. Virtually all of the lines are horizontal except where cross-hatching was used to establish darker tones. A careful pencil drawing of the trees was done first. The background was then done in ink, with the trees done last so that the bright areas representing the sunlight hitting the foliage could retain their prominence. Examine the detail study to see how the white areas were left for later completion of these trees.

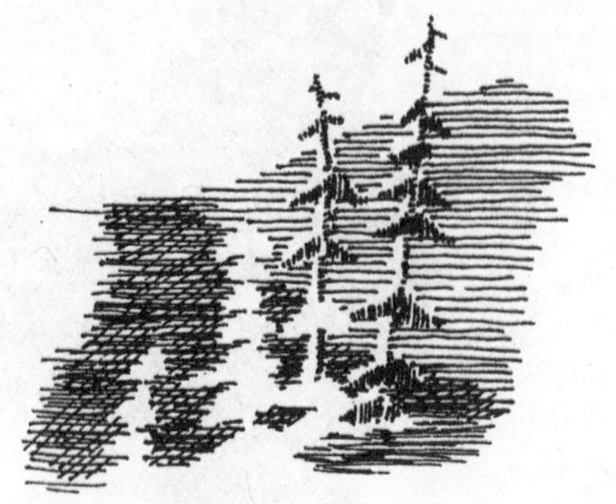

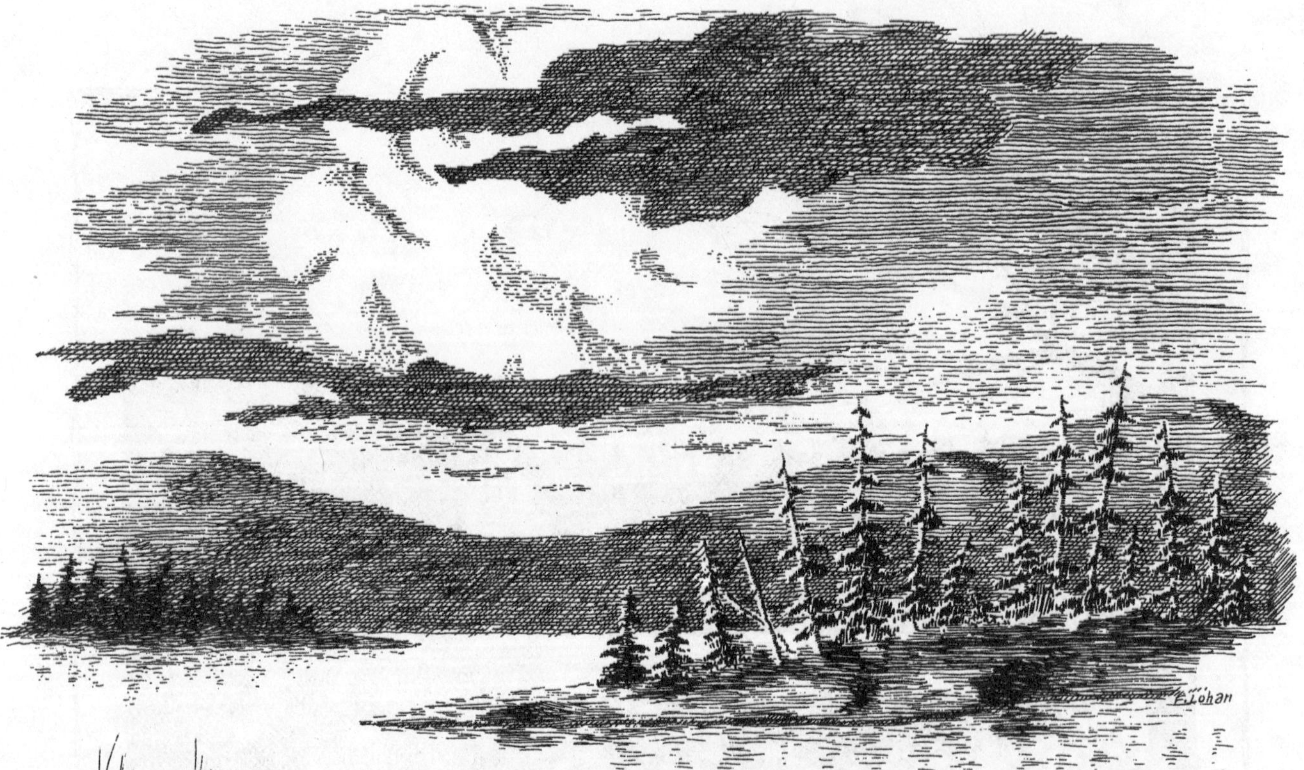

Foggy Day

Fog tends to make all objects appear as flat monotone silhouettes. Only the closest objects show any gradation of tone due to deep shadows and surfaces that receive no reflected light.

For this sketch the structure, rocks, boats, and seagull shapes were first sketched in pencil. Then the dense patches of white fog toward the lower left foreground were

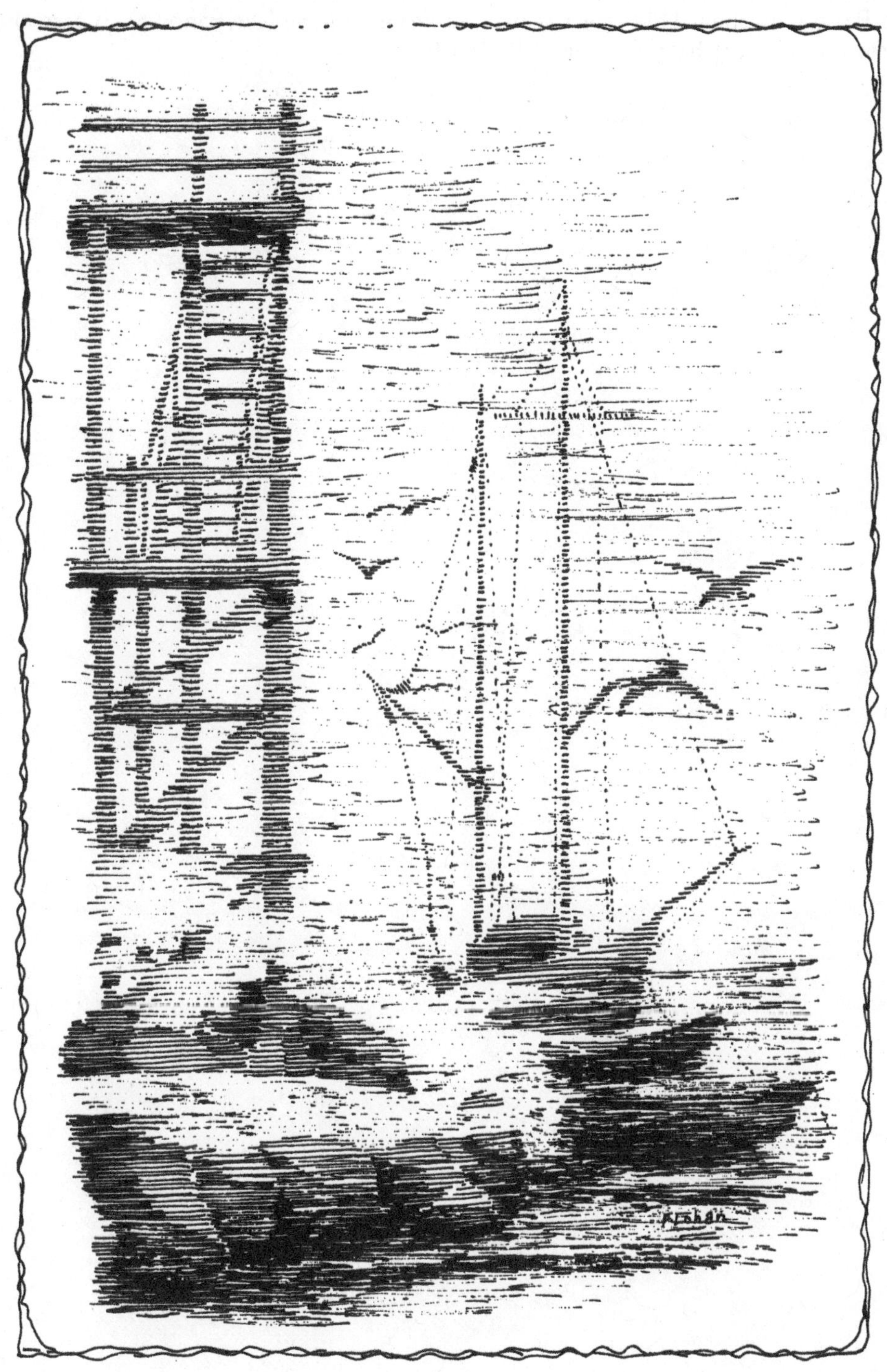

indicated in pencil. The rest was a matter of using horizontal ink strokes exclusively, emphasizing a deep shaded area here and there to give form to the closer rocks and to show a little shade under the two platforms on the wharf structure. The final step was a series of rapid horizontal strokes across the entire sketch, black and white areas, to suggest the general overall fog.

Also look at *Fog on Cannery Row* in Chapter 4, Subjects from Photographs, for other treatments of fog.

Hazy glare in the midday sun causes the same visual effect as fog—distant objects become flat monotones. This effect is used in *Sunny Clearing* (see page 98) to give the impression of a bright hazy summer day in a forest.

4: Subjects from Photographs

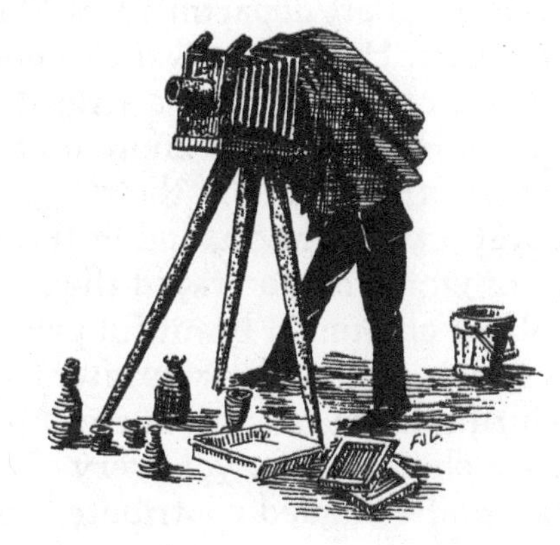

Now we come to the second most plentiful source of sketch ideas—photographs. My personal philosophy on the use of photographs as source material is less conservative than that of some of my artist friends. Some who have mastered a medium, such as oil or watercolor, hold that a photograph should be used as a source only if the real thing is totally inaccessible, and then only if the artist himself took that photograph. These artists do, however, use photographs for the study of detail that might otherwise be impossible to discern or to learn more about the structure of a subject.

This second point—using photographs for studying and clarifying details—represents an extremely valid course of action. Serious artists who are confidently competent have no need for copying. They do indeed, however, know the value of studying a subject from all aspects before they create their own composition and their own rendition of that subject.

As an example of this point, Arthur Chargois, who wrote the foreword to this book, recently showed me his very effective oil painting of a herd of zebras galloping across a hot, dusty African

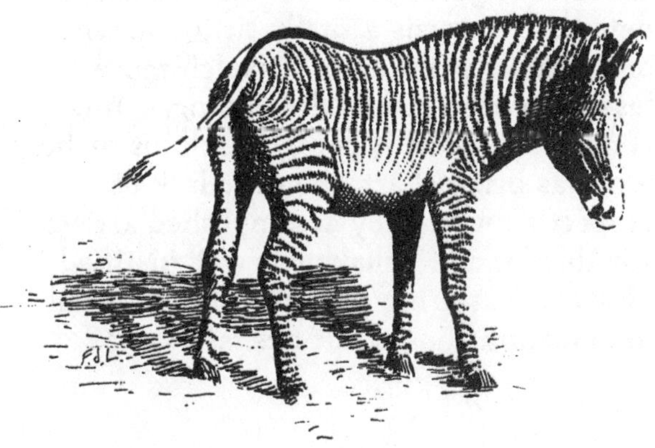

Grevy's zebra

plain. He told me that he had first researched and studied all information he could obtain, including illustrations, concerning the zebra. He learned the difference between Chapman's zebra and Grevy's zebra (the former has broad stripes with shadow stripes between them while the latter has long ears and numerous narrow stripes). He found out that while in one South African subspecies the stripes do not extend to the lower limbs, the East African zebra does indeed have the lower limbs striped and lacks the shadow stripes . . .

Enough! This is not a treatise on the zebra. My point is that he is a thoroughly accomplished artist of excellent merit, having been professor of art and head of the commercial art department of DuCret School of Art. He did not want to portray just the *idea* of the zebra as a striped quadruped. He wanted to know that his zebras were true to life in their configuration, coloration, and in the habitat in which he portrayed them. He cared about creating a beautiful painting that was also technically accurate. He did not paint his animals from one of his reference photographs, yet every photograph he studied contributed to his painting. This is the proper use of photographs for the accomplished artist.

The first point in the initial paragraph of this section concerns the use of photographs for more than just reference about configuration or for clarification of detail. It concerns actually sitting down and doing a painting or a sketch more or less composed just as the photograph is composed. If one is going to sell his or her work as original art, then the lack of respect expressed by accomplished artists for this kind of behavior is well justified. However, aspiring students of any visual art medium should not hesitate to use appropriate photographs for practice or studies of composition if the photograph inspires them. I hold that any inspiration for practice work is valid inspiration because proficiency in any medium requires practice and practice and then more practice. Whatever gets you going is great!

I stated above that my view on the use of photographs is less conservative than some. I guess I feel this way because, although I have sometimes started out to copy some photograph, I almost always have felt that a different angle or elevation, or a considerable rearrangement of elements, would create a composition more suitable to my goals. So in reality, for me anyway, a photograph really acts as a general concept for the composition that rapidly tends to become mine. I feel this is a valid use of photographs that may not have been taken by the artist. Such license, however, requires a fairly good grasp of fundamental perspective drawing in order to alter the viewpoint from that which the photographer used, especially if structures are involved. A second point I want to make is that it is usually a particular detail in a photograph that attracts my attention rather than the total composition. Again, the photograph acts as a catalyst rather than as a ready-made composition.

The availability of photographic work is limitless if you read newspapers and magazines or have access to a library. In increasing your proficiency with the pen, do not hesitate to use this almost universal source of subject matter.

I started this chapter by indicating that photography is the second most plentiful source of sketch ideas. The most plentiful and best source, of course, will always be the real thing.

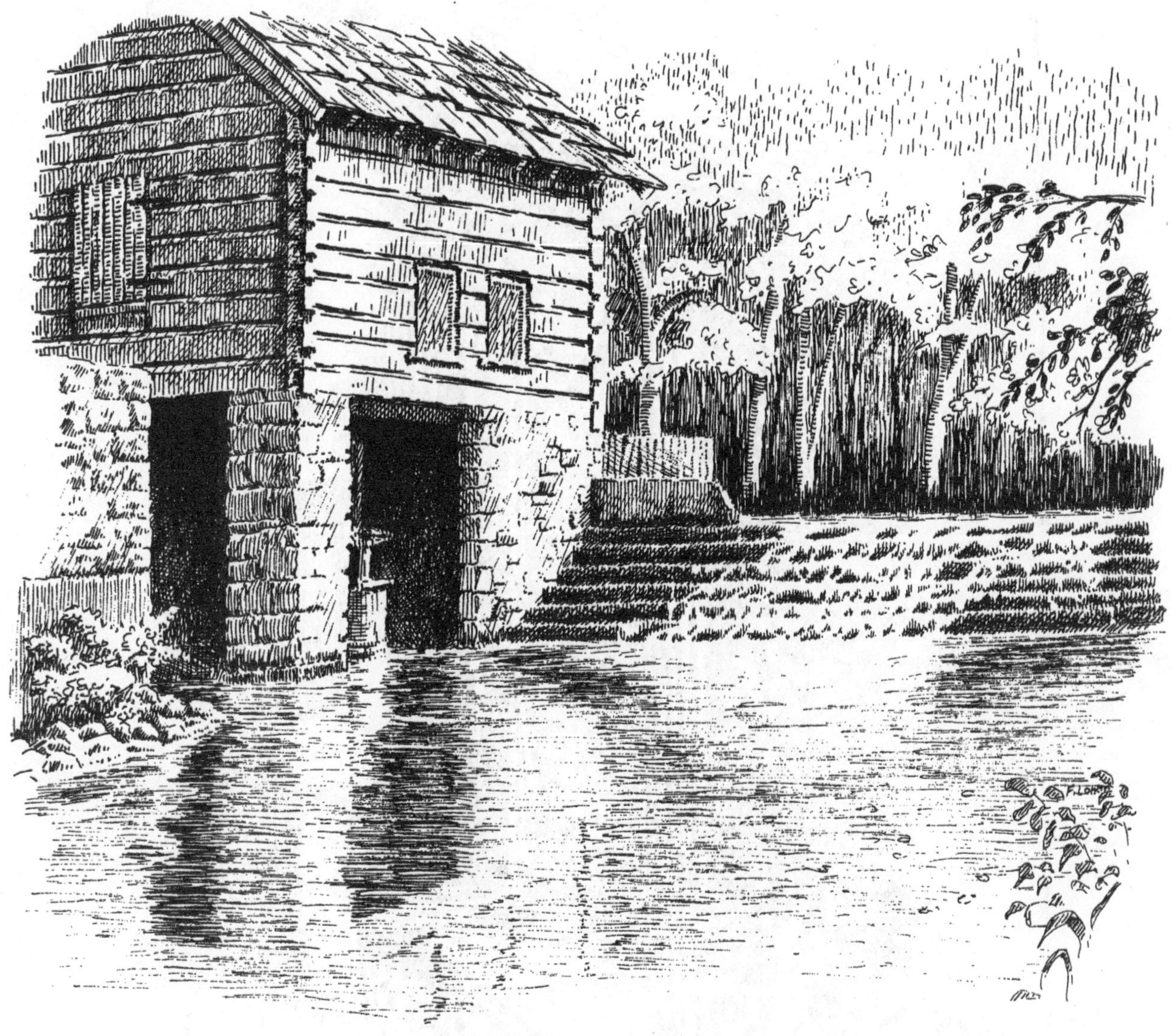

Below the Millpond

This sketch was based on a photograph that was printed in a magazine. The photograph showed much more of the surrounding forest on both sides of the mill. I really wanted the water cascading down the stepped dam to be the center of interest, so I eliminated quite a bit of the forest and simplified a lot of the visible detail on the mill itself.

I used a fine pen to do this sketch, with good pencil guidelines that were later erased. I took special care in placing the few strokes in the white water cascade, since there was a real possibility of overdoing it and spoiling the effect.

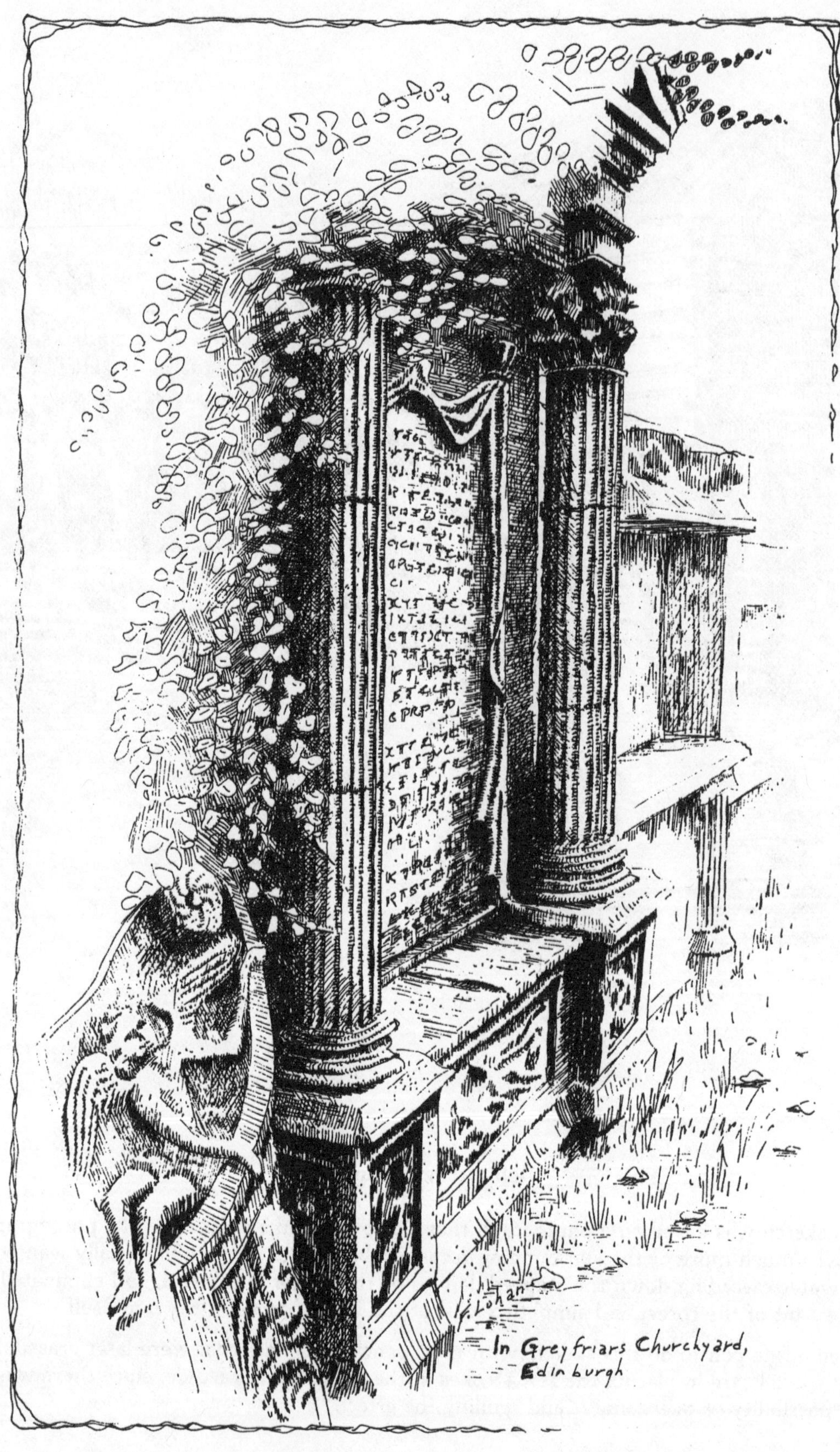
In Greyfriars Churchyard,
Edinburgh

Greyfriars Churchyard, Edinburgh

This elaborately carved mausoleum was part of a photograph in a book on Scotland. The photograph showed much more of the burial ground and included a good bit of the city beyond; I chose to ignore these details.

The ivy-covered stonework of this one element of the photograph attracted me. You too should look for some element, some detail, which you can abstract from a photo. This selection process is similar to what you must do when sketching on location anywhere—you must zero in on a single subject and eliminate all else. On location, of course, you have full vision in all directions so selecting a single subject is perhaps a bit more complicated than when looking at a photograph. Still, a photo will generally show much more than you need for a sketch, thus offering you an opportunity to practice being selective.

In this photograph a mass of intricate detail was presented to the eye: the thousands of ivy leaves, the fluted columns, the high relief panels on the base of the mausoleum, the carved lettering and drapery between the columns. Adequate suggestion of such detail is all that is required to guide the mental process of the viewer to complete them. Do not attempt to include too much detail in your sketch. After all, you really are only trying to put forth a suggestion. You should not try to impart the same detail that a photograph would.

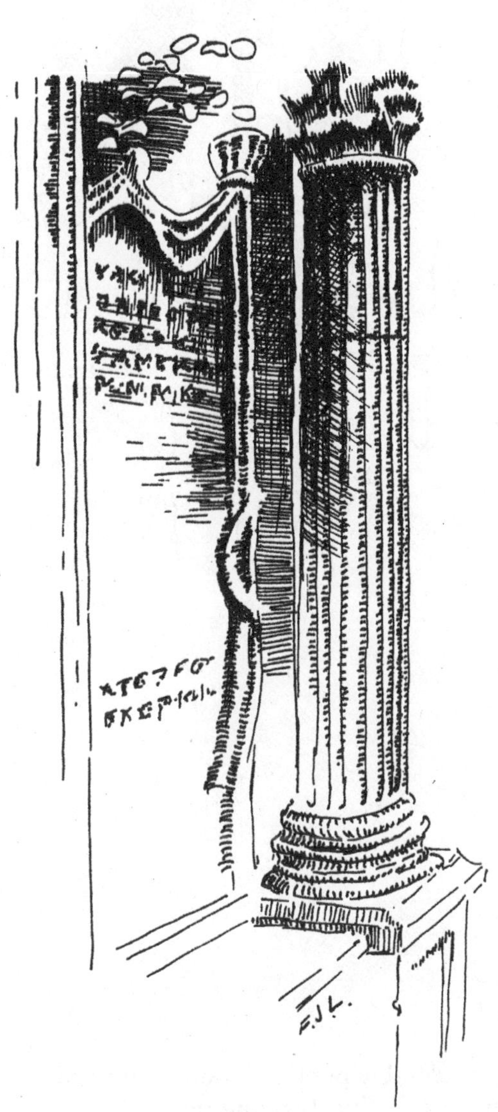

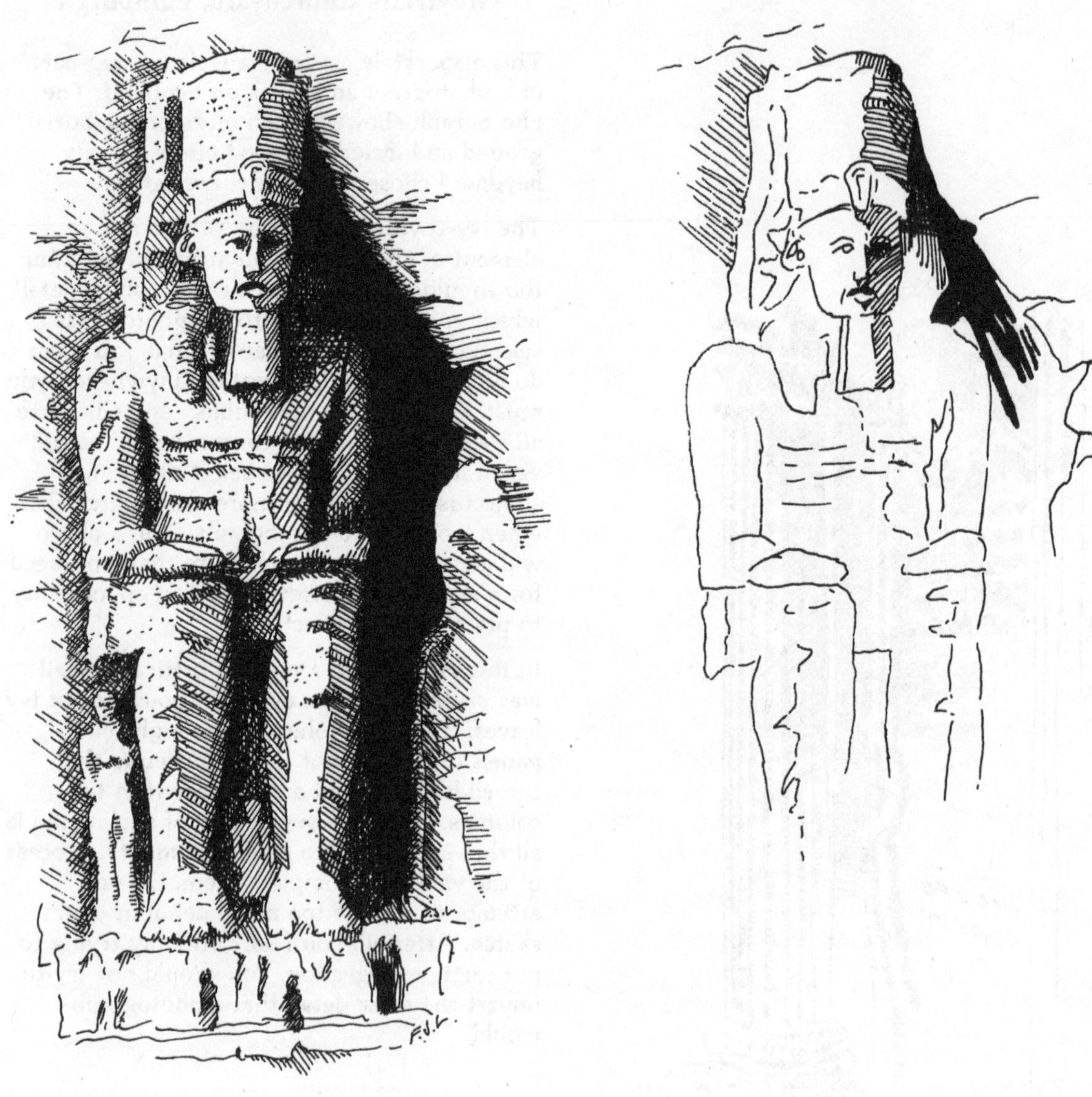

Abu Simbel

This magnificent temple along the Nile received considerable publicity some years ago when the proposed Aswan Dam threatened to inundate it. But, through one of the most challenging engineering feats ever, the huge cliff that housed the temple and its gigantic seated deities was cut into sections, raised, and reassembled above the proposed water level. This sketch came from one of the myriad photographs taken at that time.

Basically this is a four-tone sketch—solid black done with a brush, two gray tones using the pen, and finally the white paper. Lots of dots and squiggles, as well as irregular outlines representing the chipped rock, were used to help indicate the texture. By the way, just as every rule has its exception, my frequent admonition to avoid outlining does not hold here. This is an outline sketch enhanced by the four tones mentioned above.

Colt

This fuzzy little fellow was sketched from a small photograph. I enlarged it by first laying a grid of squares drawn on an acetate sheet over the photograph and drawing larger squares on my paper so that I had an easy reference for obtaining an enlarged outline.

Just as with the bear in *The Old Timers* (see page 2), the fuzzy texture of this colt is suggested primarily by the broken, fuzzy outline treatment, which is done first. After depicting the lips, eye, and nostril, I began showing the shadows. Then I put just enough texture marks on his face and neck, taking care not to make the colt look too dark.

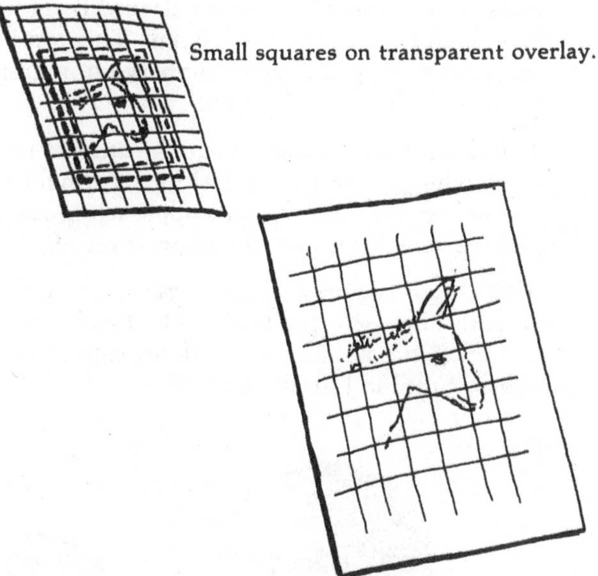

Small squares on transparent overlay.

Larger squares on sketch paper to enlarge from the photograph.

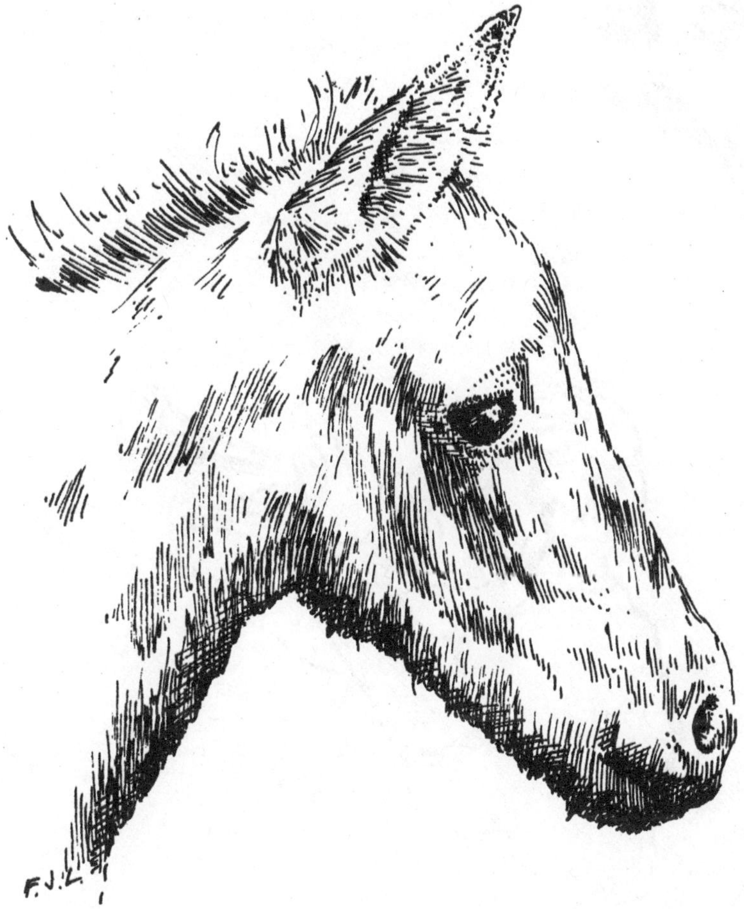

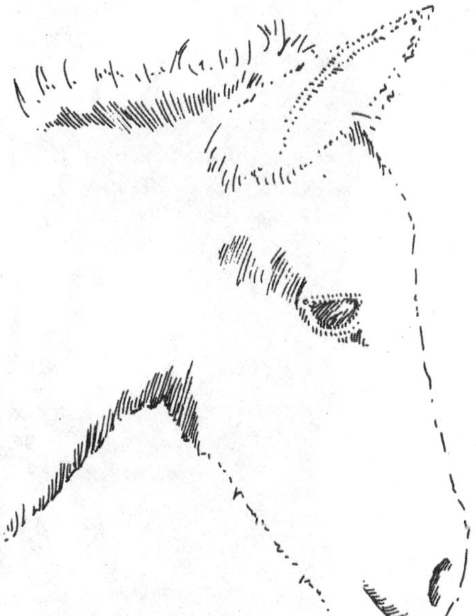

People in the Newspapers

Both of these sketches were enlarged from newspaper photographs. Such photos often have high contrast and lack detail. This can be beneficial if you are using them as subjects, since you have to simplify photographs and eliminate a lot of detail anyway when you sketch from them.

The horn player was a very high-contrast reproduction—virtually just solid blacks and stark whites. It was a natural for treatment with a brush rather than with a pen, since I wanted to use this two-tone approach in my sketch. The exclusion of detail on the horn player's face helps give the impression of a bright spotlight flooding him with light.

This sketch required a careful pencil outline of the horn and then carefully executed smooth lines with the brush. The figure was done loosely and quickly with the brush and ink. The outlines of the figure and shadow shapes were done using a 000 watercolor brush; to fill in I used a 0 brush.

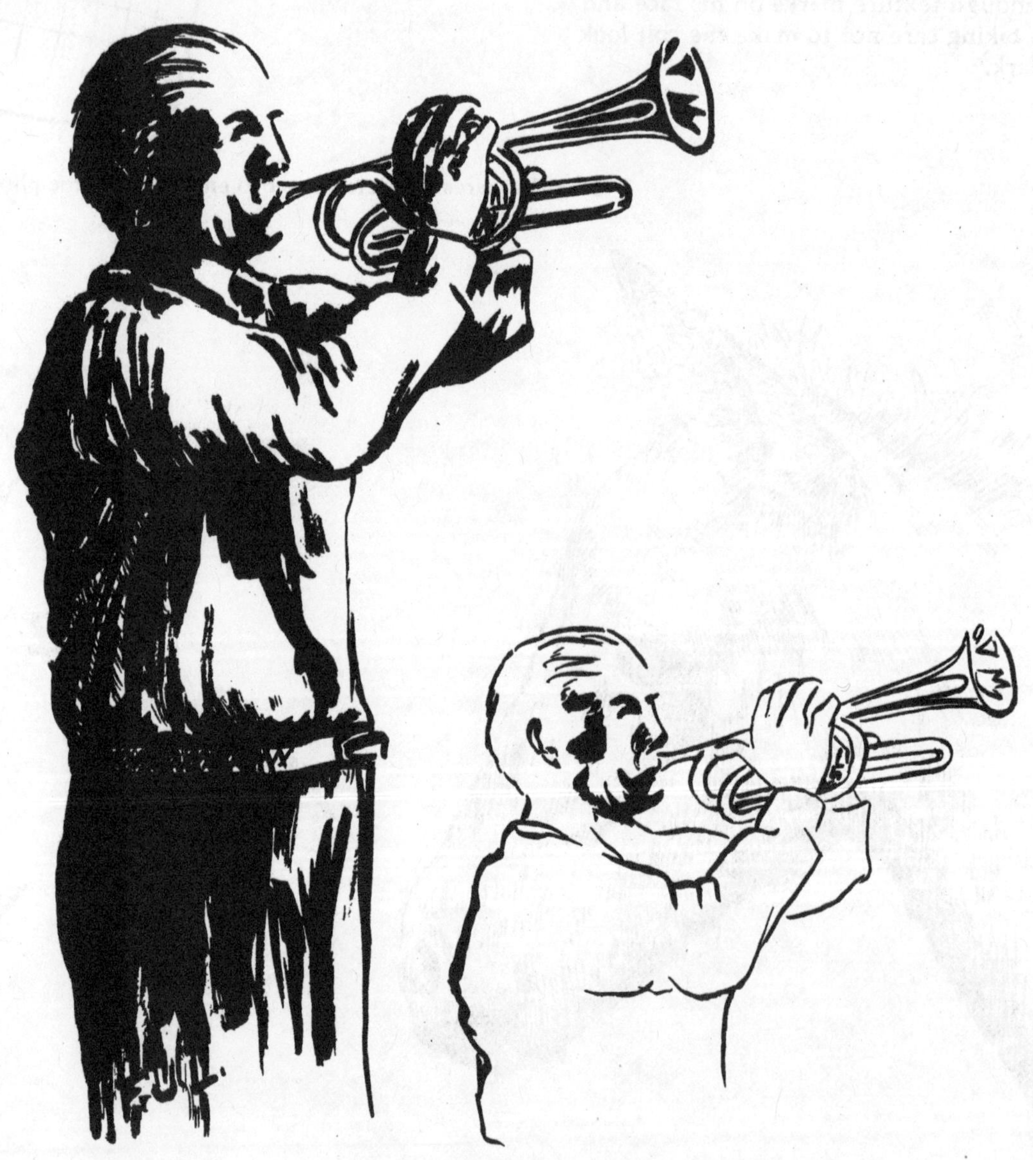

The telephone lineman and utility pole formed a simple but interesting V-shaped composition. In this case I chose to do the sketch with a pen, although it would also come off well as a three-tone sketch done with a brush—solid black, hatch work with the brush for gray, and solid white. Why don't you try that with this composition? Just about everything in this sketch is merely suggested by a few strokes—look at the lineman's face and the wires hanging out of the junction box. This is an outline drawing created with a continuous back-and-forth squiggle line for most of the dark tones.

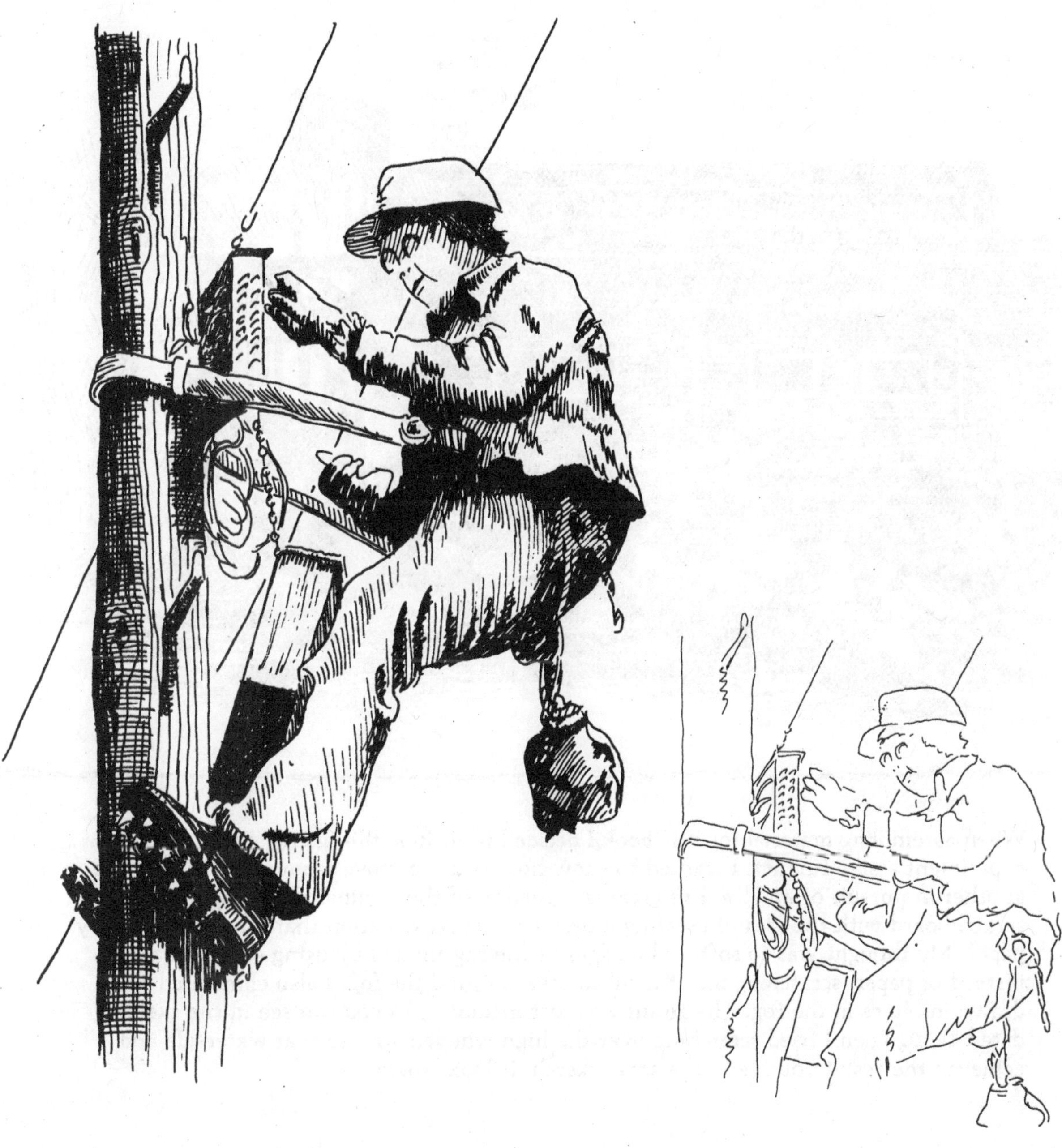

Fog on Cannery Row

I did this little sketch about two years ago. It shows one of the old buildings on Cannery Row in Monterey, California. I had been there earlier, but I did no sketching on that trip. Later, at home, I saw a photograph showing fingers of fog creeping in from the sea and grasping one of the buildings I had seen not long before. This sketch illustrates my attempt to suggest that kind of fog. I was not totally satisfied with the result, but I kept the sketch to show students at least one way of attempting to sketch fog.

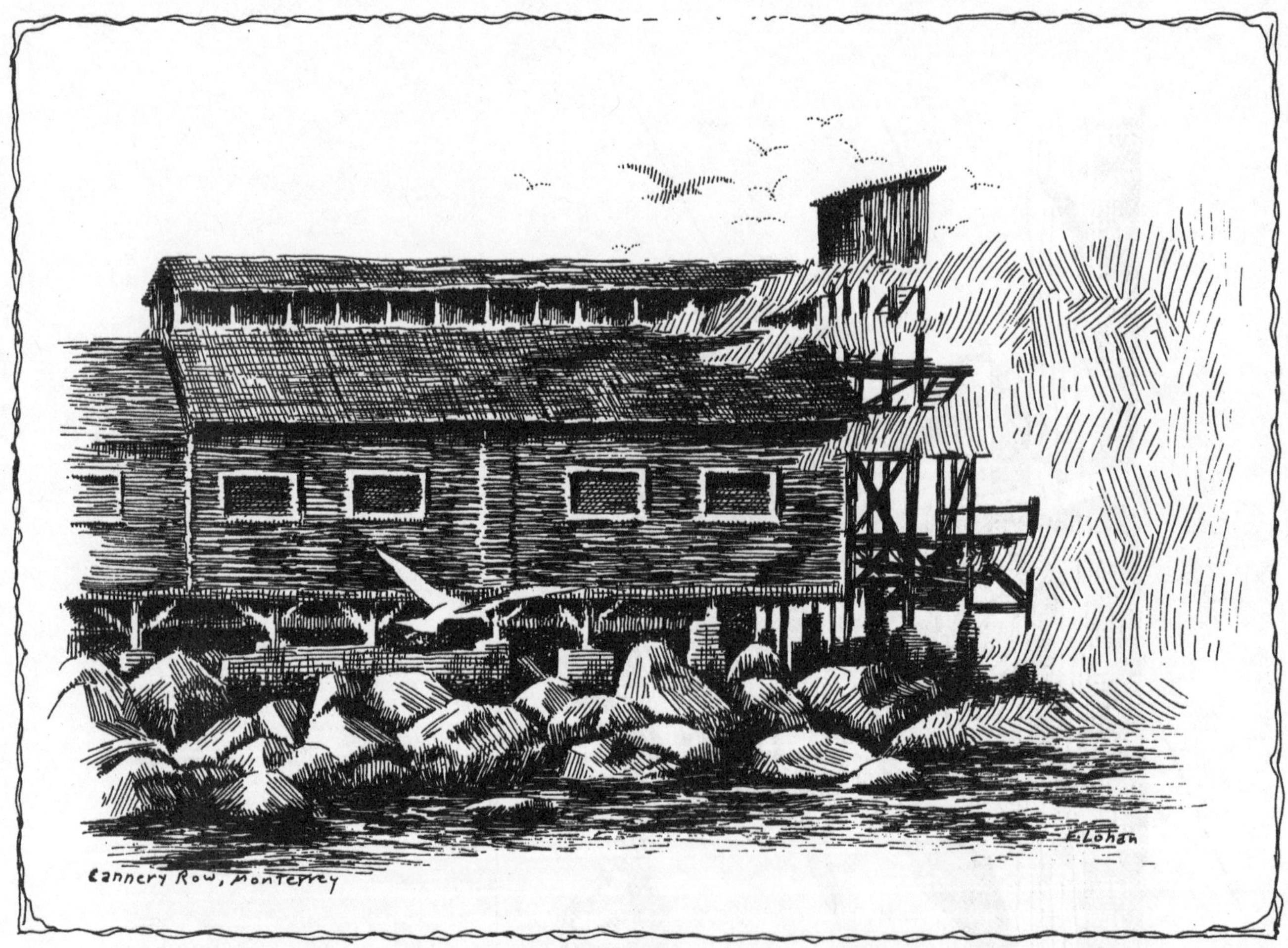

When assembling material for this book I decided to include this sketch and to carry the experiment a step further. I wanted to show how you can move from one treatment to another in pursuit of an idea. I re-created a portion of the original sketch on scratchboard with the idea of creating a better fog representation than I had on ordinary paper. My thought was to soften the edges of the fog fingers by using scratchboard instead of paper, scratching into the inked areas around the fog. I also eliminated the drawn ink lines in the fog. The result was just mediocre, as you can see in the sketch dated 1980. Then I tried scratching over the high wooden structure at waterside and achieved the result you see in the same sketch. It looks foggy.

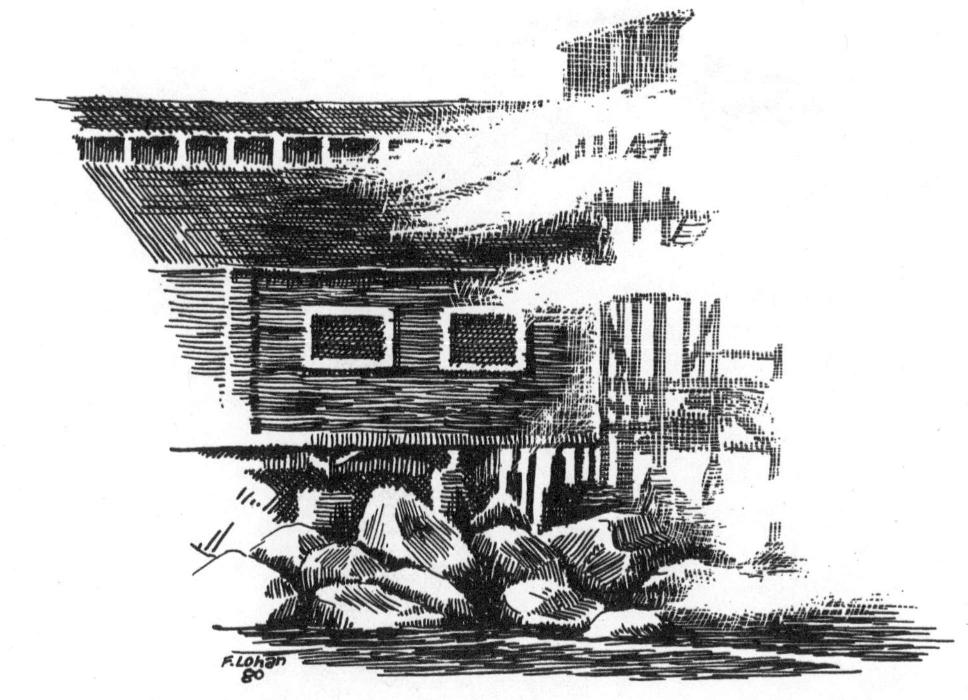

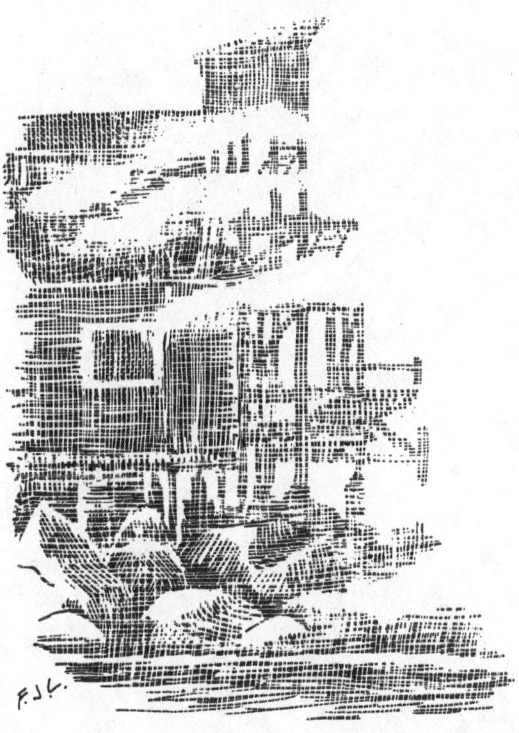

The effect of this scratching led me to imagine that if I scratched over the whole sketch it would certainly look more like the fog had moved in completely. So I again re-created a portion of the sketch on a piece of scratchboard and scratched all over it. The result was interesting, as you can see in the smallest sketch.

Scratchboard is a lot of fun to work with. Compare this use of it with the *Scratchboard Blizzard* (page 34). In that sketch the ability to alternate black on white and white on black was also used to achieve an effect that would be rather difficult on plain paper.

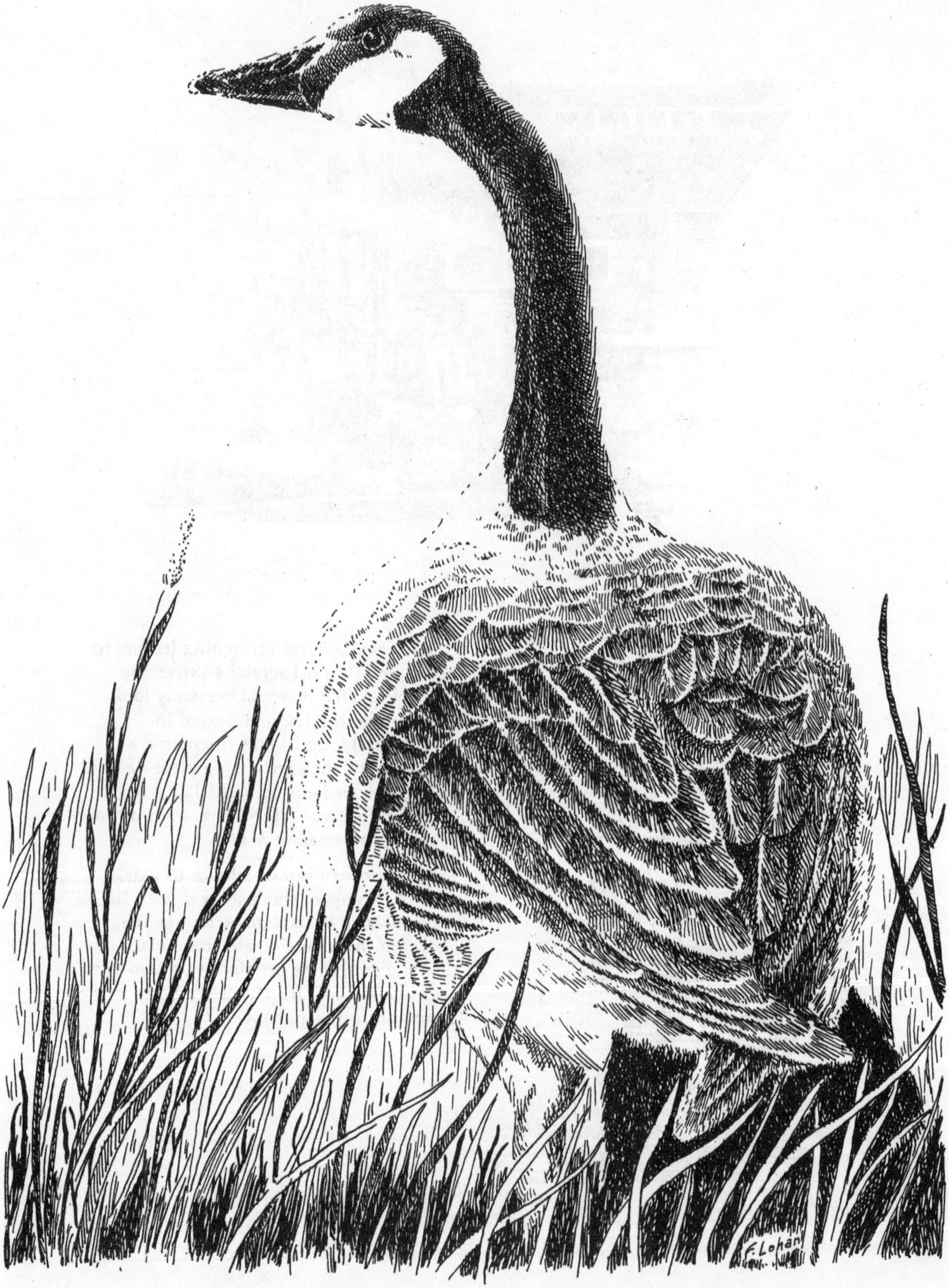

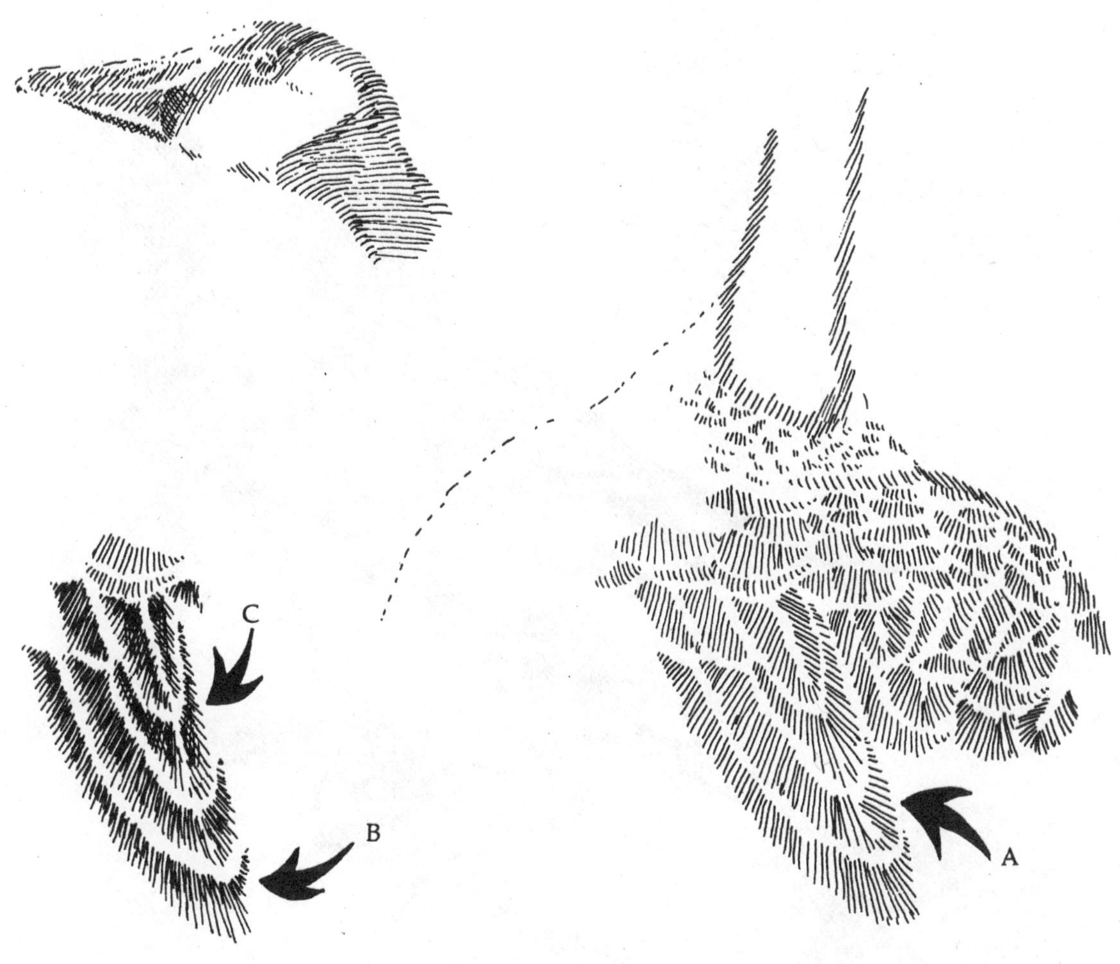

Canada Goose

The photograph I used as a model for the sketch of this goose was large and had enough detail to show the structure of the feathers on the bird's back. I made a careful pencil sketch, placing each feather on the bird and showing the quill running down the length of some of the larger ones.

The first ink work was done as shown on the bird's head and beak in the detail sketch. Then I did the neck and the first layer of ink work on the large back and wing feathers as shown at **A**. The second time over these feathers, I used strokes in the same direction as the first. You can see this at **B**. The third time over these feathers, I placed just a few strokes of cross-hatching, as shown at **C**.

When building up dark tones, such as on the head and neck of the goose, it is best to follow the principle generally used with watercolors—proceed from light to dark. Therefore, I first made a single layer of hatching over the goose's neck—this set the lightest tone in this black area. Then I used cross-hatching to build up the darker tones, being careful to leave some of the first, single hatch work for the highlight that runs from the head to the body. The darkest areas on the neck were achieved with three superimposed layers of ink.

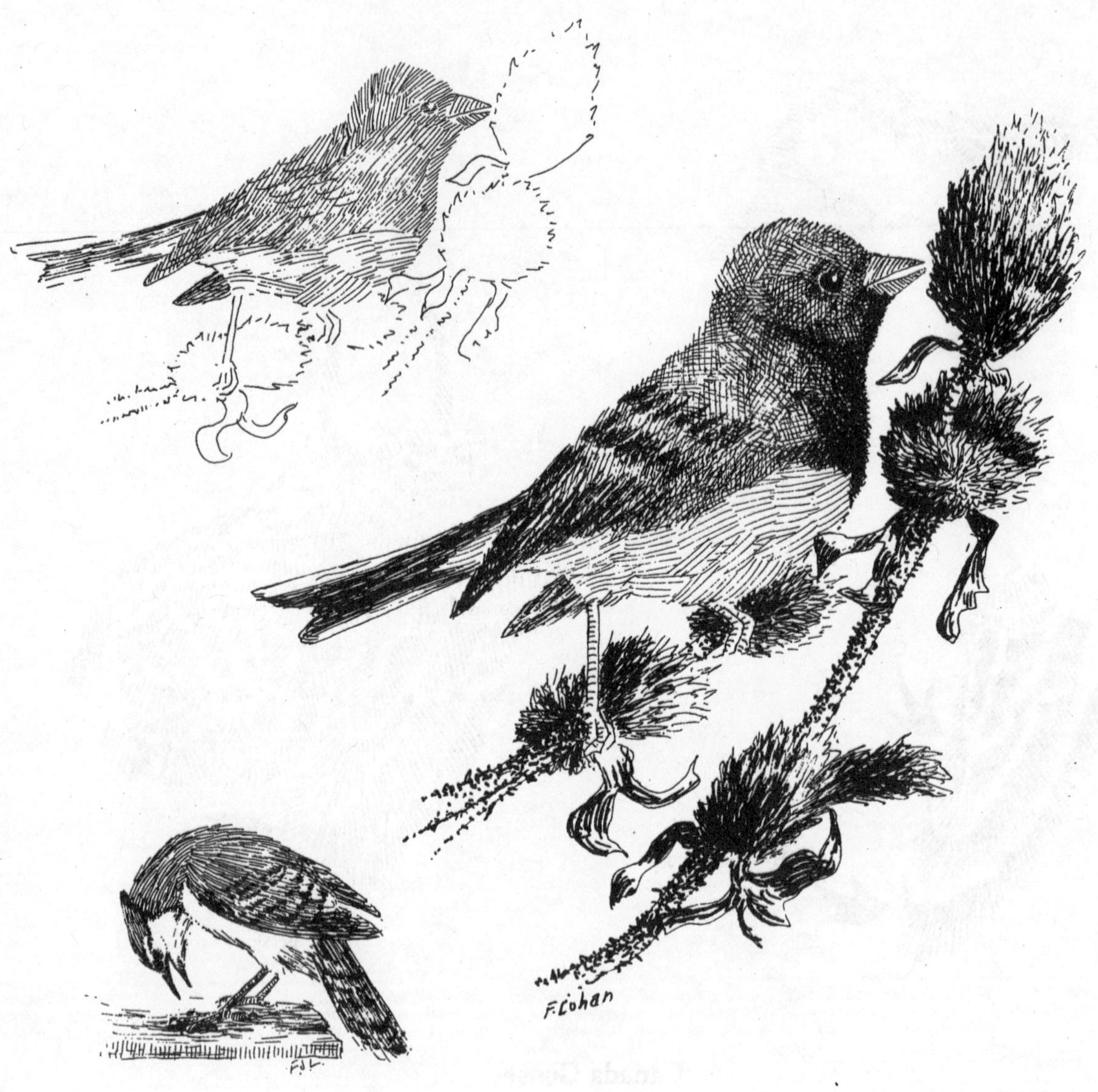

Junco

These sketches were not done from photographs but are included here to supplement the preceding discussion on the much larger Canada goose.

The little junco, or snowbird, is a frequent winter visitor at our bird feeders. The beak, undersides, and outer tail feathers are white, while the rest of the bird is a dark slate gray with some of the wing feathers and tail being even darker.

I did the light colors in this sketch with one layer of fairly loose hatching. I did the overall gray with two layers of tighter crosshatch. The darks received a third and, in some places, a fourth layer of ink. The shapes of the dark wing feathers were drawn first with the overall gray hatching and cross-hatching superimposed over these lines, as you can see in the partially completed detail.

The amount of detail you include in any sketch depends on the size of the sketch. The smaller one here that shows a bluejay has almost no fine detail in the wing and tail areas other than suggestions of black bars and white feathers.

Bodiam Castle

These sketches and the stone barn sketches that follow show how I treat relatively smooth stone—just a few indications of the cracks between the stone blocks on the sunlit surface. For contrast, look at the sketch called *Progress* (see page 26). This subject had rough, irregular stones forming the barn foundation and required more texturing to indicate the roughness.

The sketch of Bodiam Castle was done with a Hunt 104 point—a very fine, inexpensive replaceable nib. I did the small detail using a much heavier fountain pen point to show the various effects that different point sizes have and to demonstrate how a bold pen stroke can also indicate texture and shade very effectively.

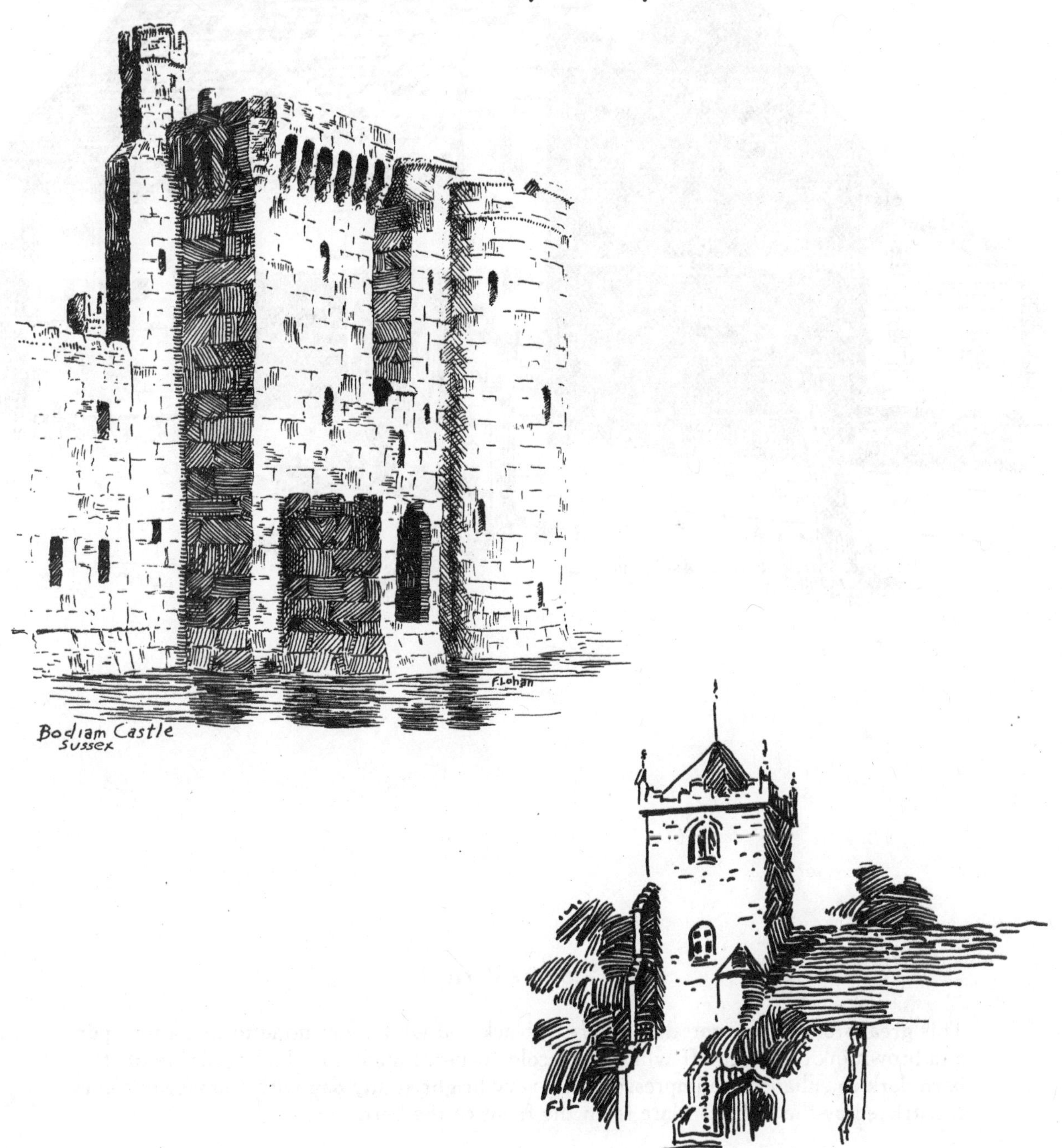

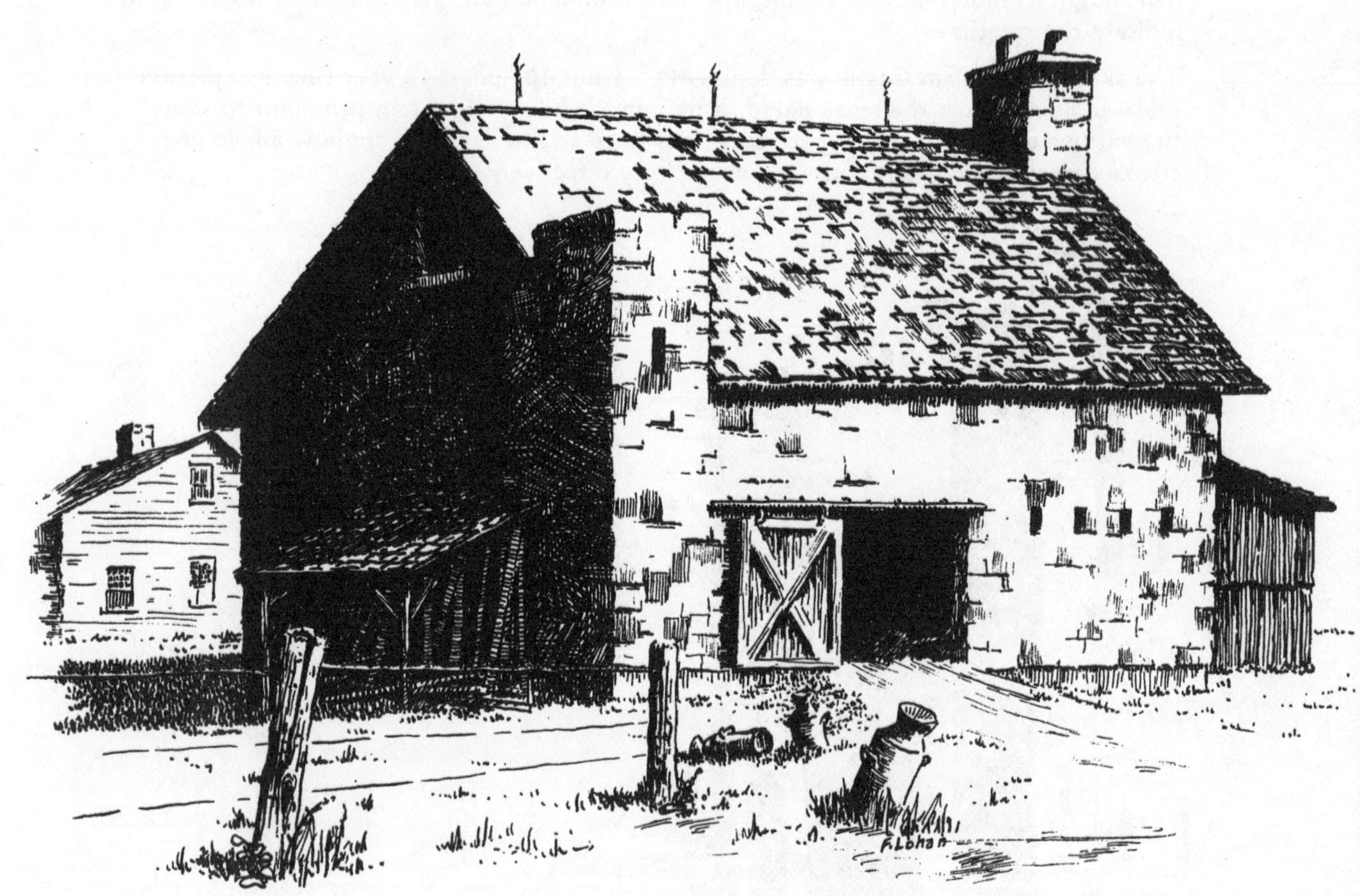

Stone Barn

This great stone barn, reproduced here in black and white, was done to test a new pen and brown ink on rough off-white watercolor paper. I made the shadowed side of the barn dark to enhance the impression of a very bright sunny day with the viewer's eyes constricted by the brilliant glare from the front of the barn.

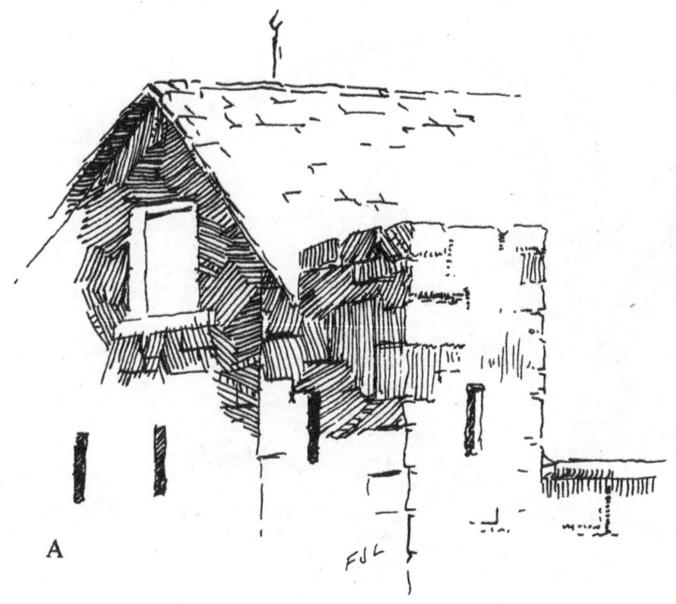

As shown in the partially completed sketch (sketch A), I first indicated some of the stone work on both the sunny side and the shady side of the barn. Then I built up crosshatches over these indications on the shady side. On the sunny side I simply darkened some of the stones here and there.

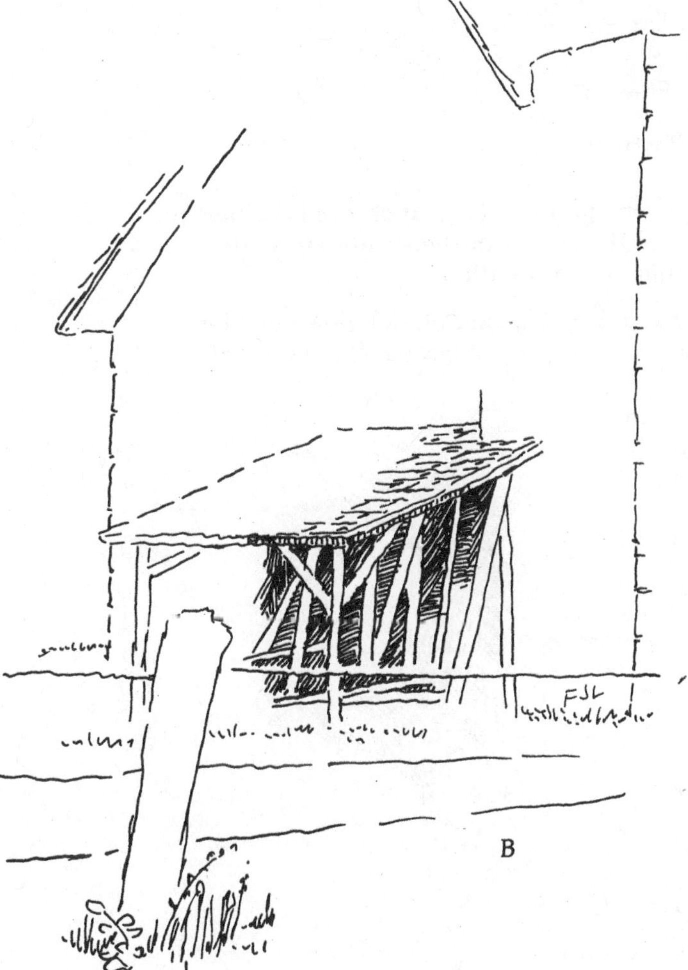

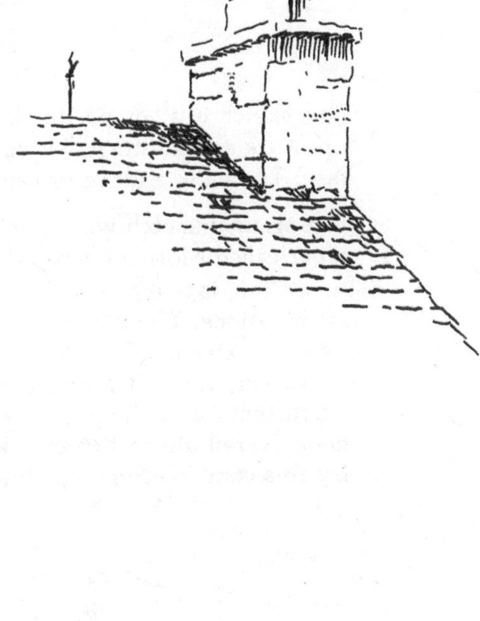

I left the wood standing and lying under the small roof on the left untextured (sketch B) until the shade was completed around it. Then I could tell just how much to darken it with hatching without losing it in the surrounding dark area.

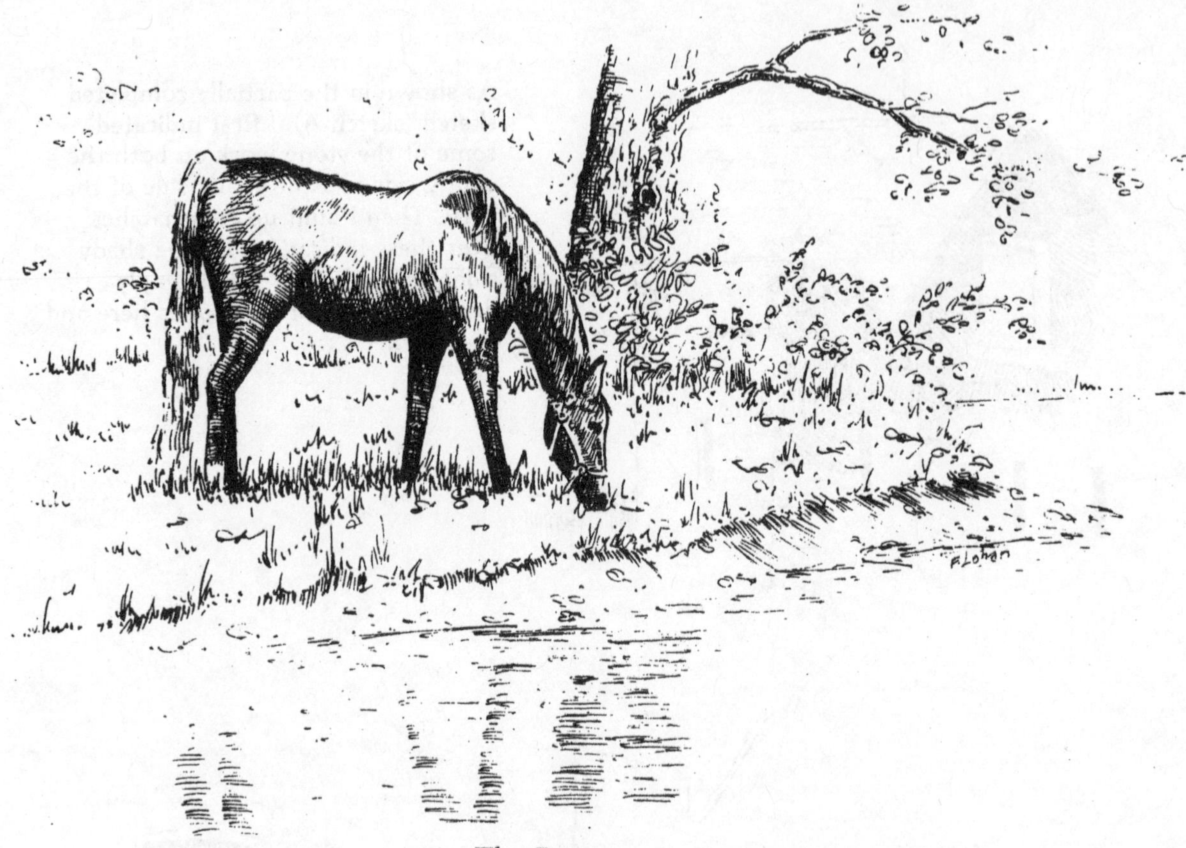

The Pasture

This sketch is a composite based on one photograph that showed the horse in a pasture and another that suggested the tree with the shrubbery at the base. The bank and water came from my imagination.

The original sketch was done on a rough 140-pound off-white watercolor paper called Morilla board. This paper, used with Winsor and Newton peat brown ink, is one of my favorite combinations. The very dark brown ink gives an extremely rich look to sketches on the slightly buff paper, while the rough texture of the paper itself lends overall interest to the sketch. Try this combination sometime.

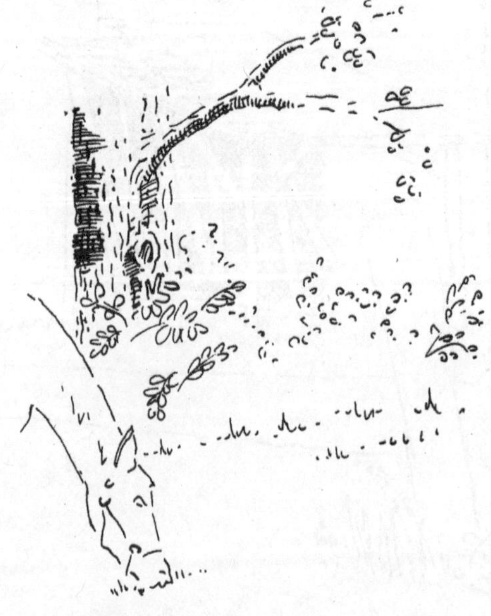

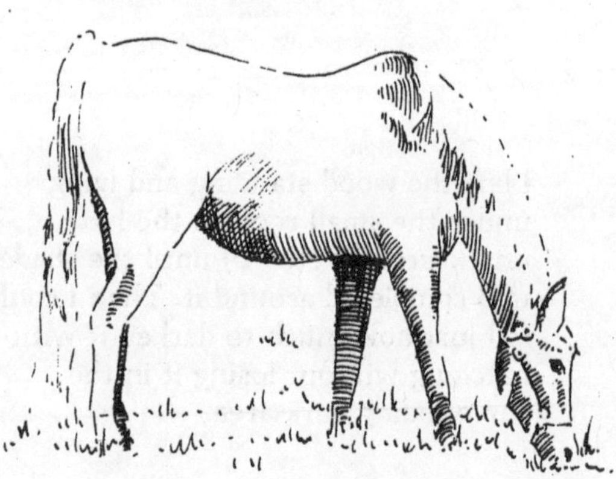

A Word About Pens

It may be beneficial to stop a moment and look at some of the many ink effects that can be produced with different tools. The subject of horses will be used for this discussion.

The full sketch shown here was done using a technical pen, a Mars 700, equipped with a 000 point. This produces a 0.25-millimeter line. For those of you not familiar with the nomenclature, this is a fairly fine line. When properly used, it produces lines such as you see in the horse's face. I used it properly on the face since I wanted the viewer's attention to be drawn to that area—hence some of the greatest contrasts are on the face. When the pen is barely touched to the paper (improper use), however, the little wire, which comes through the tube that actually is the point, deposits the ink rather than the tube. When rapid strokes are used, this makes an interesting broken line, which I used to shade the horse's neck, body, and legs.

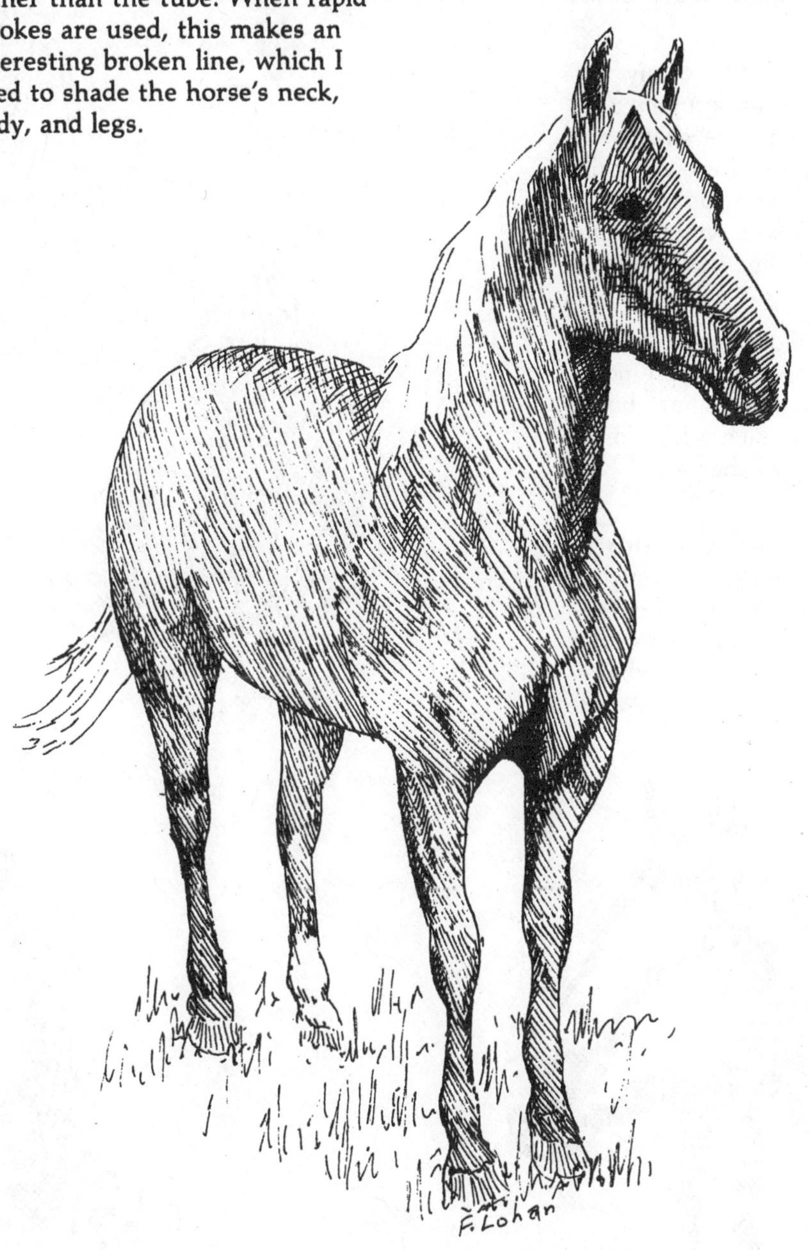

Sketch A was done with the finest point I have—a Pelikan Graphos style S, which makes a line about 0.10 millimeter wide. Note how you can build up dark tones to whatever degree you need with this delicate tool. When you really want detail and are in the mood to spend time developing it, an extremely fine point like this is just the thing.

For sketch B I used a Pelikan Graphos round-point lettering pen, with a 0.5-millimeter point. There is no flexibility to this point, so it makes a line of just one thickness.

Sketch C was the product of my favorite sketching fountain pen, a Pelikan 120. This has interchangeable points. The one I used here was called "extra fine." When you apply pressure to this pen it delivers a wider ink line. I used this variable line width feature in sketch C.

I used a 0 watercolor brush for sketch D; for sketch E I used a square-point lettering pen that made a line about one sixteenth of an inch wide. For the thin lines here I used the pen edgewise.

None of these pens—nor, for that matter, any of the infinite variety of other tools you might use—is more correct than any other. It all depends on what your purpose is and what your taste tells you is right to serve that purpose.

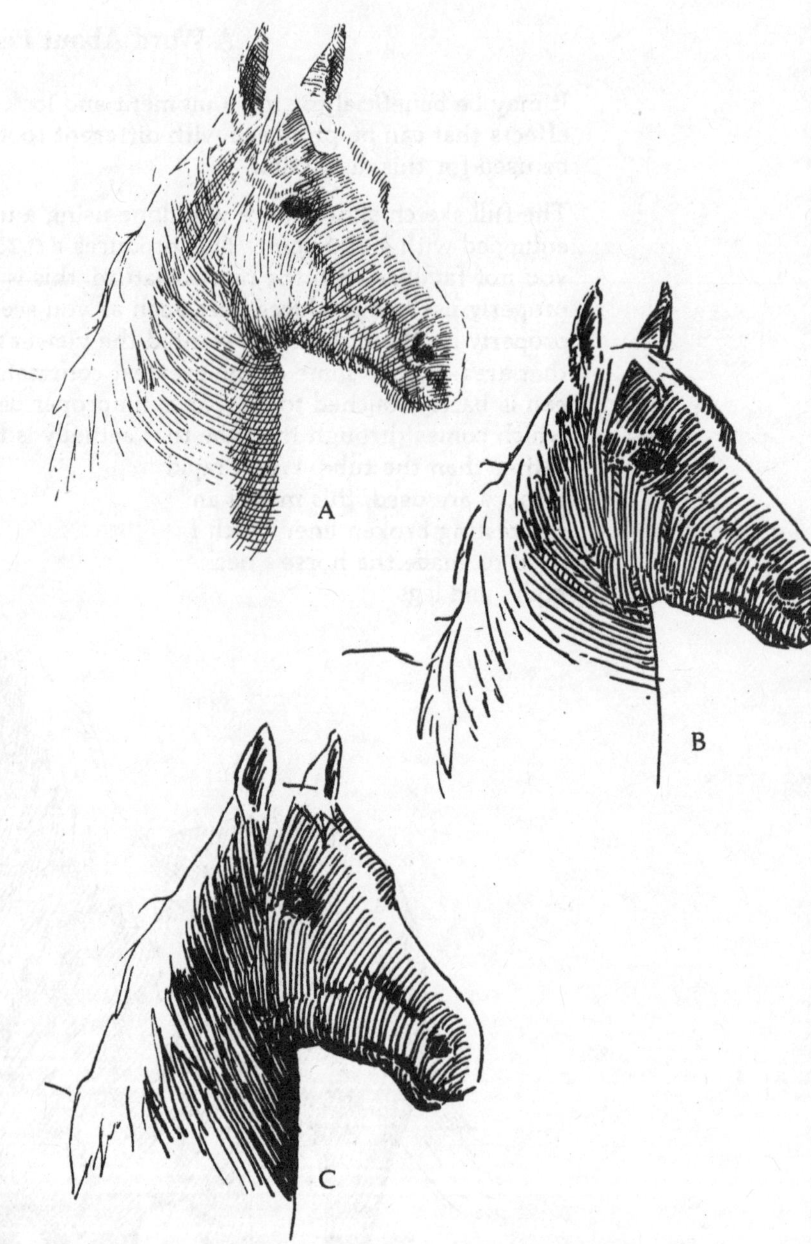

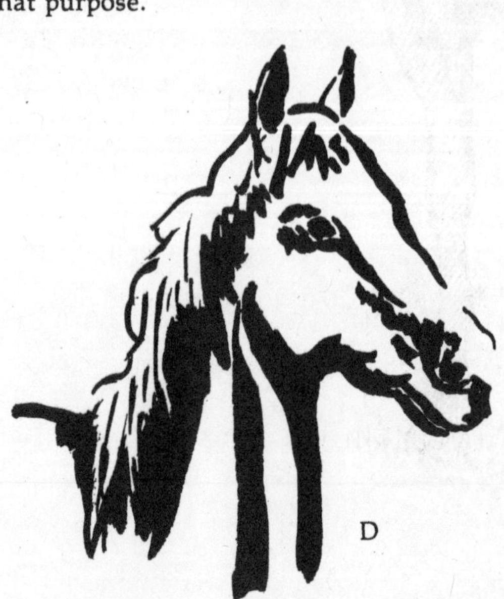

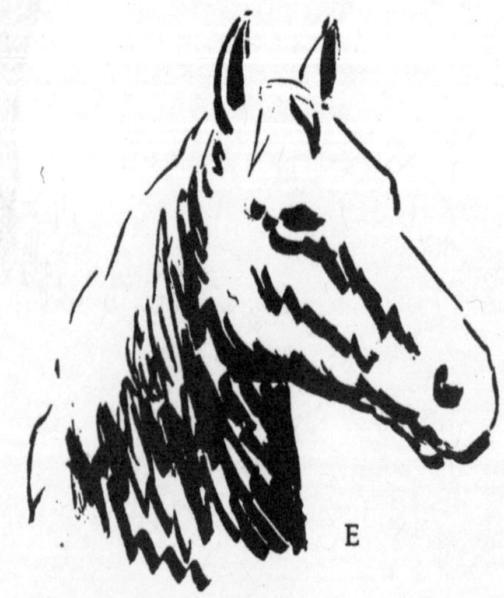

Maine Harbor

This sketch represents a tremendous amount of simplification from the photograph that prompted it. I eliminated literally hundreds of houses on the background hillside, dozens of craft in the harbor, dozens of people, and half the New England population of gulls.

My interest was focused on the strong tension brought on by the perpendicular masts and the horizontal hulls of the two ships that form the center of interest. I believe I even exaggerated the height of the masts to enhance this feeling.

The beautiful orderly clutter of rigging on the two ships required very careful handling. Naturally, the first step was a very tight pencil drawing. Then I proceeded by inking the rigging, which allowed me to start over without abandoning too many hours of drawing if I did not achieve the effect I wanted. One problem was to achieve the effect of dimension with the fine weblike lines of rigging. I had to make it visually obvious that some of these lines were closer to the viewer, with others passing behind them. The key to this was to start with the closest rigging and depict them through very fine broken lines. Then I decided what was just behind these lines and very carefully indicated this, making certain that I left clear uninked paper on both sides of the rigging that was closer to the eye. This does not look unnatural in the completed sketch, yet it definitely gives the three-dimensional effect I wanted. Look, for instance, at the nearest boat, just to the right of the dock where the ratlines come down from the top of the masts to the side of the ship. There is no detail shown behind these lines at their lower end. The slightest detail, even a dot or two, would have visually destroyed the effect. The same holds true where the prow of the white ship lies in front of the darker ship. In this case it is what is left out of the sketch that tells a lot of the story.

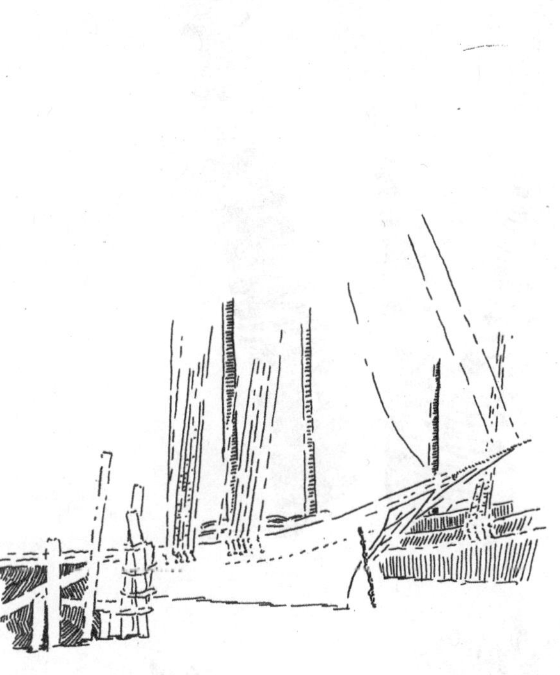

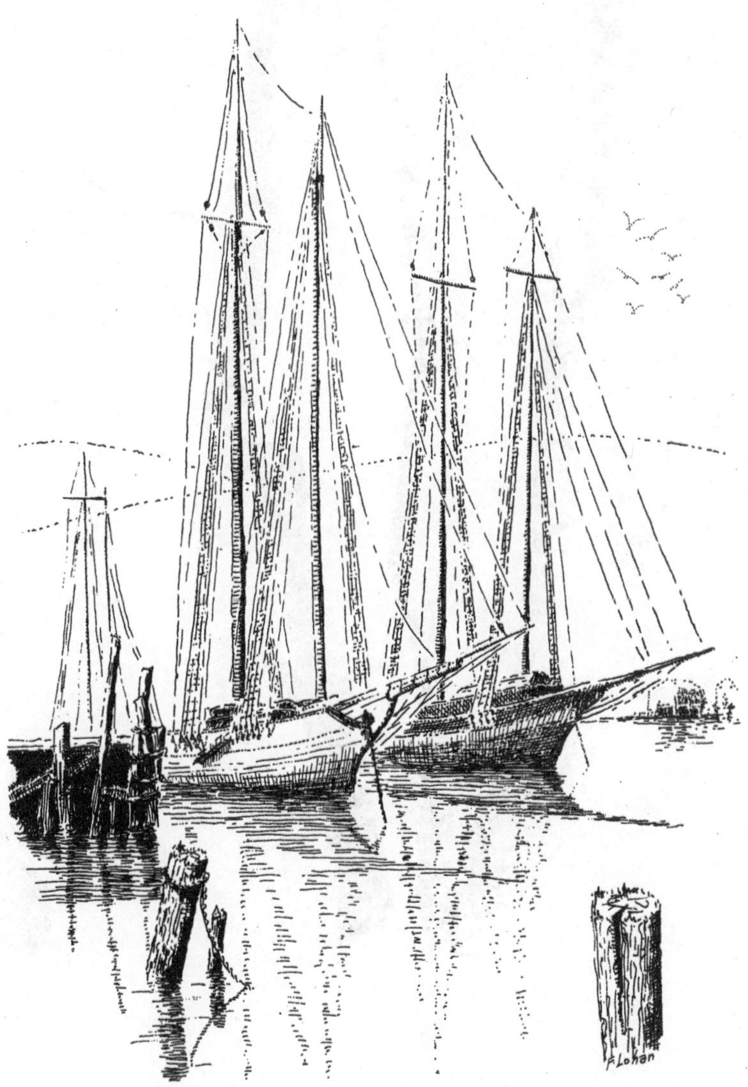

Birches

Anyone who does much sketching in pen and ink feels an occasional urge to tackle a clump of birches. So it was with me as I was selecting material for this book. I had no birches that I wanted to include, so I did this sketch.

This snow scene allows me to point out once more that you should always be on the lookout for opportunities to eliminate outlines. In this case, except for a couple of the branches, there are no outlines at all. It is only your imagination that sees an edge on the left-hand sides of the trees where the sunlight strikes them. I used more pen work to define the right-hand edges of the trees since they were in shadow, but still there is no outline per se. Striped or spotted subjects also offer an opportunity to eliminate outlines.

Isn't there a hillside behind the birches that slopes downward to the right? Again, it is only your imagination that sees it, because it is simply suggested by the weeds and bare shrubs that appear to show just over the crest.

I took these three birches from a photograph of a grove containing about fifteen visible trees. I selected these for their interesting shapes and "replanted" them into my own grouping. I used my finest pen point to render these birches.

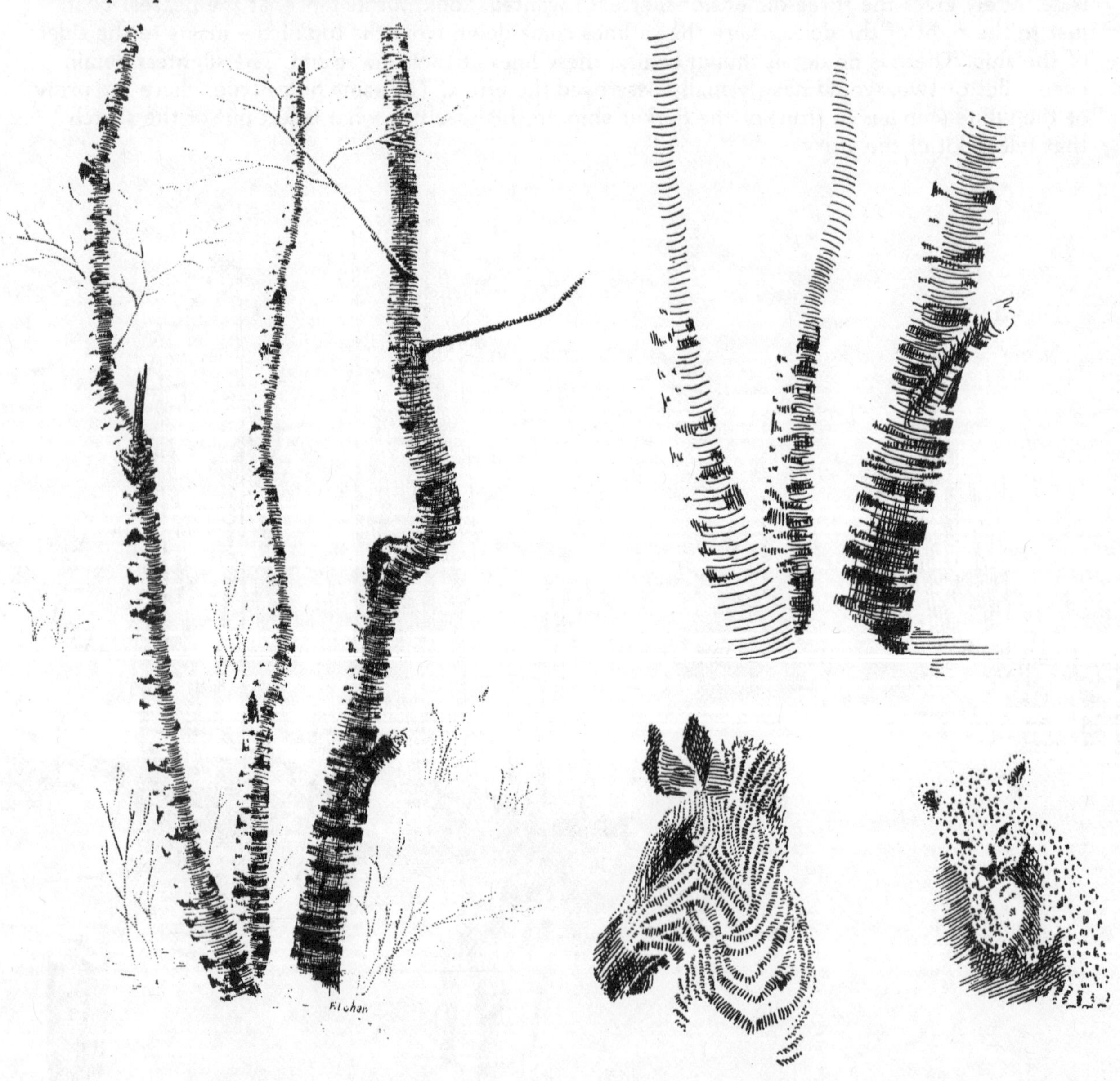

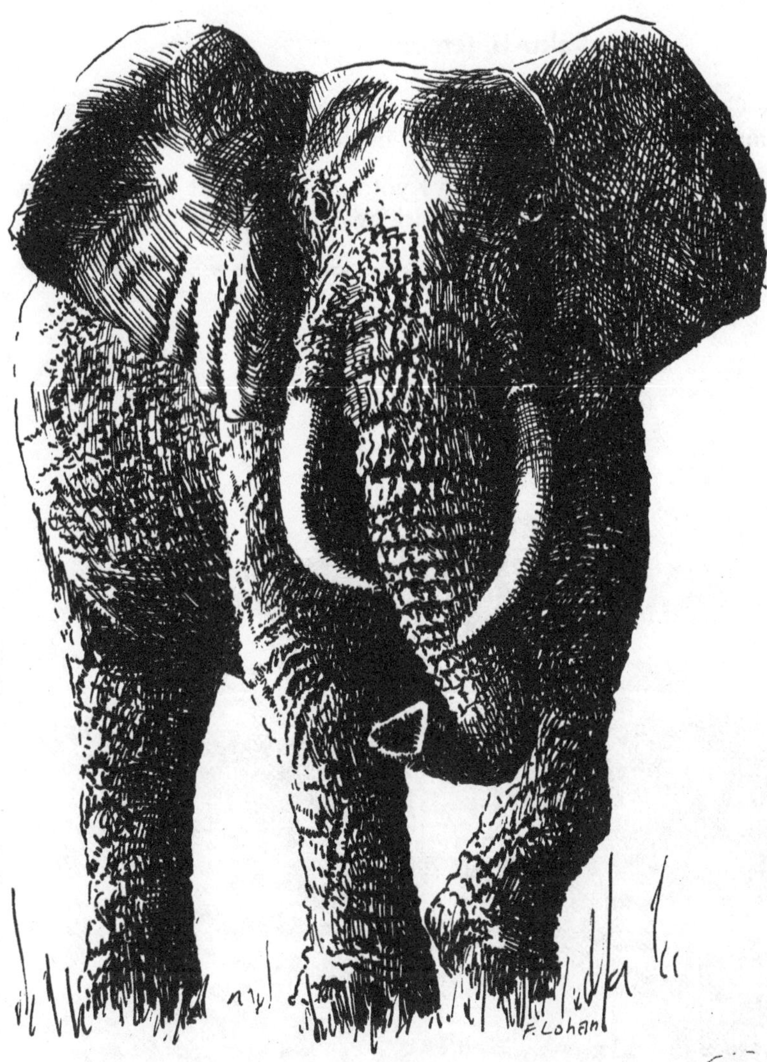

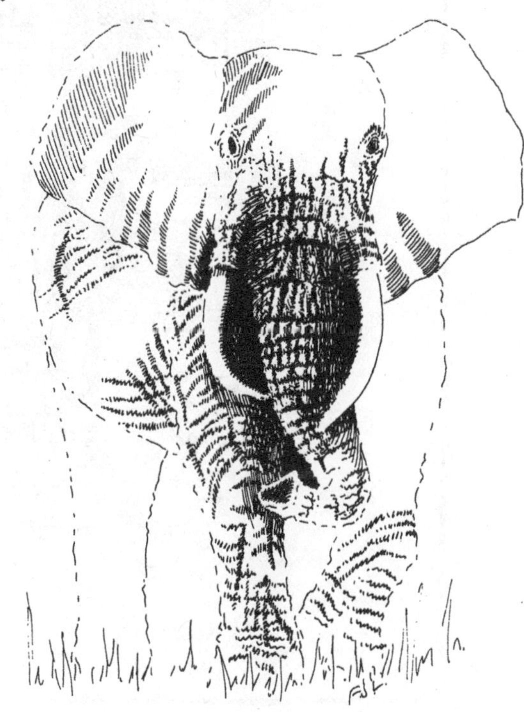

Elephant

The inspiration for this sketch was a beautiful photograph that showed a great deal of the structure of the wrinkles in the animal. It was quite obvious that the photographer was the object of the elephant's curiosity.

This kind of texture is not difficult to render. I first indicated the pattern of wrinkles all over the animal, then started building up the dark areas over these. As the wrinkle features began to disappear into the dark areas, I reemphasized them as I went along. The dark tones were a matter of piling on crosshatches until I was satisfied.

Kinkaku-Ji Temple

This temple is called the Golden Pavilion in Japan. Many Japanese feel it is the most striking of the many temples and shrines that abound in that beautiful country.

I visited Kinkaku-Ji and numerous other shrines in Kyoto on a trip that took me more than a thousand miles southwest from Tokyo and back again.

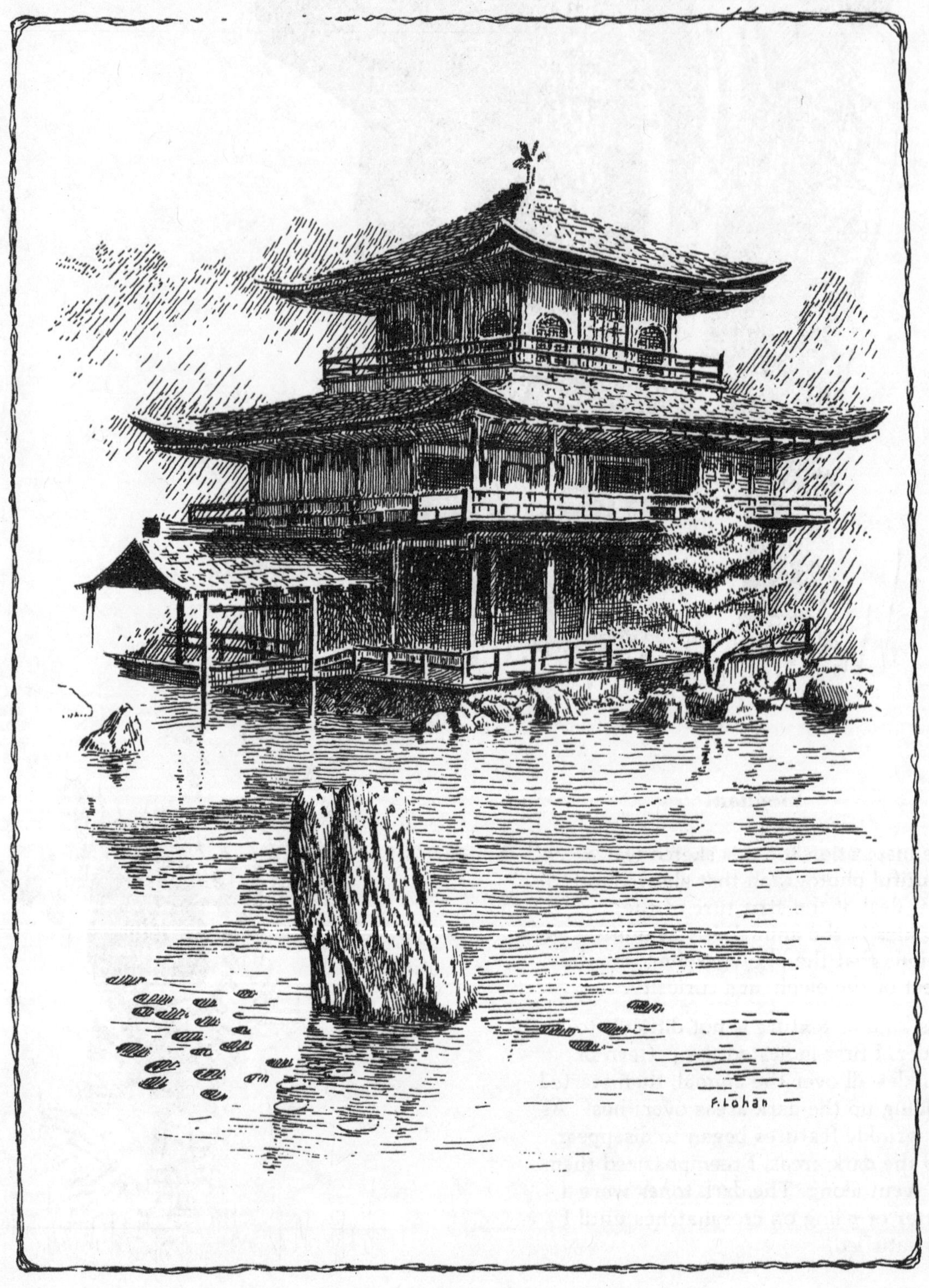

This temple is on the edge of a man-made lake constructed more than a thousand years ago. Visitors follow a path around the perimeter of this lake and get a view of the temple from all angles. The view shown here is one of the two most popular that are generally seen in photographs.

The strong geometric symmetry of this structure required careful and accurate perspective drawing before I started to apply ink. Naturally asymmetric subjects allow for all sorts of variation in proportion and line without looking unnatural. This does not hold with buildings and faces, however. Here the structure is primarily built up of several boxes or cubes of different sizes and shapes piled on top of one another. This is illustrated by the detail sketch. My initial pencil sketch looked like this before I began to place and define the details.

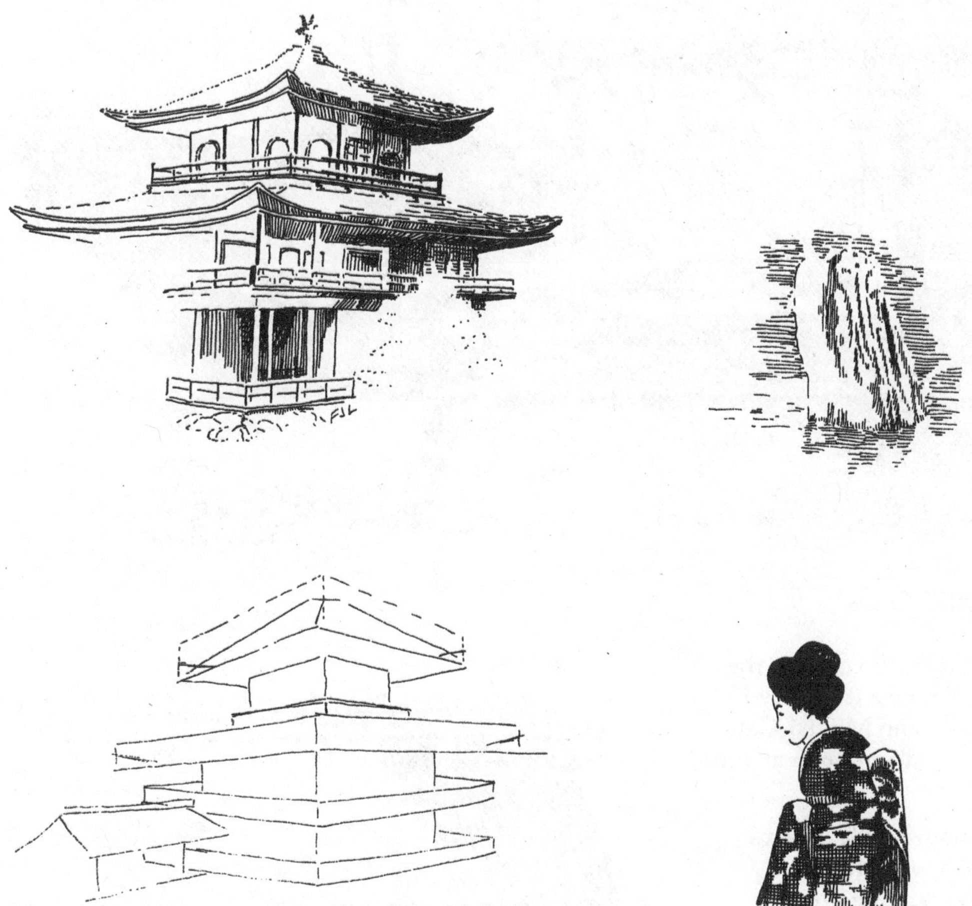

From my personal experience, this sketch could just as easily be placed in the nostalgia category. I made a lengthy visit to Japan and soaked up much of the country's cultural charm, as evidenced by temples, shrines, and gardens. These abound in all cities and suburban areas. I do not know if I will ever be able to return to see more of Japan. But I did see enough that I am able to appreciate the beauty of many locations I did not see through photographs and descriptions of them. I came back with enough photographs, sketches, and a wealth of reference material to keep me busy over the years making small sketches and vignettes of the many things of incredible beauty that exist in Japan. Don't you have memories you can renew by sketching them now?

The vignette of the pretty girl also came from a photograph.

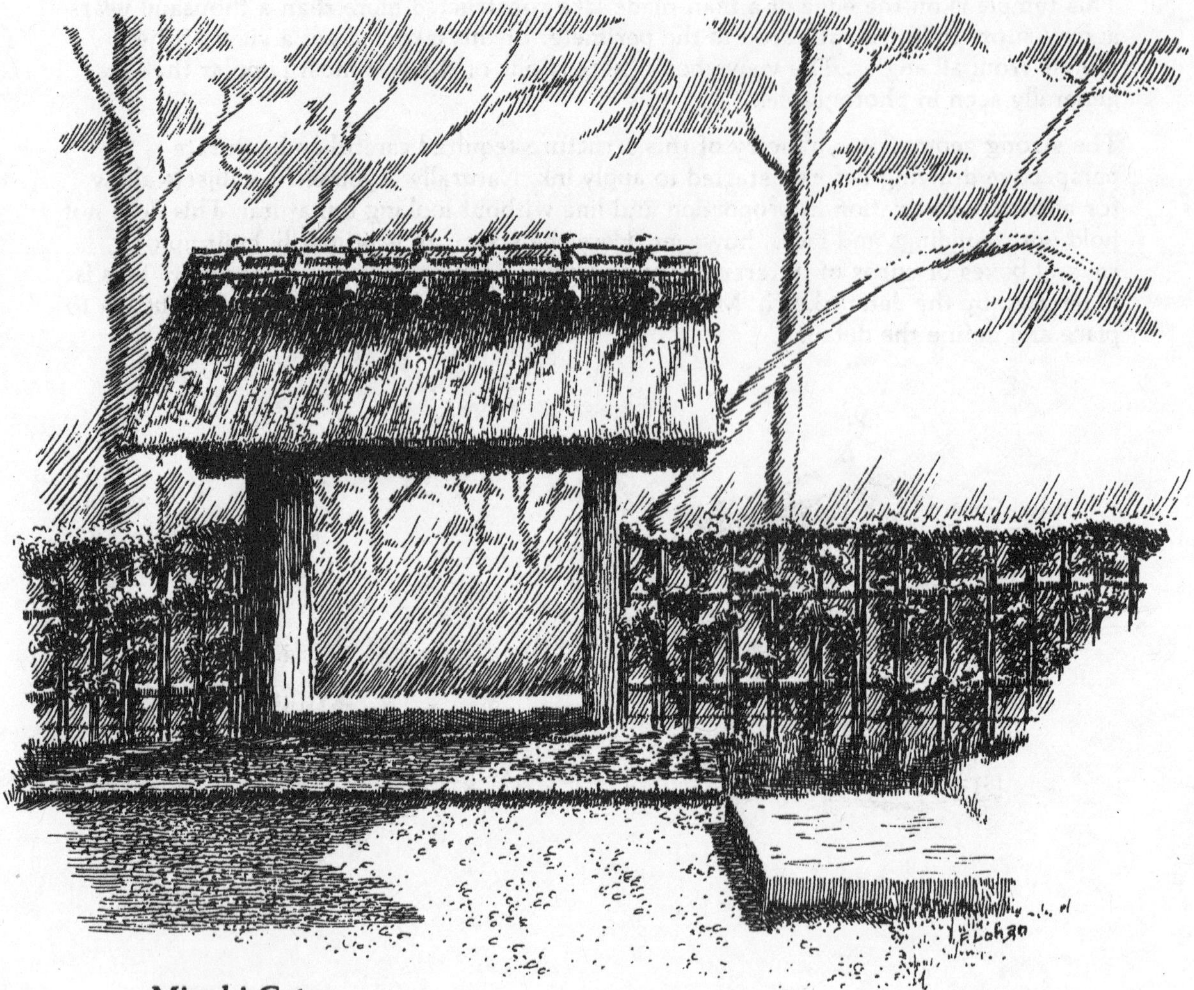

Miyuki Gate

Early in the seventeenth century the Imperial Villa at Katsura (near Kyoto, Japan) was created. The Miyuki Gate pictured here was built in 1658 at the villa.

I did not visit Katsura Villa when I was in Japan, but I was given a beautifully written and illustrated guidebook by a friend there. These sketches are based on photographs from that guidebook.

So much of the beauty of things Japanese is based on both symmetry and asymmetry. This gate is symmetrical, just as Kinkaku-Ji on the preceding pages is basically

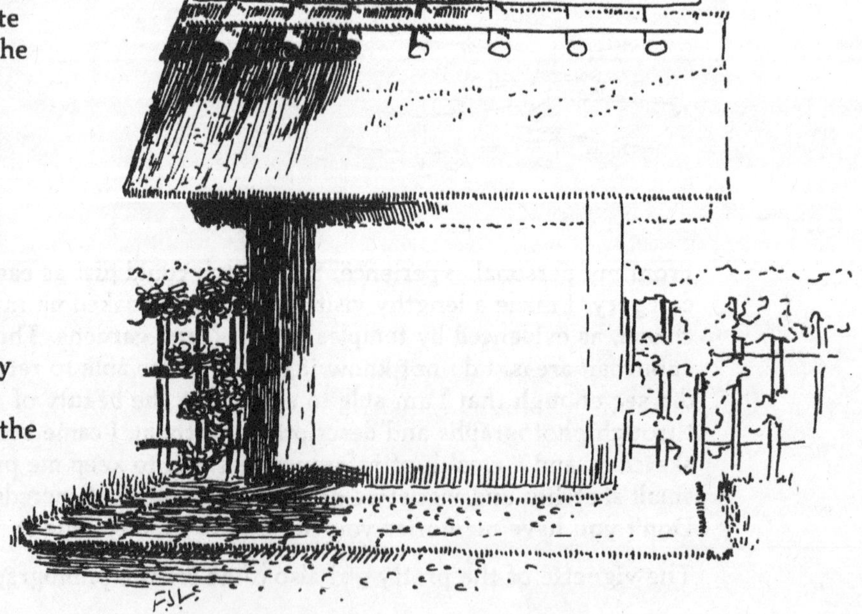

symmetrical. However, a symmetrical space can be subdivided asymmetrically with taste—this is the basis of all good design. As an example of such subdivision of space, I have sketched the pattern of Shin Walk, one of several cut-stone pathway segments on the Katsura grounds. The principle of graceful, interesting division of space is seen not only in fabric, rug, and wallpaper designs but in *all* well-composed visual artworks. Any good painting or drawing starts as an abstract division of the space with the artist's initial consideration of the proper placement and relationship of the compositional elements.

The basic design of any well-composed painting—that is, how the space is divided—would provide a good compositional base, regardless of the subject matter of that painting.

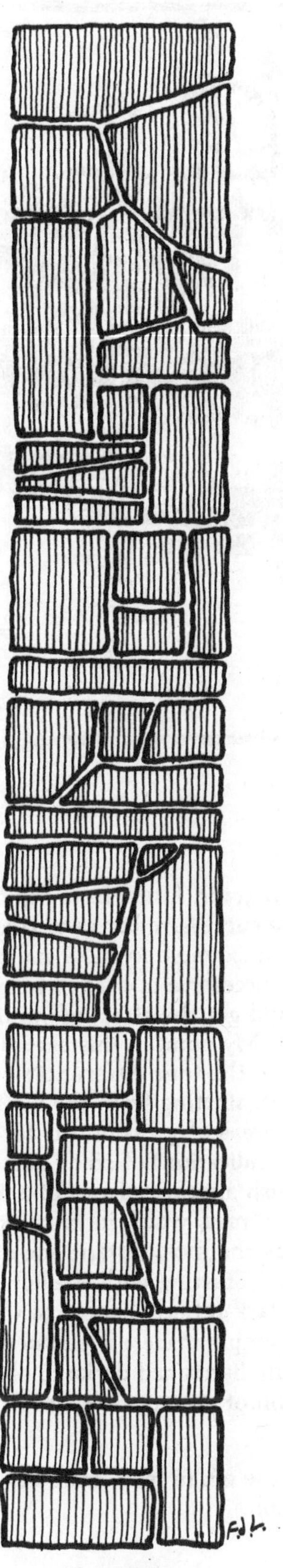

Shin Walk

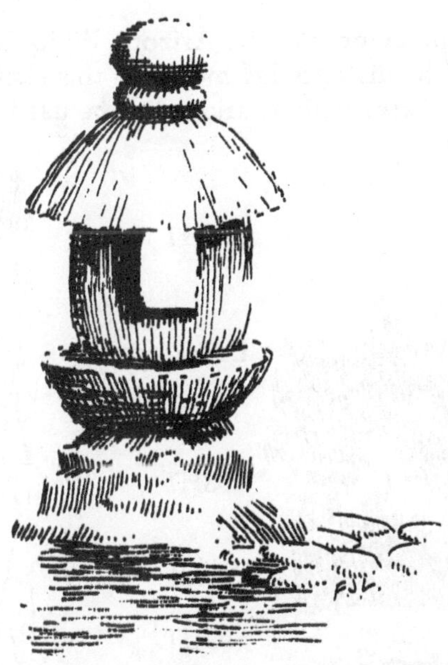

One of twenty-four stone lanterns.

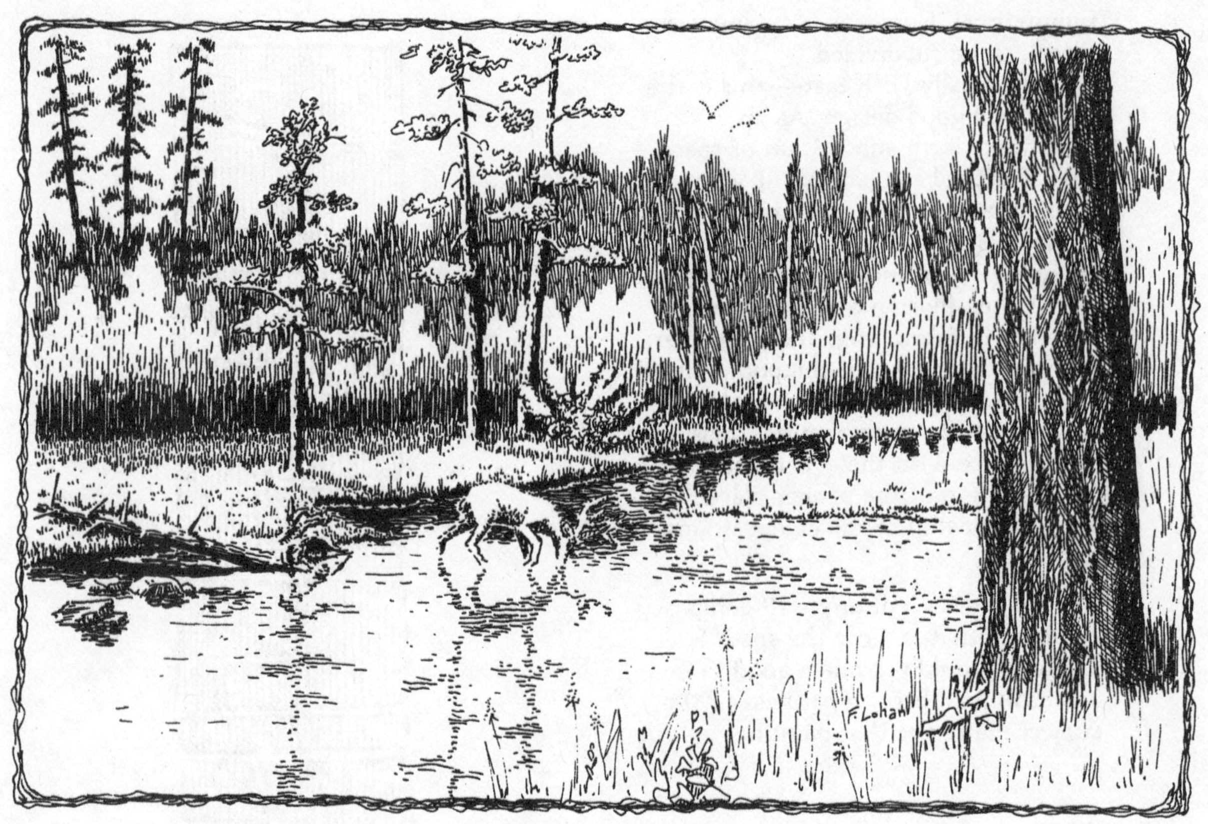

High Country

The photograph I used here depicted a beautiful lake somewhere in the Arizona White Mountain area. The successive banks of trees stretching off into the distance led me to do this sketch. I wanted an example to show my classes how tone (and texture) alternations can be used to indicate successive masses of foliage—to separate these masses and get the effect of varying distances. My point in this sketch was to exaggerate the tone differences somewhat, starting from the light, then shadow, areas of grass on the far side of the lake. Indications of some darker underbrush appear in front of a line of very light trees, which in turn are framed by the most distant line of fairly dark trees. Starting with the light water, and the dark-reflected shore in this water, I simply made a succession of alternating lights and darks to obtain the impression of objects in front of other objects.

I moved the elk in from another photograph.

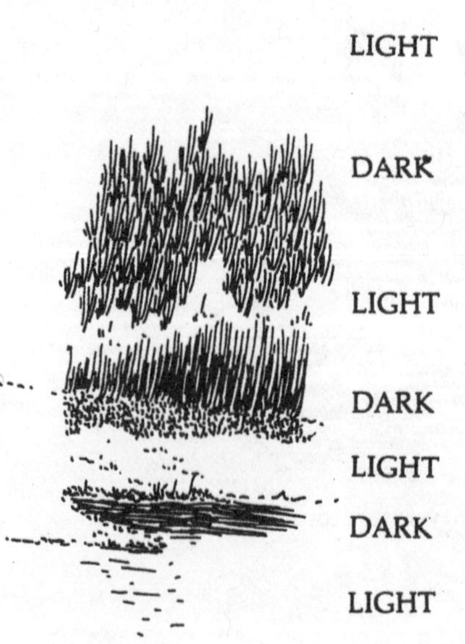

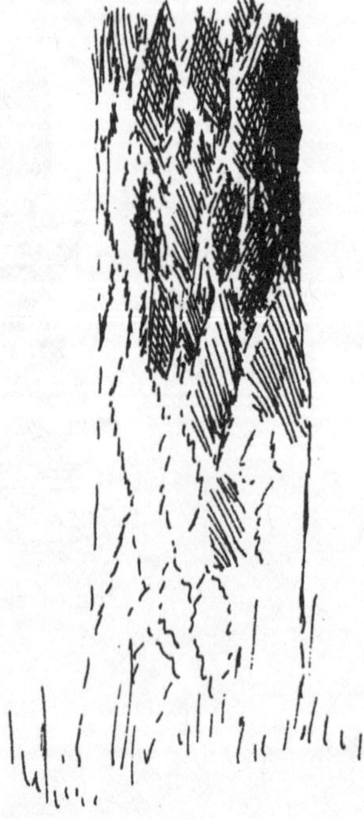

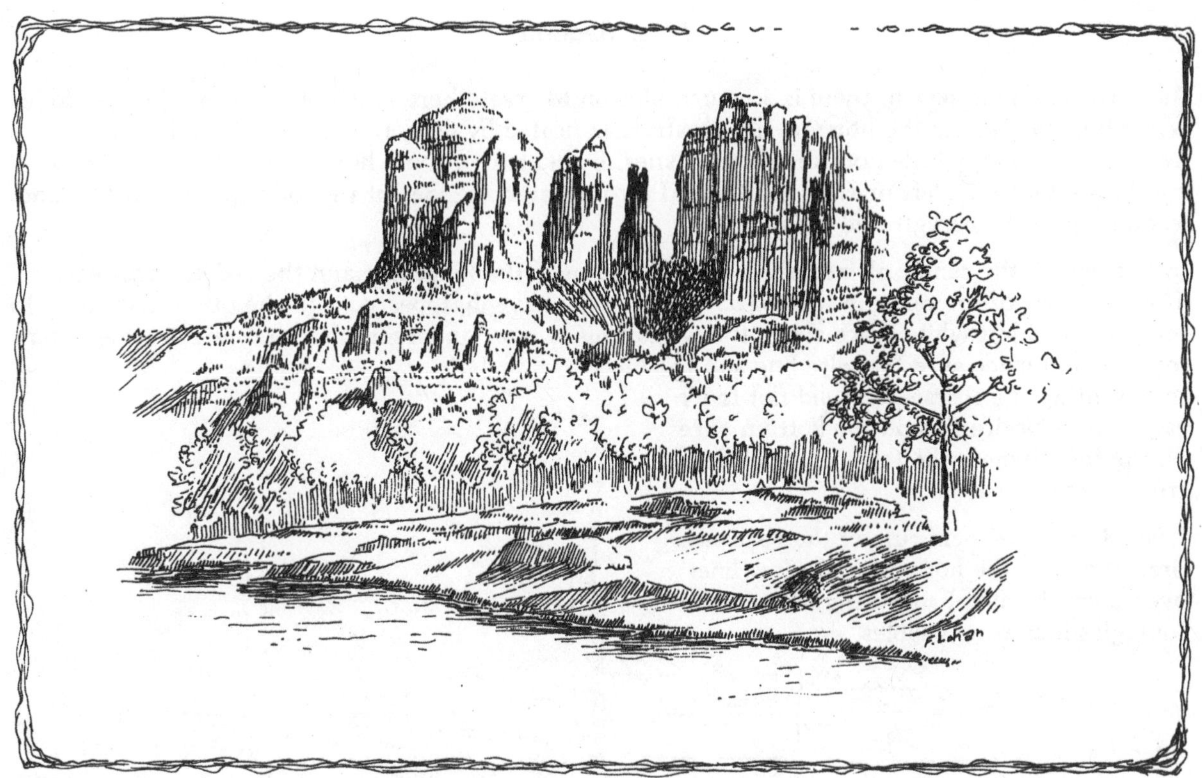

Cathedral Rock, Sedona

Next only to the Eiffel Tower, Cathedral Rock, near Sedona, Arizona, is one of the most frequently painted and photographed and therefore most recognized shapes.

Sedona is located between Flagstaff on the high plateau and Phoenix at desert level. It gets neither the severe winters of the one nor the ovenlike summer heat of the other. It is to me one of the most beautiful places in our country. After several visits to Sedona's Red Rock Country, this has become one of my favorite sketch subjects.

Cathedral Rock was a familiar backdrop for Western movies made in the 1930s and 1940s. The classic view is the one shown here, close to a shallow ford in Oak Creek.

In this sketch and the one that follows, economy of ink was vital. Every dot and line had to work for me because there was so much to suggest on the small piece of white paper. A few well-placed rows of dots establish that the rock masses are stratified horizontally. Less regular little clumps of dots and dashes suggest the scrub growth that sparsely covers the slopes. Then careful shadow indication, followed by a once-over to strengthen any lost features, and I was finished with the sketch.

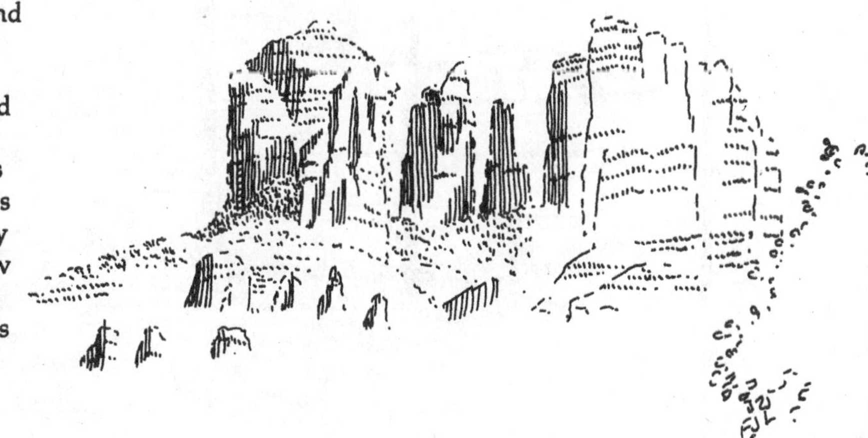

Near Sedona

As in the previous sketch, there is so much illusion to create here that not a dot or a line could be wasted. In addition to the horizontal rock strata indicated by dots, the scrub growth is also indicated by clumpy little dots and short dashes. By sketching these horizontally in some places and tilting up to the left or right in others, I incorporated the idea of the hilly contour of the land leading up to the background mountains.

In this sketch the center of interest is the foreground—the fence line and the red dirt roadway. The thin wire of the fence in this sketch could easily have disappeared into the other ink work. To prevent this I left white space above the wires (this is most apparent where the wires cross a dark feature) and made sure the wire line and the lines representing the sparse grass did not touch each other. Notice this on the bottom wire on the fence where the taller grass blades cross in front of it.

I established the main ruts of the roadway first, then put the horizontal shadow lines over them. Finally, I added the dots and squiggles indicating pebbles.

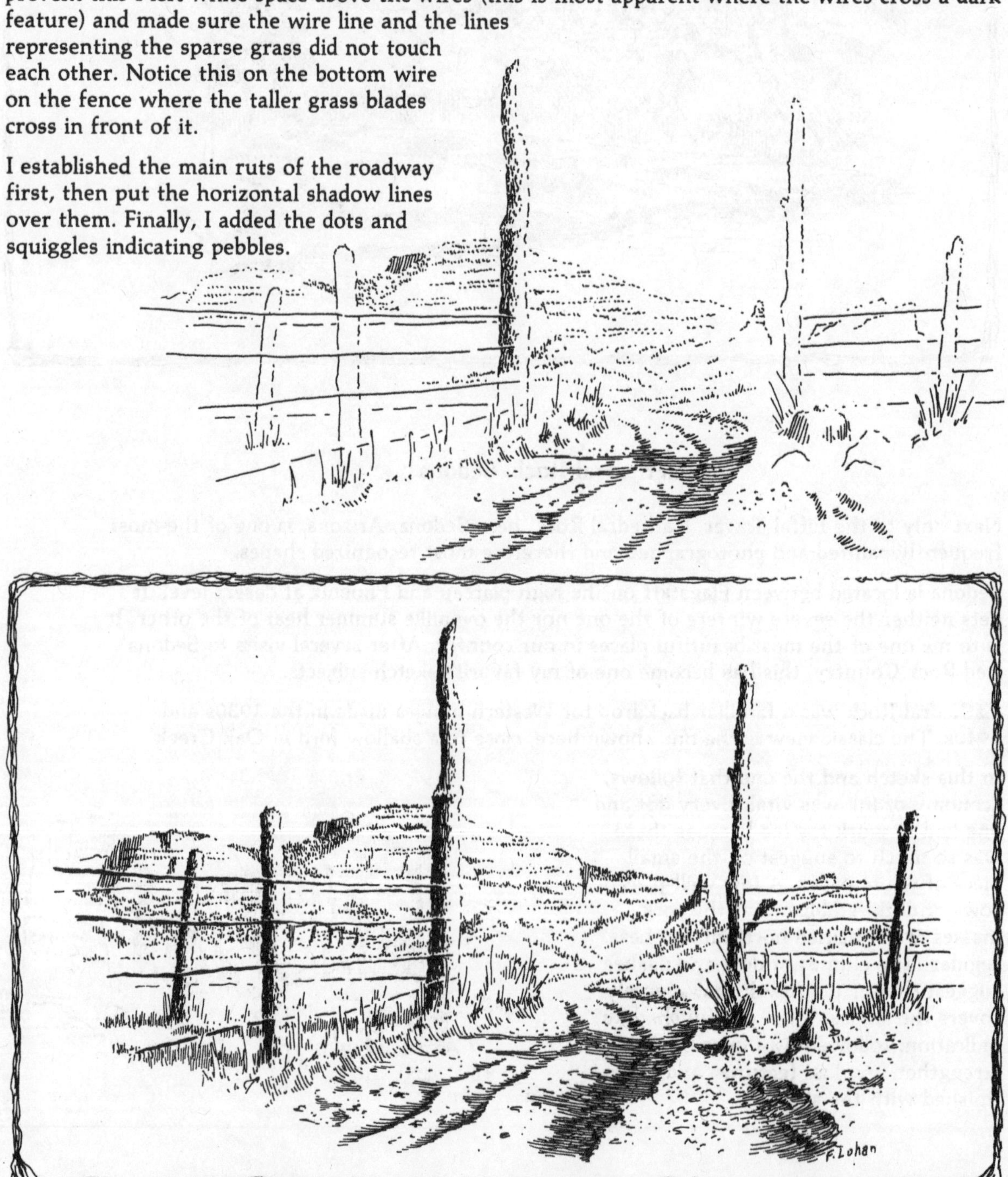

Joshua Tree

There is so little life in the deserts of our Southwest that what *is* there really stands out. This allows an appreciation of the individual beauty of plants, for instance, which might be lost to the eye if this plant life existed in crowded profusion as it does in the tropics or even in part of the dense growth of our forested areas.

The Josua tree is only one of the many species of desert plant life, and it presents a unique challenge to the artist. This sketch is one approach to that challenge.

The Joshua tree's leaves grow in porcupine fashion in clumps at the ends of branches. In order to show this, I indicated each clump of leaves with lines aimed in the direction of the growth. Some of the clumps are in profile and some face the viewer head-on. The head-on clumps are indicated by line work that radiates from the center of the clump in all directions. Once the basic line work and directions of these clumps were established, I did the trunk and then went over to darken here and there to get the definition I wanted for each clump. Finally, I put the shadows on the trunk and branches.

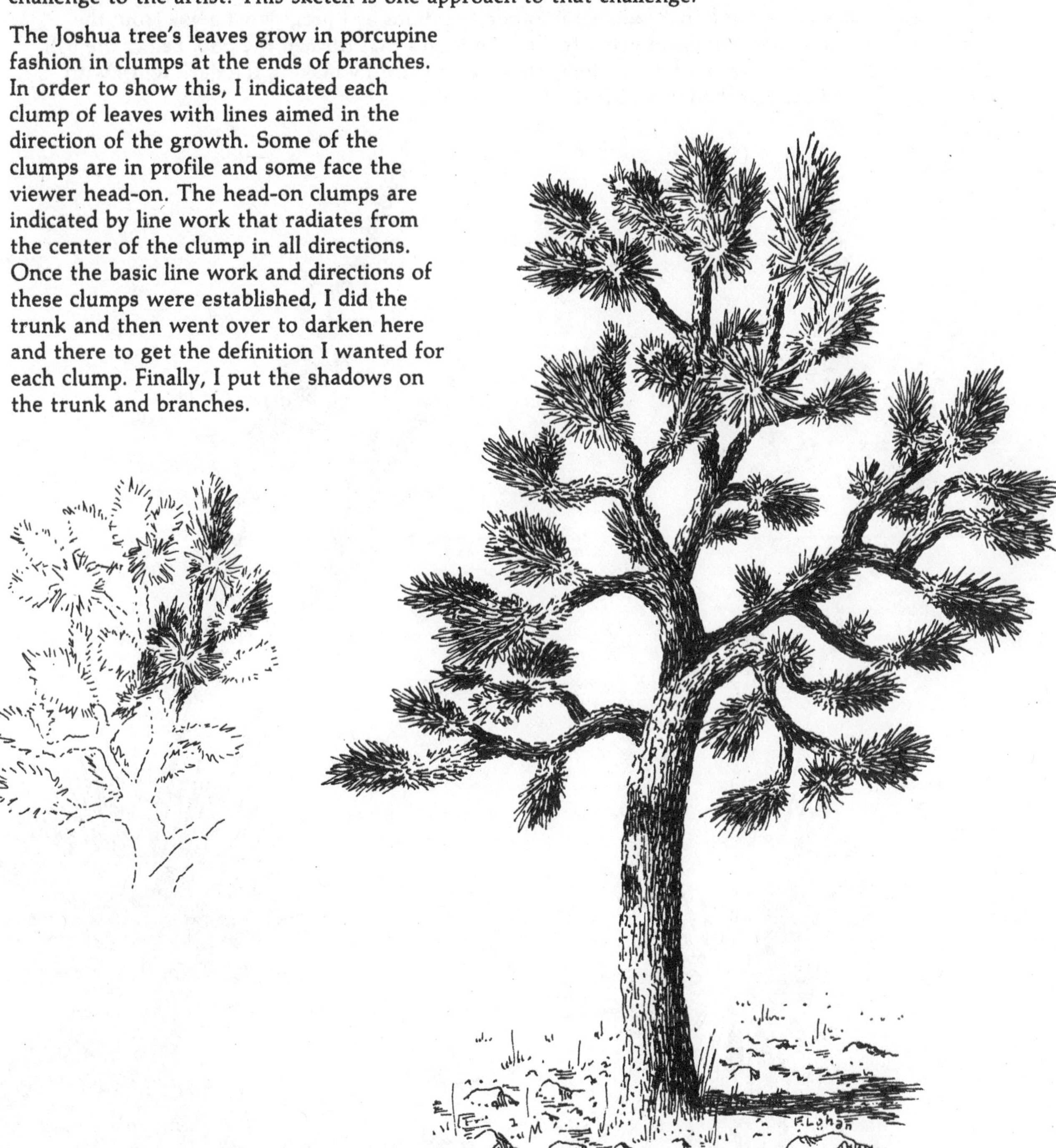

Yucca Plant

Here is one of the desert beauties—the yucca. It is familiar as a garden plant to homeowners all across the country because of its tolerance for cold weather. There are many yucca plants in my Michigan neighborhood.

The primary challenge with this sketch was the spiny ball of leaves. As you can see in the auxiliary sketch, I started by defining the outline of this ball. Then I established a few of the leaves in the center in full outline. This central core of leaves included those coming straight out at the reader as well as some that radiated in other directions as I progressed away from the center. At the same time I outlined just a few of the leaves that formed the boot below the ball. The remainder of the lower portion of the sketch was created by making the dark tones with lines that showed the direction in which the foliage grew.

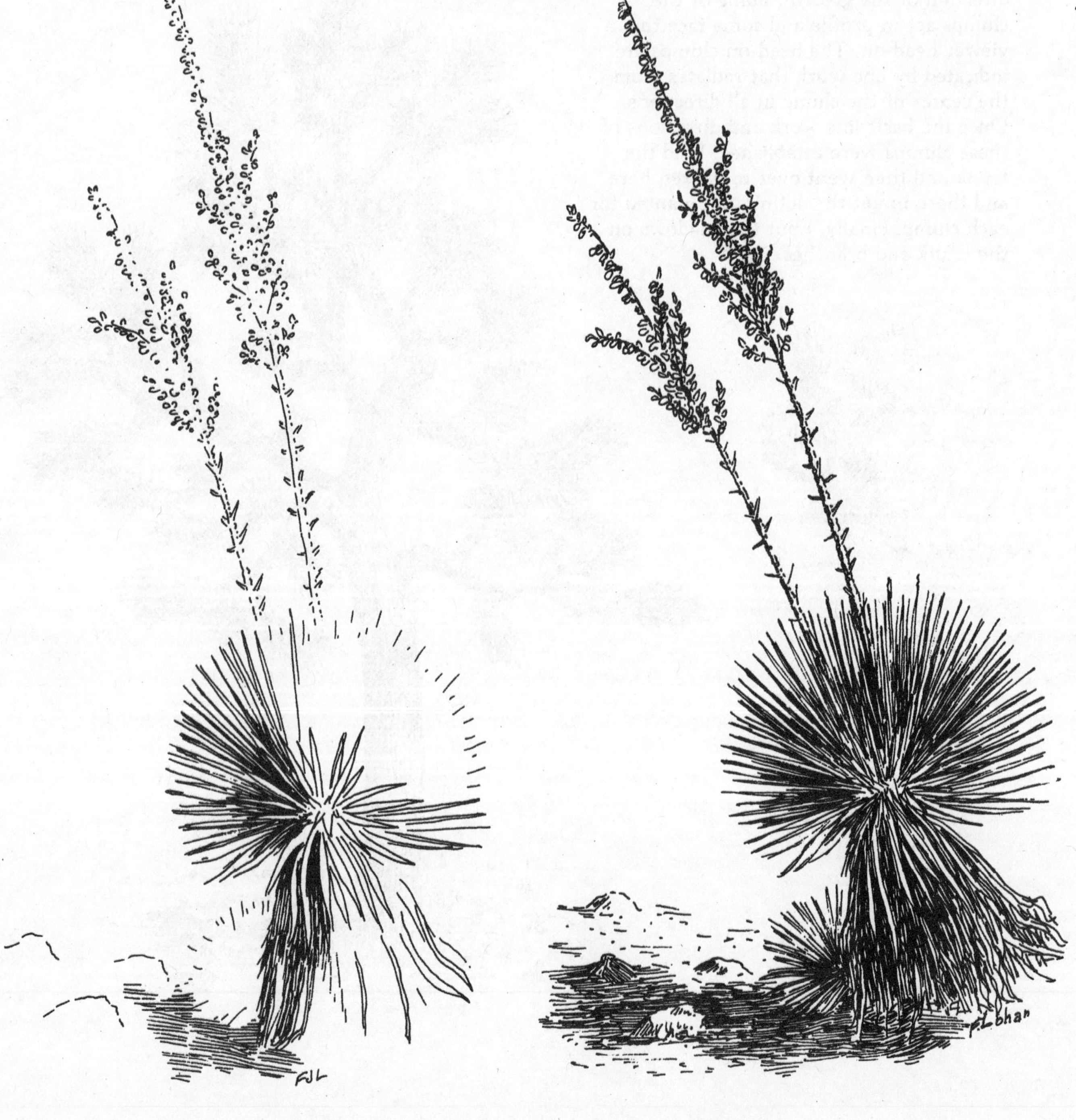

Saguaro Cactus

This symbol of Arizona, the tall, deeply ribbed saguaro, is actually a tree. The outline of this tree is simple enough; creating the ribbed effect required only my technical pen, a series of vertical lines to start with, and some patience.

After getting my pencil outline down, I sharpened the pencil and drew a series of lines about one sixteenth of an inch apart on the saguaro. Then I inked a broken line on these guidelines—as you can see in the auxiliary sketch. I then drew the little hatch marks like teeth on a comb, touching one side of the broken lines and being certain to leave a pure white area between them and the adjacent line. This pattern created the fluted or ribbed impression. When this was finished, the last thing I did was to hatch over the areas I wanted shaded in order to help achieve the feeling of roundness in the cactus.

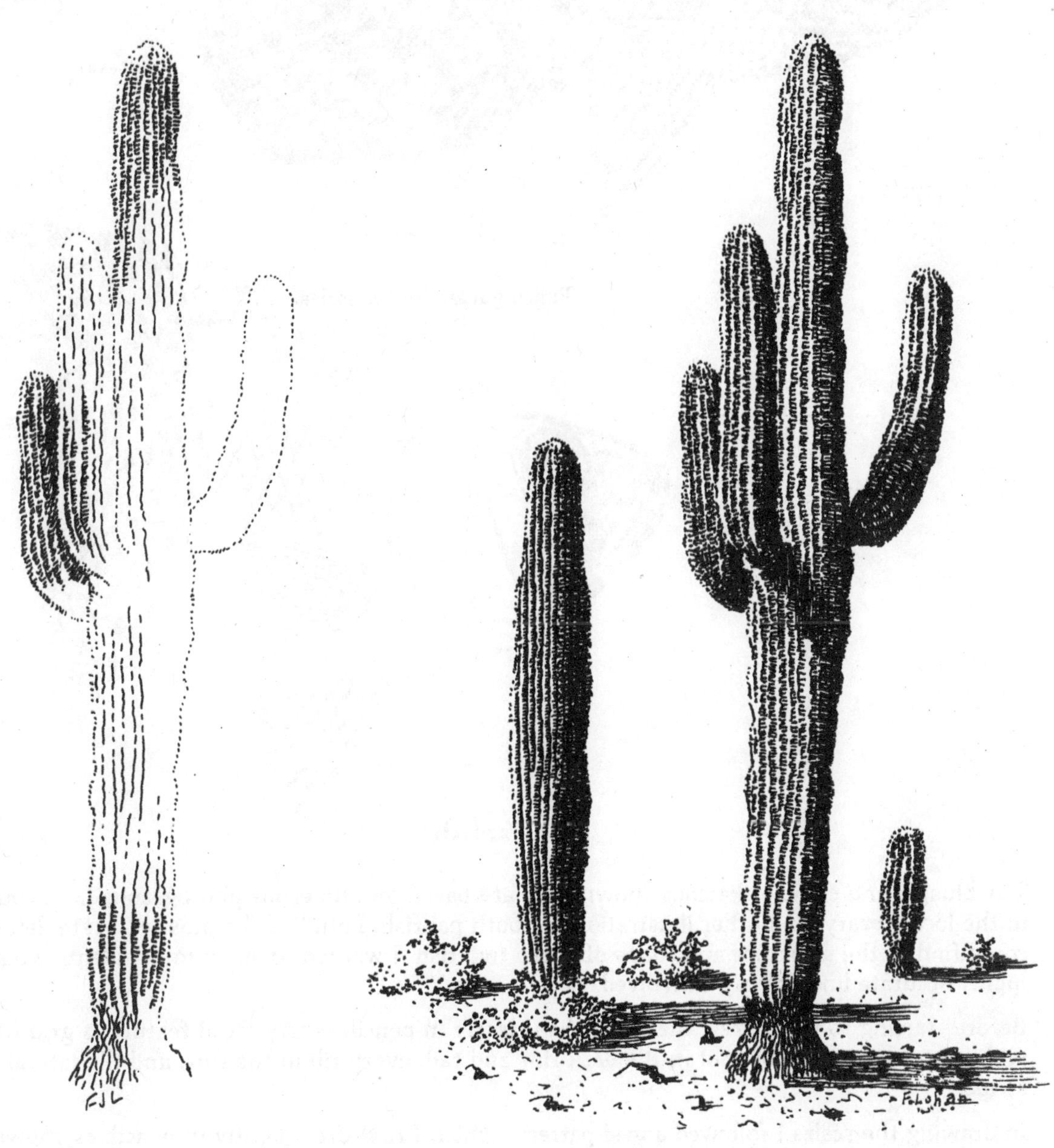

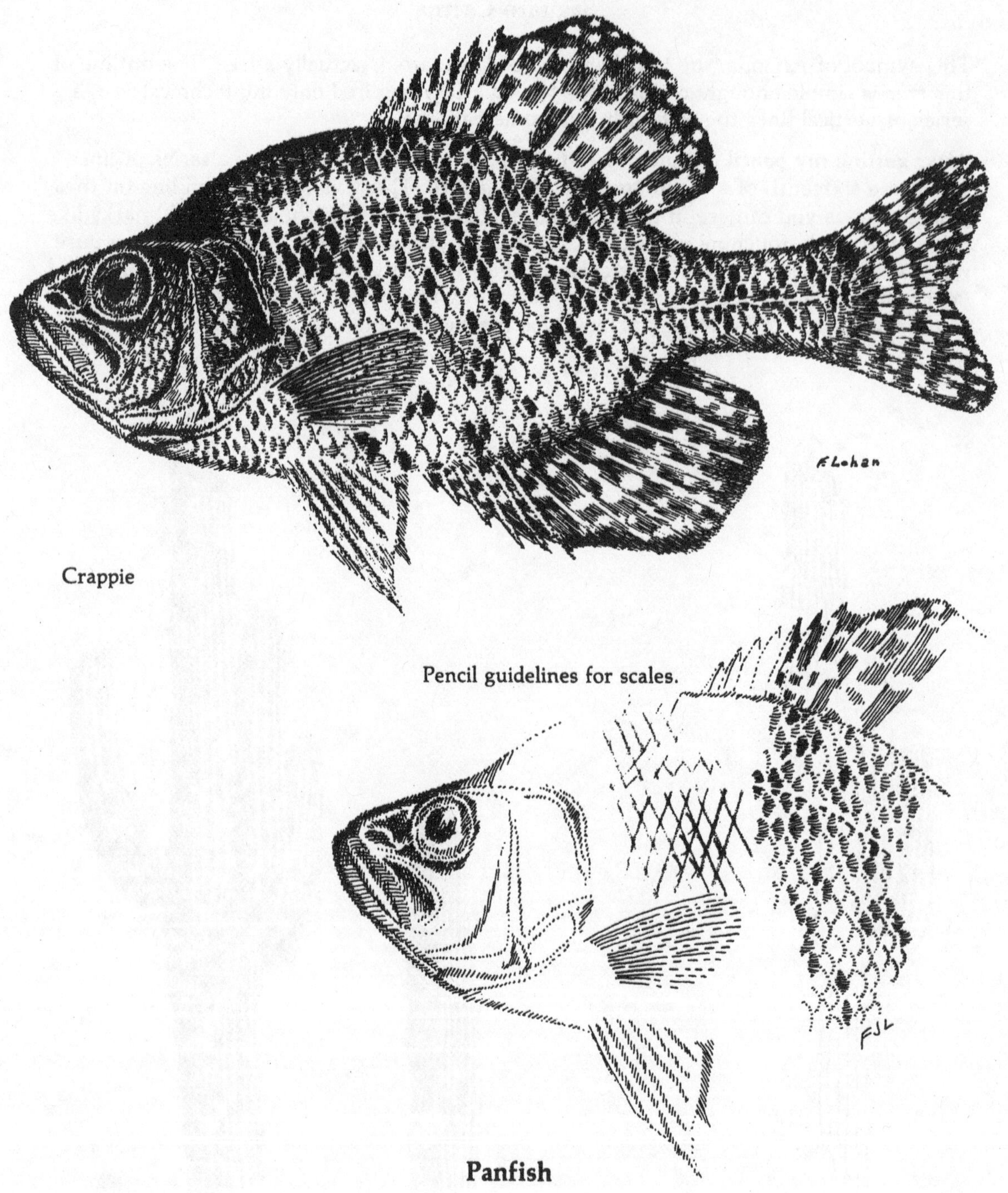

Crappie

Pencil guidelines for scales.

Panfish

The bluegill and crappie sketches shown here are based on numerous photographs (all I could find in the local library) and other illustrations of both panfish. I studied the most accurate details I could find of the structure and shape of these two fish. I wanted to show my students what a highly accurate line portrayal involved.

Before starting to ink, I drew the entire fish clearly in pencil—every facial feature, a grid for the scale pattern, every light spot in the dark fins and tail, every rib in the fins, and the lateral light stripe.

In drawing the scales I followed a grid pattern, which I first drew lightly in pencil, as shown in the auxiliary sketch of the crappie.

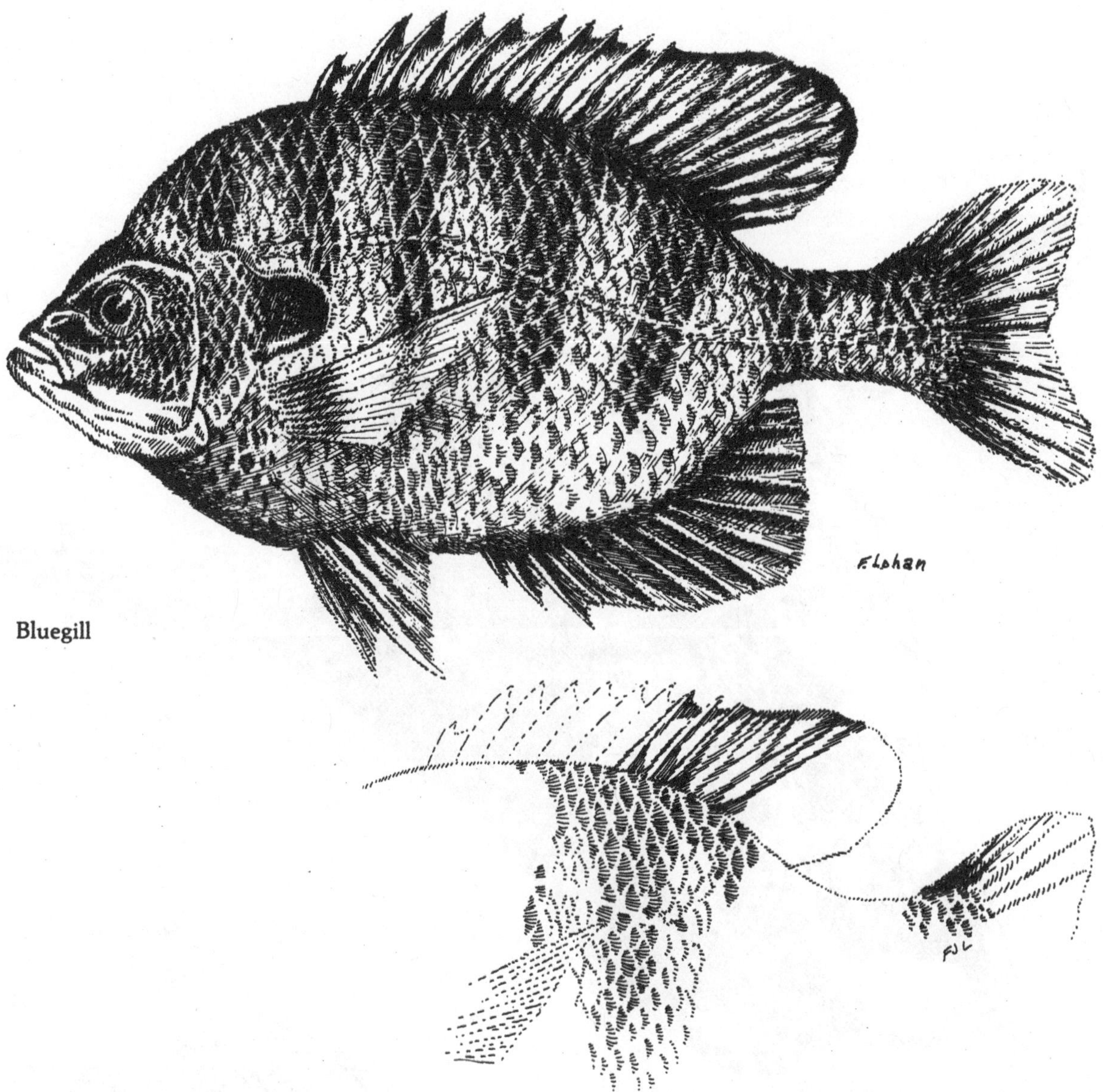

Bluegill

For each fish I started with the head, as shown by the partially finished crappie, making sure I defined every feature in ink. At this stage I erased the pencil lines in the head area to eliminate the clutter and to allow me to see better for the next step—that of adding the scales in the head area and building up the dark tones. I brought the head to about 90-percent completion before I moved over and started on the scales.

In inking the scale pattern I made a first pass over the entire body, pretty much as you see on each of the auxiliary sketches. With the bluegill I made sure the dark fingerlike pattern was established and each light scale indicated, not in their final tones but approximately as you see in the unfinished details. Then I erased the pencil guidelines from the scale area and proceeded to develop what I felt would be the final dark values on each scale. Notice that the crappie has three scale tones and the bluegill just two.

Then I moved to the fin and tail areas where the light and dark patterns were still carefully outlined in pencil. When these features were developed to the extent shown in the detail sketches, the pencil lines were erased and the final tones established and balanced.

I did the bluegill sketch first and decided when I started the crappie to try for a more rounded impression by incorporating the bright highlight between the head and the dorsal fin.

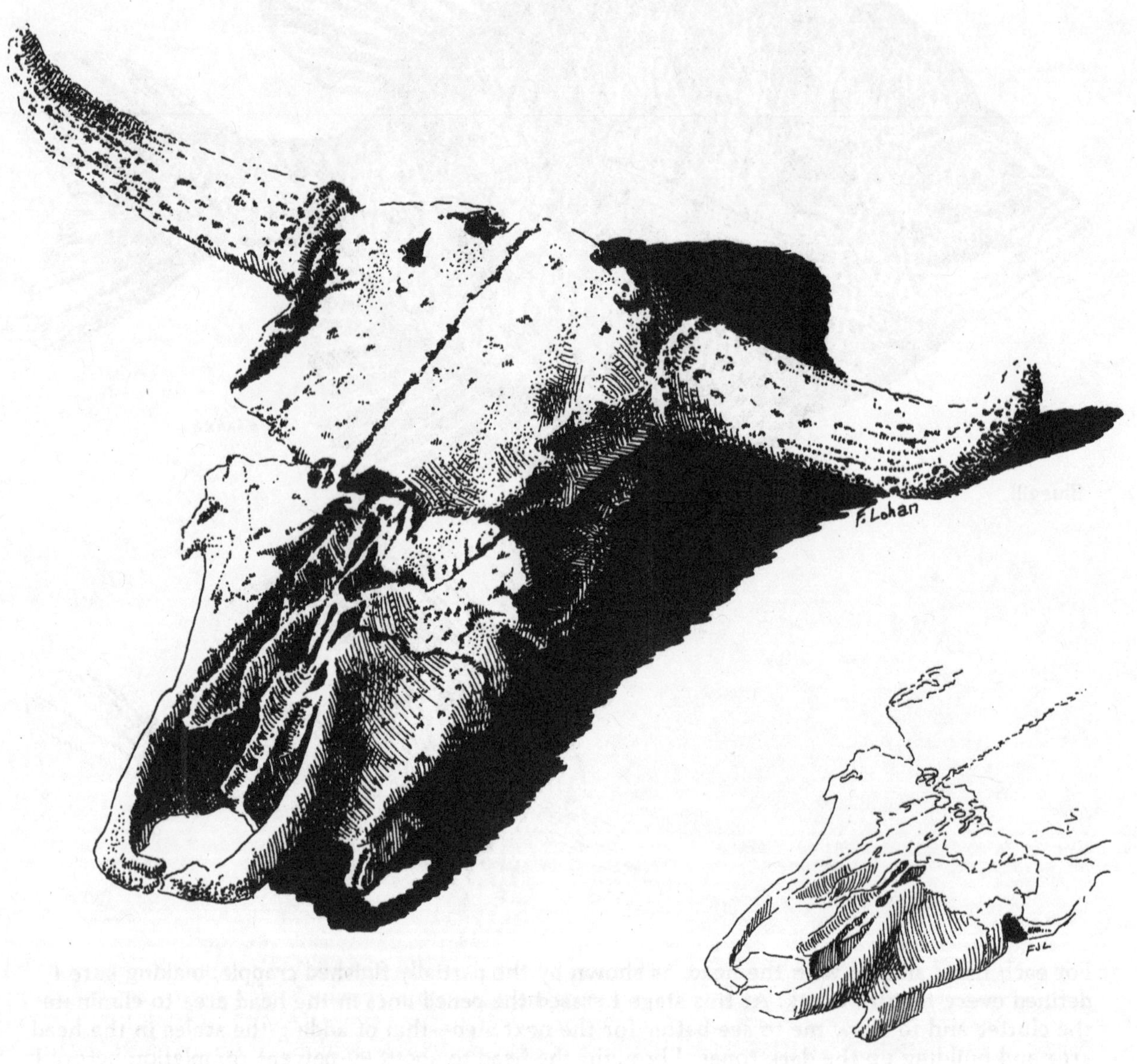

Bleached

This is an example of another characteristic element of the southwestern desert. The dried cow skull sketch started as an outline drawing, as you see in the auxiliary detail. I first located the major dark areas, cracks, and larger holes in the outline. Then I started to indicate the form of the skull through hatch marks with which I molded the surface—curving them appropriately to indicate concave or convex surfaces and making them straight for flat surfaces. Then I placed the fine dots, or stippling, to put the finishing touches on the more subtle surface indications. I finished up with the larger dots that indicate small holes in the bone and the horns.

5: Subjects from Life

Whether strolling through your backyard or sight-seeing thousands of miles from home, you will find countless subjects—some panoramic, some insignificant—that are naturals for your sketching repertoire.

This section contains some of the subjects I have sketched from life. They may provide some help for you should your travels near or far give you the urge to sketch something that has a particular appeal for you.

Do not underestimate the problems of sketching a feathery sprig of grass. The matter of organizing the sketch so that the space on your paper is used in a pleasing manner is the same for such a simple subject as it is for a river with a million rocks in view. Every subject you select to sketch must be simplified and some portion of it composed on your paper before you can begin to draw or paint it. This is the point at which, consciously or unconsciously, you decide how to organize that space on your paper.

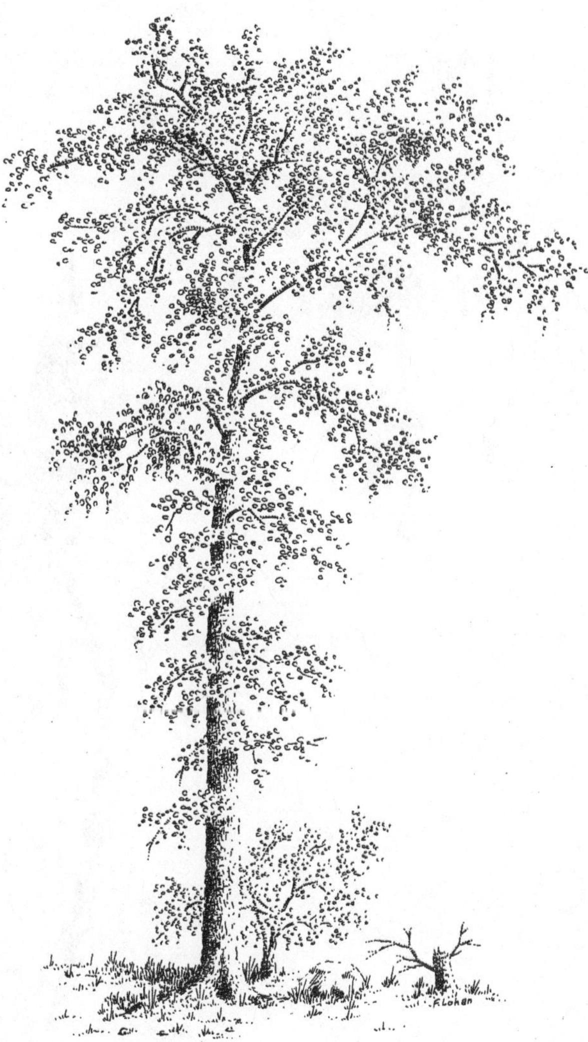

Milkweed Pods

Hard brown milkweed pods spilling their loads of seeds into the air are a sure sign that summer is gone. These pods are favorites in dried flower arrangements. The interesting texture of the shell and the silky softness of the seeds make them a good subject for sketching. The pods often group themselves in beautiful clusters on their curved and twisted stems and give you many excellent ready-made compositions.

I first organized this composition by selecting two stalks of opened milkweed pods. Then I lightly drew the stalk pattern and roughly indicated the pods. For the next step I more or less outlined the whole sketch in ink, placing a few seeds here and there. I had to know where the seeds and their white fuzz were to be so that I could develop the dark shell around the whites that I wanted to highlight. After putting in the little groups of hatch marks to indicate the roughness of the shell, I hatched over the whole shell to darken it and thereby emphasize the white seed fuzz.

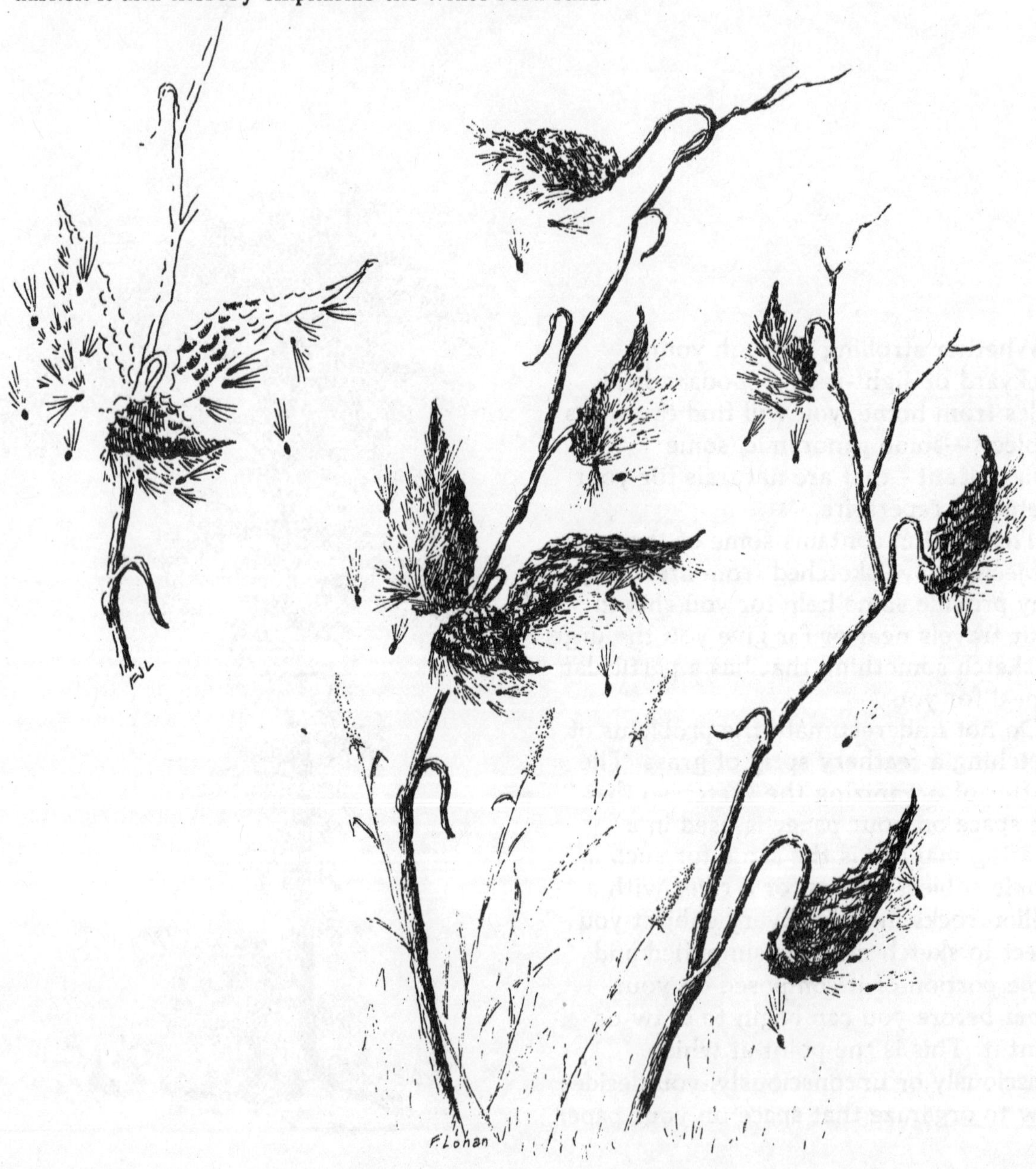

Field Grass

When I sketched this simple little sprig of grass, I first made a few indications of the stem structure with the pencil, pinpointing the way the little branches radiated in groups from the stem. Then I put in the arrangement of the leaves. I proceeded with the ink work by first doing those features that were in front, that is, closer to my eye. I made sure that any feature that passed behind did not touch the feature in front. With a very fine, delicate subject such as this, the illusion of depth would have been lost if all the elements crisscrossed and touched one another. Leaving that little space where one thing passes behind something else makes it quite obvious to the eye which of the features is in front. These white spaces are not apparent through a casual look at this sketch. In any event, the illusion is always effective.

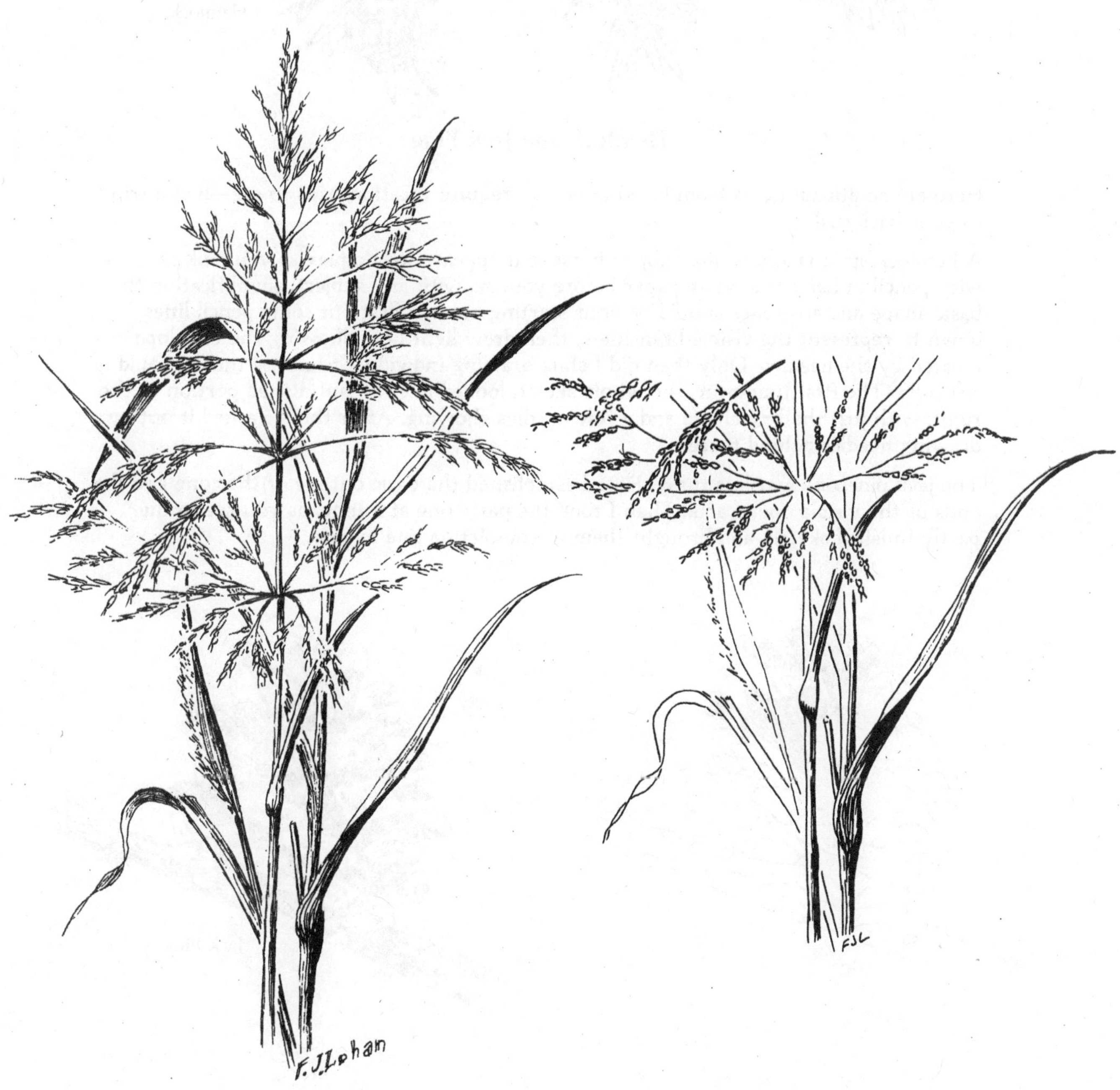

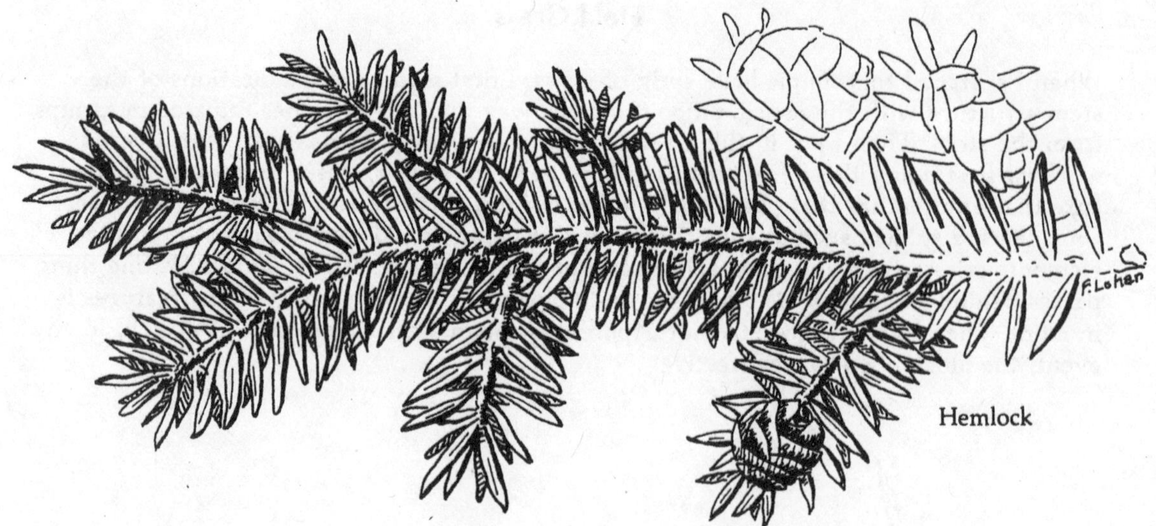

Hemlock

Hemlock and Jack Pine

Here are additional items from life that do not require vacation trips to see—just a trip to your backyard.

A hemlock sprig is a good life subject because it appears so complex as you look at it with pencil in hand and white paper before you. As with any subject, simplification to basic shape and structure should be your starting point. I first put some pencil lines down to represent the visible branchlets, then drew light lines showing the envelope created by the needles. Only then did I start drawing individual needles—those I could see fully. The first time over, the whole sketch looked like the unfinished portion to the right, with just the branchlets and a few needles showing. After this I fleshed it out by drawing needles behind these.

The jack pinecone was less fussy. First I established the basic outline of the cone and the ends of the visible open parts. Then I took the parts one at a time, as you see in the partly finished sketch, and brought them to completion one by one.

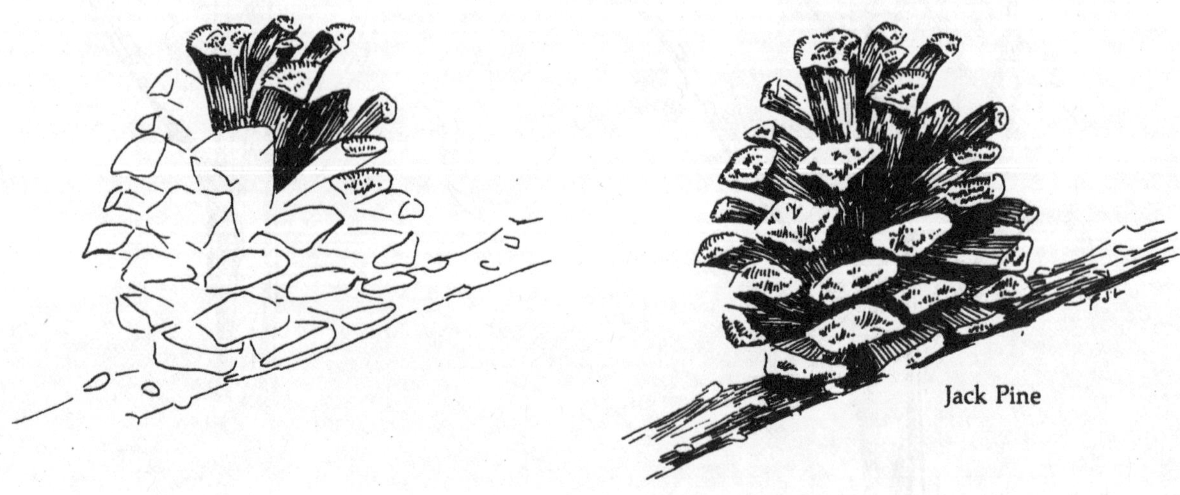
Jack Pine

A Favorite Tree

For years I drove to work each morning along five miles of rural road. Several trees along the way continually caught my attention—they became favorite trees, so to speak. Their shape, the way they stood by themselves—whatever it was, I felt pleasure every time I saw them regardless of the season.

The tree sketched here represents one of these favorites. It stood quite alone so that the small branches growing from the trunk created their own leafy masses in springtime, partially blocking out the trunk. I tried to capture that feeling—not by sitting at the side of the road and sketching, but by using those years of mental notes to do the sketch in my studio.

I first sketched the trunk and basic placement of the leaf masses and branches in pencil. Then I started to develop the crown shape with little circles and partial circles. I worked from the top of the tree down, doing a foliage mass first, then the branch indication, and only then putting in a portion of the trunk. As the last step I went over each of the foliage masses to place some larger circles and smaller dots here and there to break up the monotony. At this point I also made sure I added leaf indications at the edges of the masses to get that loose leafy effect.

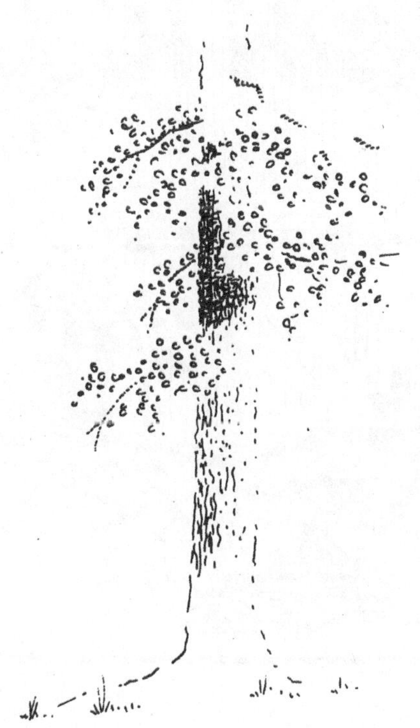

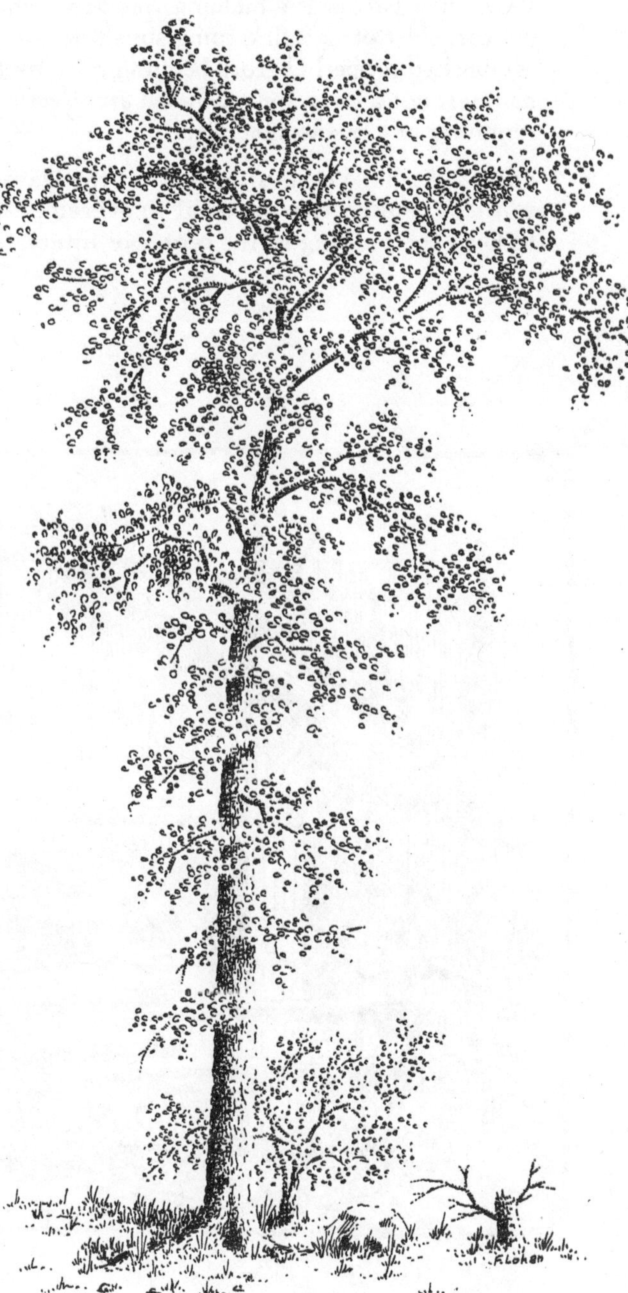

Chalet 316

I have several favorite places in the world. One of them is Gatlinburg, Tennessee, where our very good friends have a beautiful chalet. My wife and I spent a week there with them one spring, during which time I made several on-location sketches. Keep in mind how easy it is to take your fountain pen, pencil, and some bristol board (or even large index cards) with you on your vacations—you can capture little essences of a memorable trip in sketches that may mean far more to you over the years than fully detailed photographs.

Chalet 316 here is, as are all chalets in that area, built on a hillside. The sketch that shows just part of the building was done while I perched comfortably on the fender of my car, shirt off, getting some sunshine. As with all structures, the proportion must be established properly before beginning to ink the textures. I did this sketch in loose manner, not aiming for a detailed architectural-like rendering but rather a nice little reminder of a memorable place.

I inked the building first, then I did the leaves, fence, porch railing, and background trees so that I could better see what to overemphasize and what to underemphasize in order to keep the building as the center of interest.

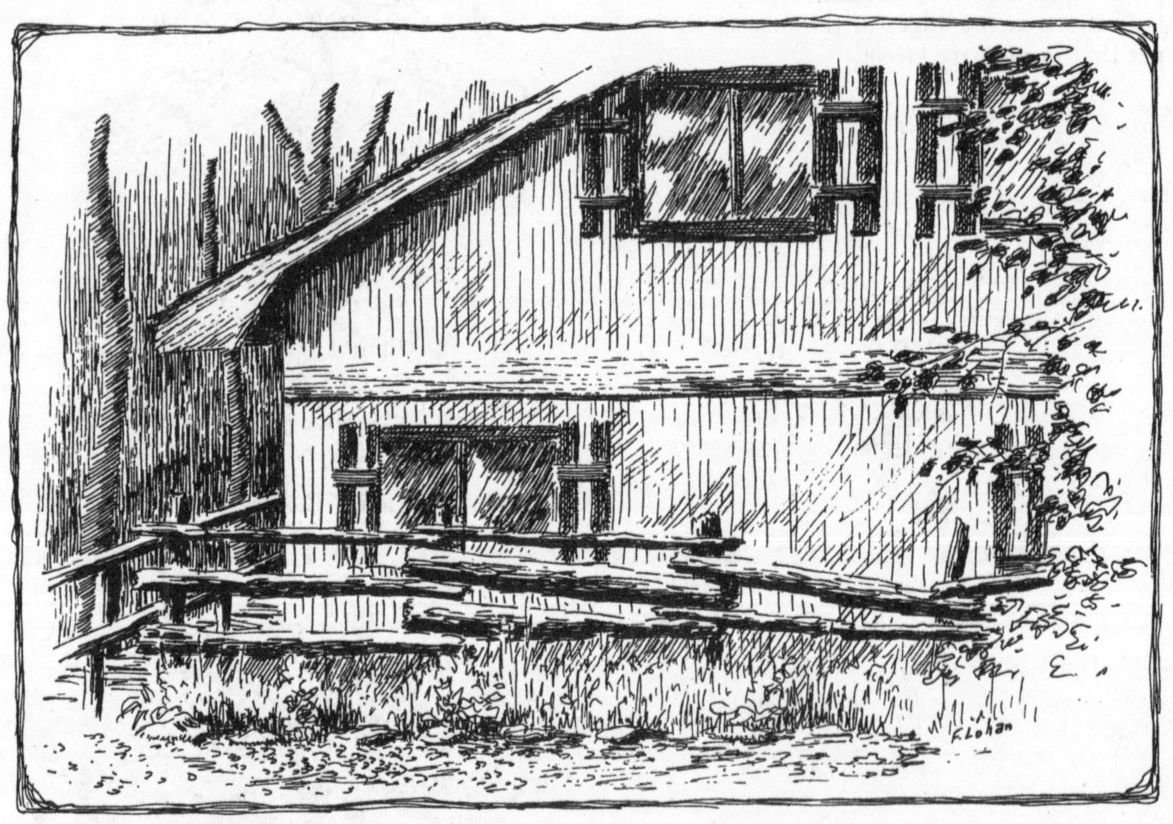

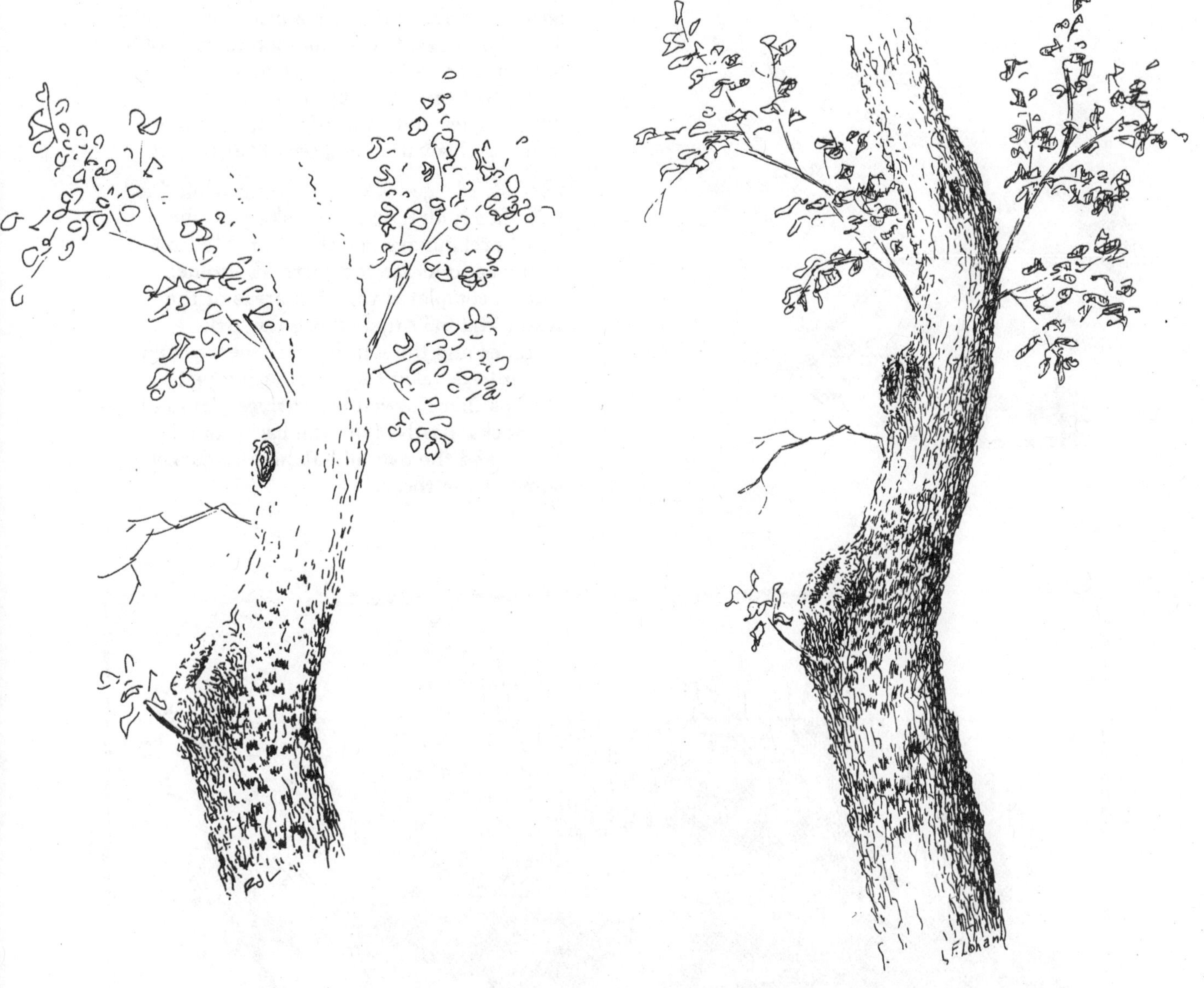

From the Porch

On the opposite, downhill side of Chalet 316 is a porch that overlooks the valley in which Gatlinburg was built. There are many trees on this side of the chalet, with part of one that is close to the porch being shown here.

What attracted me to this subject were the curve in the trunk, the knot holes, and the fine-patterned, deeply rutted bark. I used my technical pen on this sketch (000 point), barely touching it to the paper in some places to get the finest line I could.

When doing a sketch like this, exercise restraint. It is so easy to try to include so much that the feeling gets lost in clutter.

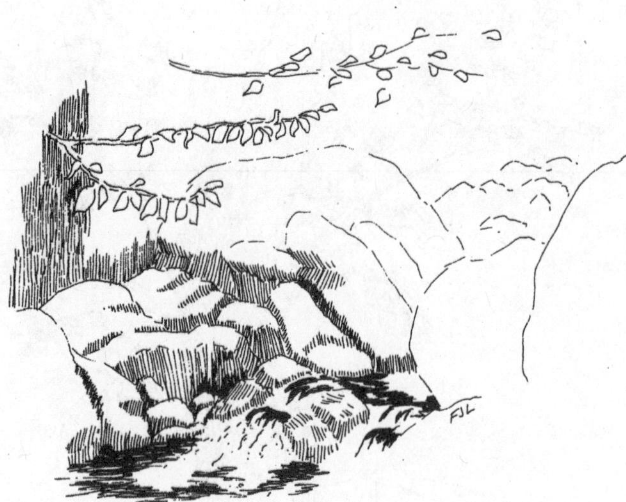

Rocky River

Near Gatlinburg there is a picnic area called The Chimneys. It runs along one bank of a beautiful rock-filled river. This stretch of river has been the subject of a number of my sketches and paintings. I am not alone in using this varied and beautiful subject.

I sat on a large rock in the river while I did this sketch directly in ink, skipping the usual preliminary pencil layout. My first step was to locate the rocks in outline. Then I completed the dark areas of the water and indicated where the little cascades and the white water were. Then I began to develop the rocks, using pen strokes that showed the surface planes of the rocks. Lastly, I did the background forest and the overall hatching to darken some of the rocks.

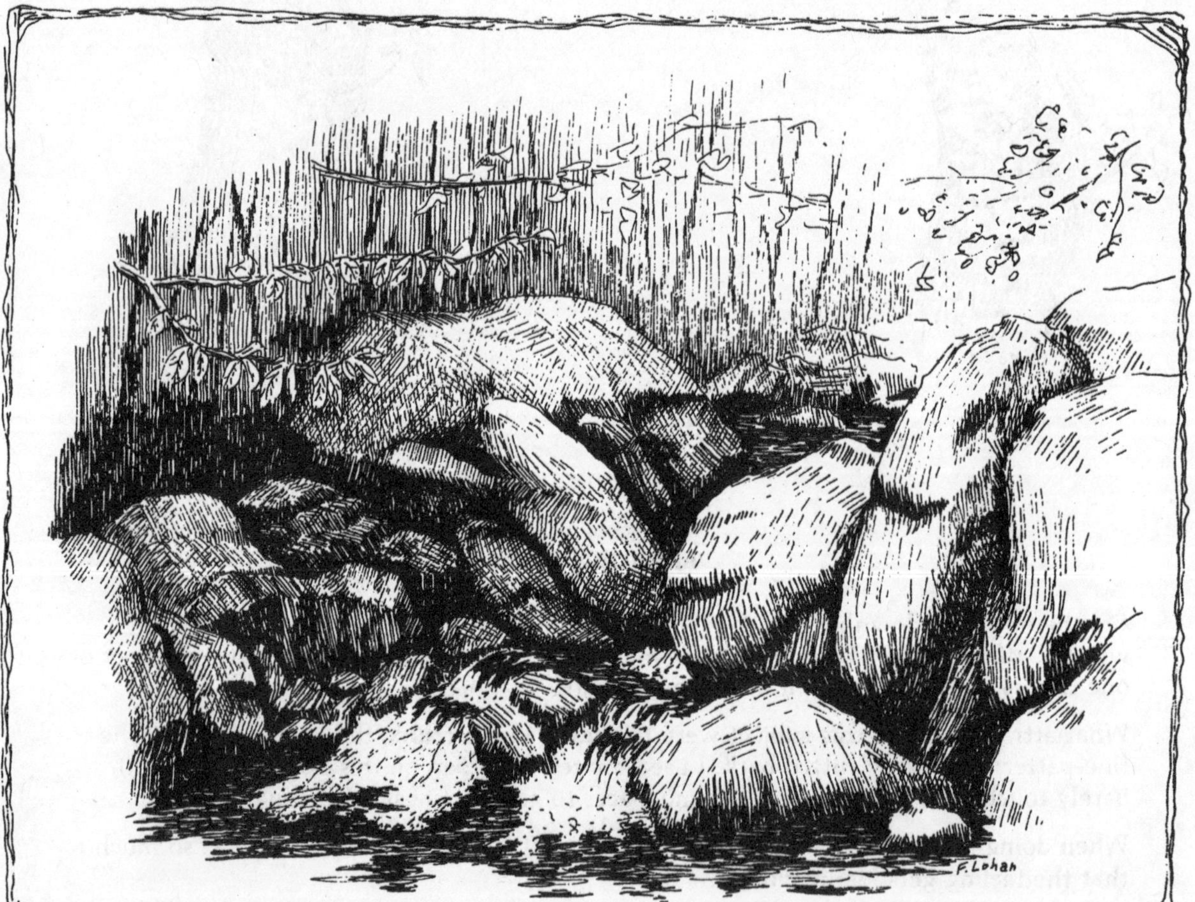

Seeds and Flowers

Your own backyard can produce a tremendous variety of subjects for practice sketches. I did these little vignettes from items on hand within fifty feet of my back patio. You may not be satisfied with the results the first few times you sketch simple little things like these. You will probably try to show too much detail at first. Keep at it—it is pleasant to spend a few minutes on a little sketch, perhaps of a couple of acorns, then try a few different ways to show the same textures.

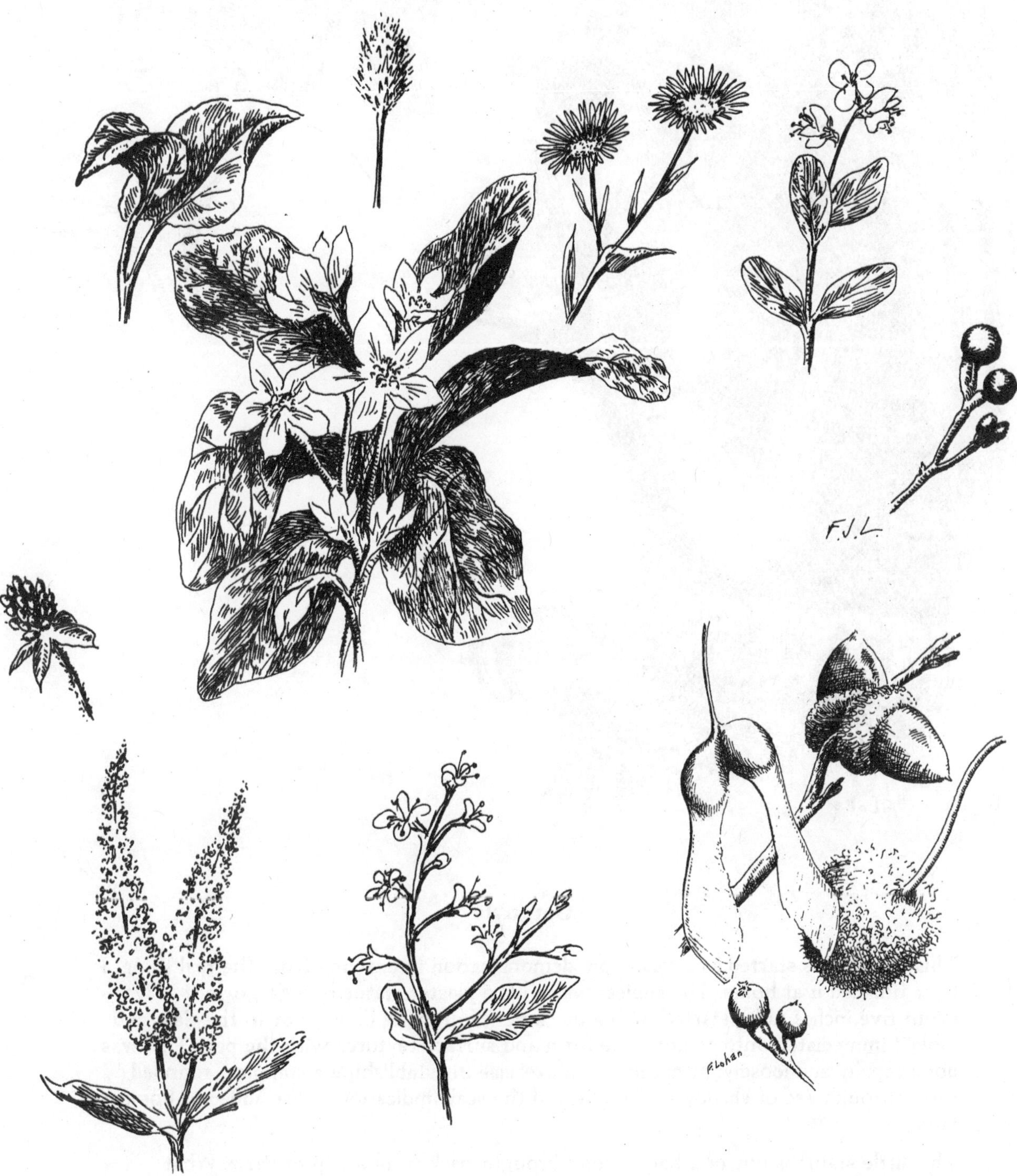

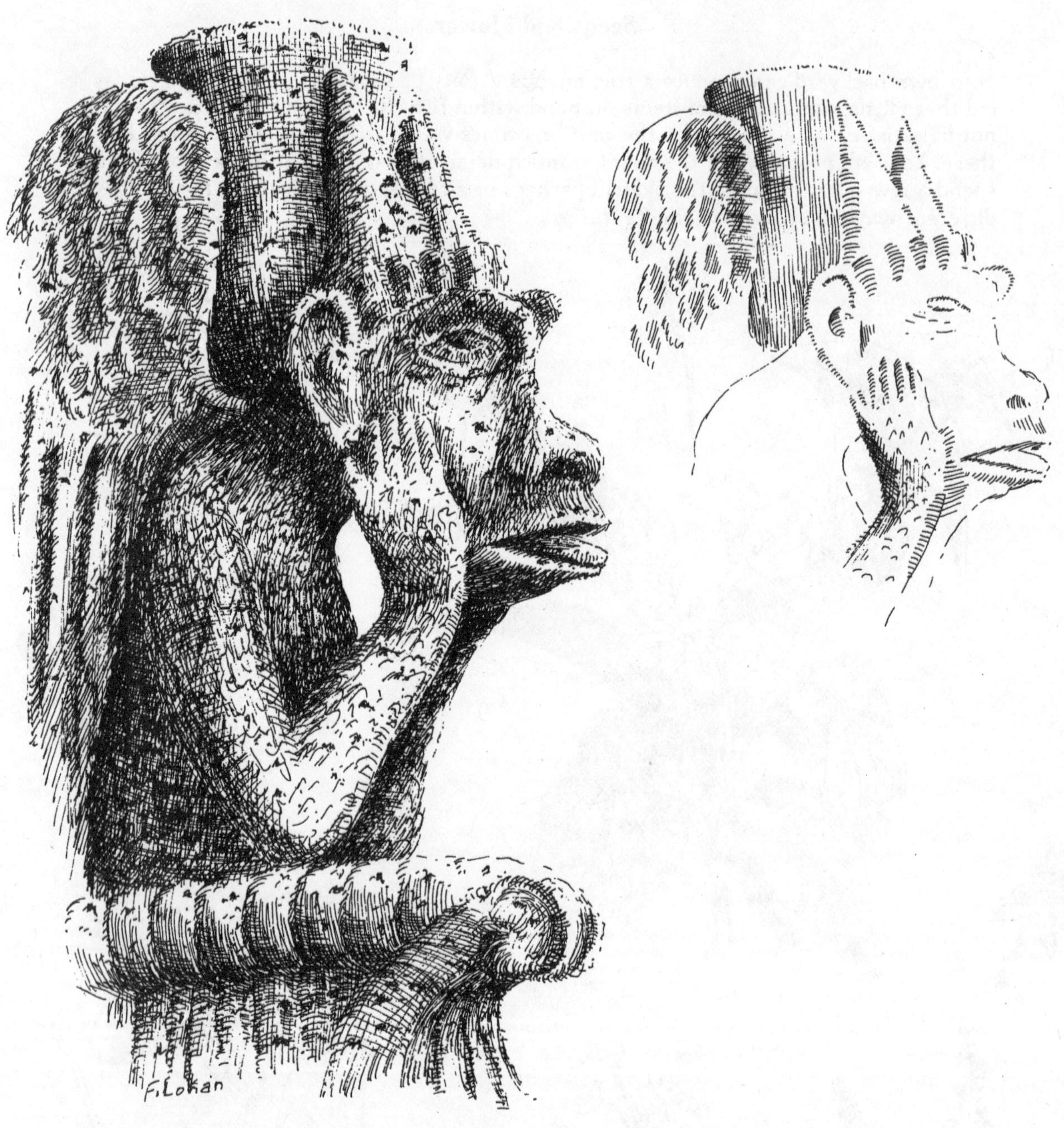

Gargoyle

This sketch was started as a classroom demonstration in drawing from the real thing. I later finished it at home. The subject was a little plaster statue of a gargoyle that was about five inches tall. I started with a quick pencil drawing done prior to the class and moved immediately into creating the form and surface textures with the pen. This was done rapidly and loosely, primarily as an exercise in establishing a complex, rounded form through use of shadows. The pits and the scale indications were added at home later.

This little statue is one of a half dozen I brought back from a trip to Paris. What souvenirs do you have that would make good sketch subjects?

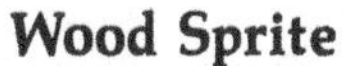

Wood Sprite

This sketch is of another souvenir—one brought back from Germany by friends. It is a face carved into a branch of wood, with the natural, uncarved wood portions acting as the hat and hair. I have often said that wood is one of the best truly natural materials for the pen artist to depict because its grain, bark, cracks, and folds are easily shown in a realistic manner. It gives me great satisfaction to create the illusion of textures such as this.

The first thing I did was to draw the overall outline and facial features, then I concentrated on the wood grain texture around and over these features.

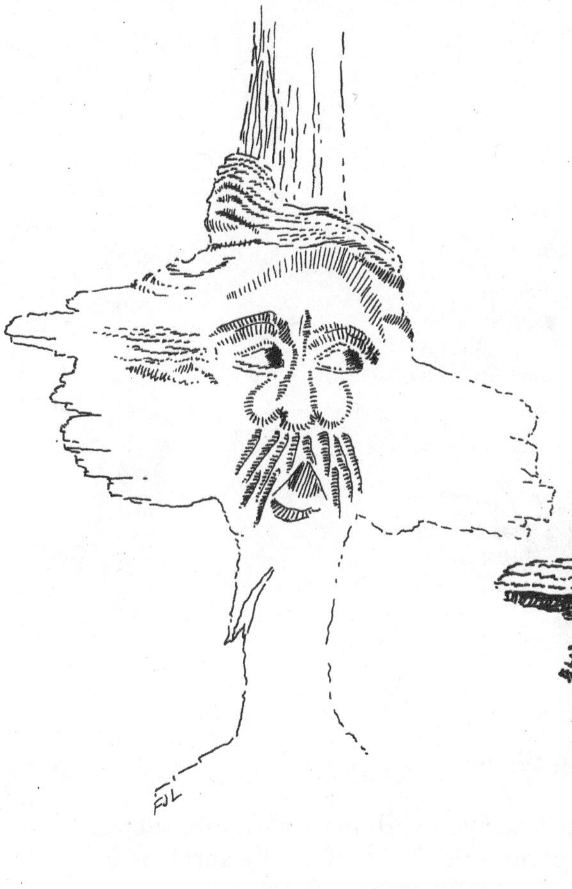

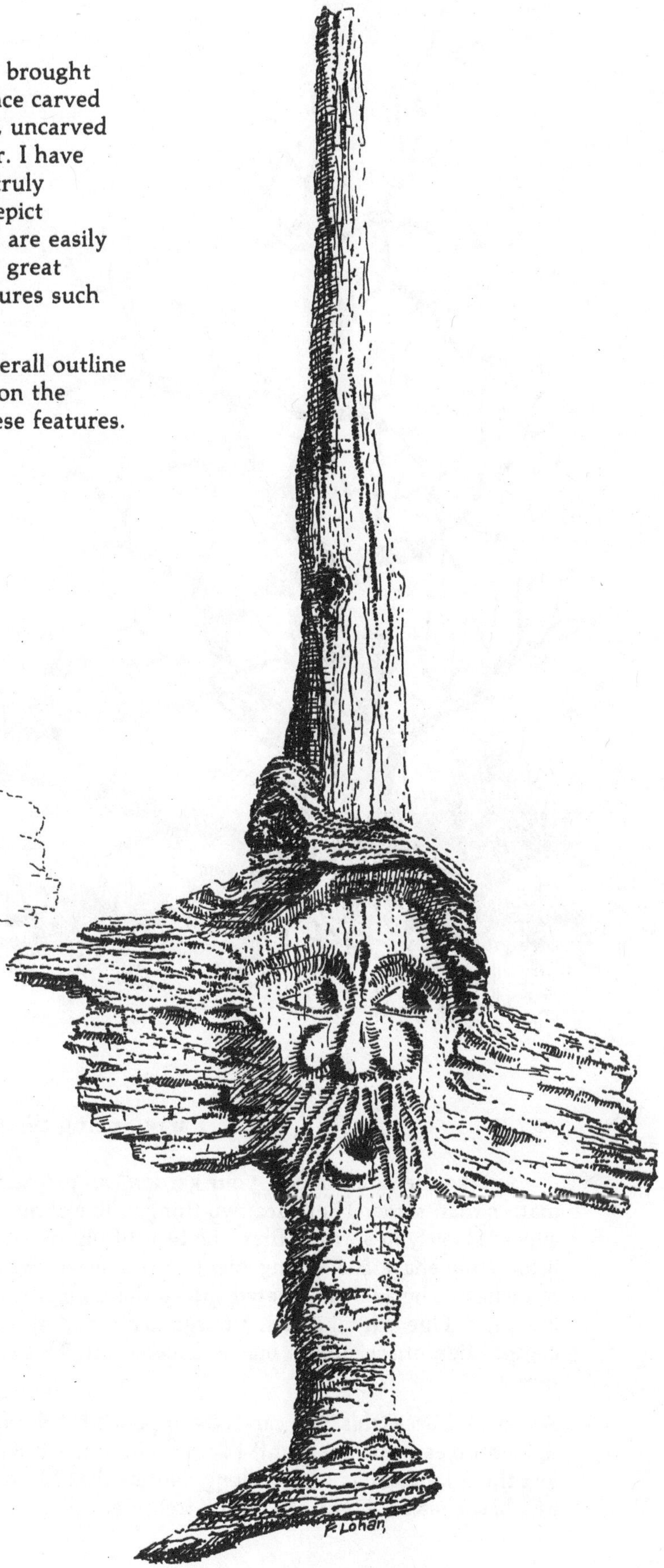

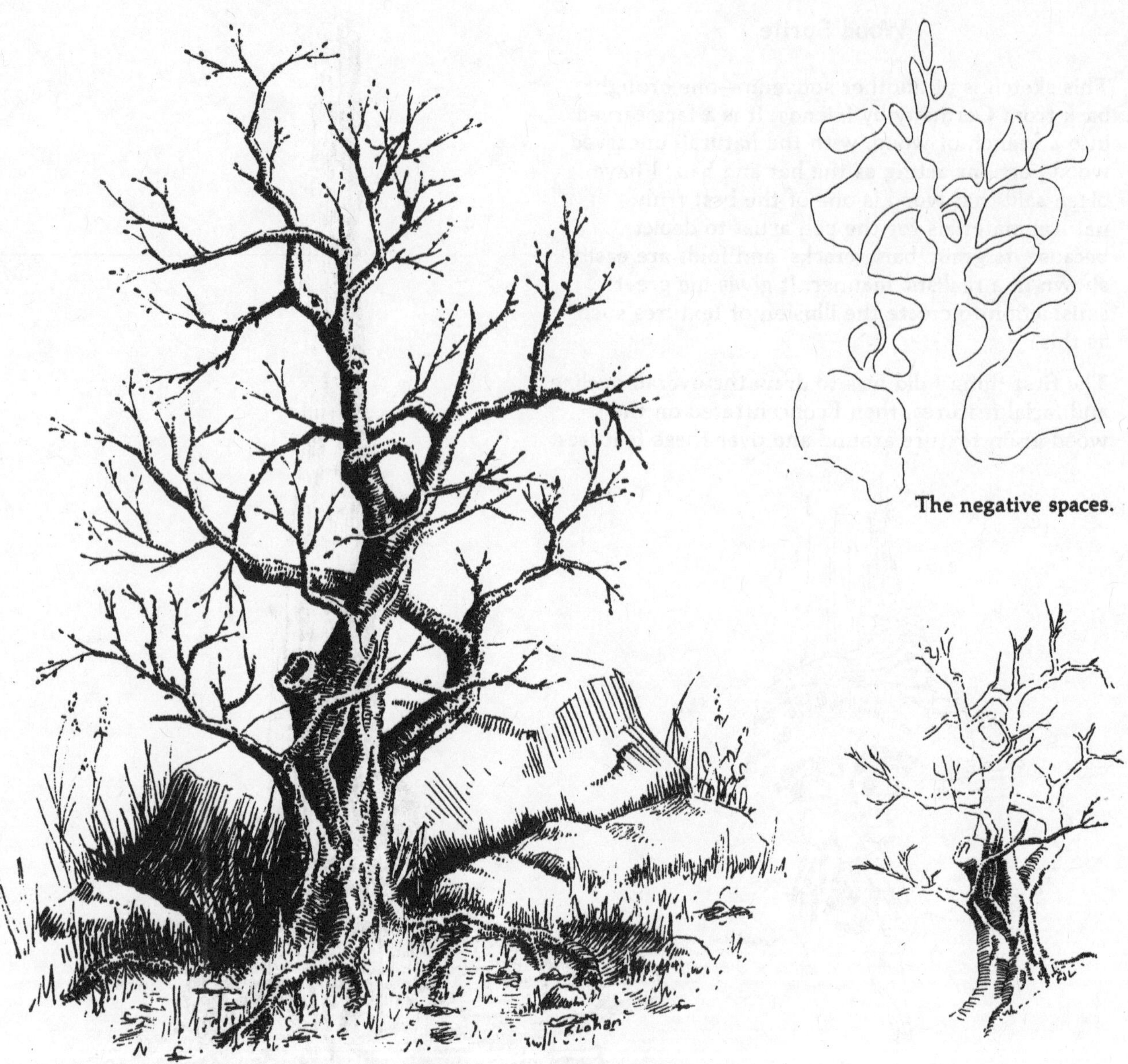

The negative spaces.

Early Spring Shrub

If you take the time to look, your garden can provide you with more elaborate subject matter than seeds. There are two things I like about this sketch of a little shrub as it appeared early in spring—first, the beautifully twisted branches and, second, the interesting shape and arrangement of the negative spaces (the "holes" between the branches). The auxiliary sketch shows these negative spaces emphasized rather than the branches. One can take such an organization of space from nature and create a composition of *any* subject matter based on it. This one suggests a floral arrangement to me.

As usual, I drew this tree carefully in pencil before starting with ink. Having selected my light sources (from the right) I knew where the bright highlights would be and carefully left them uninked as I went along. Notice that I based the method of showing the trunk and branches on Albrecht Durer's treatment of tree trunks, shown earlier (see page 32).

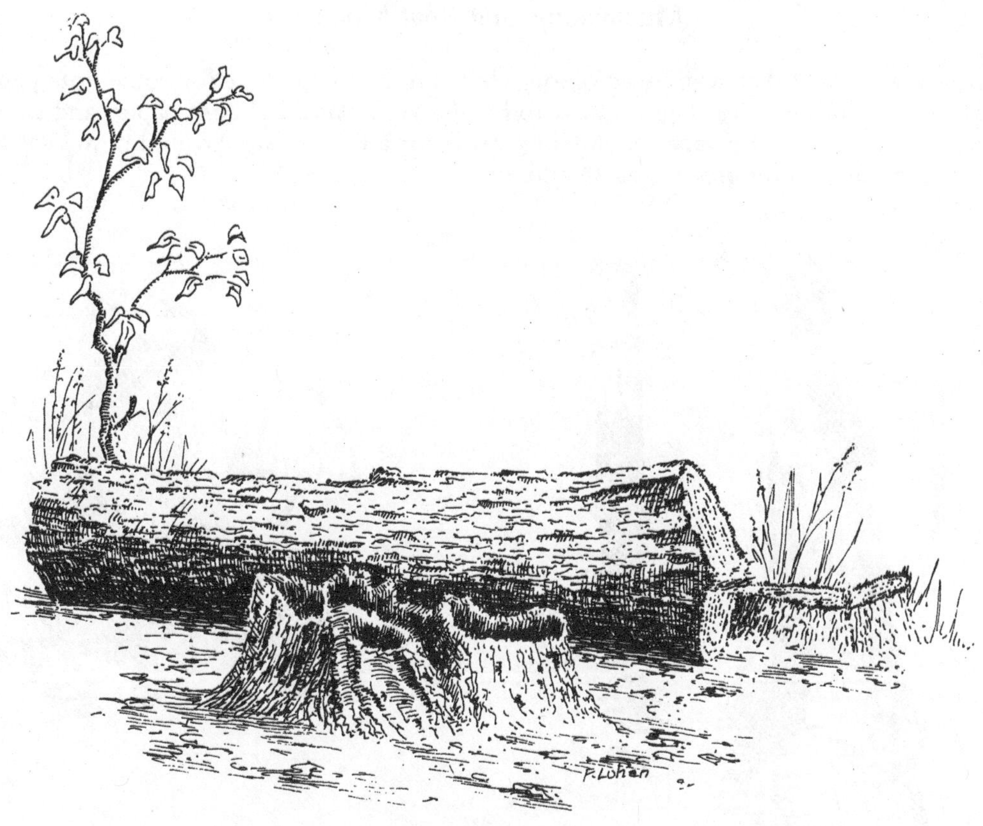

Downed Tree

An expansion program at a nearby community college required that some sizable trees be removed. Before being cut into smaller pieces, a number of these giants were left lying about for some time after being felled. On one of our customary walks (my wife, dog, and I frequently used to walk the grounds) it occurred to me that the patterns of rough bark on the downed tree trunks would make a good texture for student exercises. So after a couple of mental notes I did this little sketch to indicate a method of handling the bark.

To make a more complete composition, both philosophically and visually, I added the rotted stump that was long dead to indicate the fate of all trees, whether their end is brought about by man or nature. Life does not totally succumb to death, however, so I added the young sapling at the left to bring this thought of new life into the sketch.

I achieved the texture on the trunk by making a once-over series of irregular longitudinal lines, dots, and squiggles; then I added some small "combs" by drawing a series of short hatch marks. A final overall cross-hatching produced the shaded areas. The very last thing I did was to tone down the upper edges of the dead stump closest to the viewer. I had left these edges plain white, as they are in the partially finished sketch, so I could determine at the end how much to tone them to barely put them back into the picture.

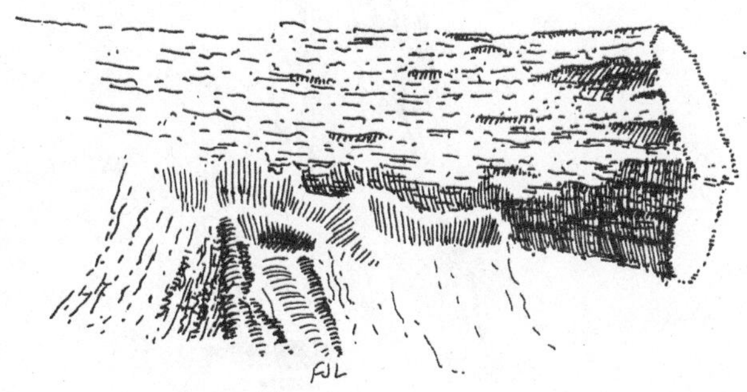

Mushrooms and Boat Moorings

These two simple sketches, based on objects from life, were done for some note paper I had printed for my wife. Tips on how to handle your sketch, choose paper, and so on, to prepare your own note paper or greeting cards for a printer are covered in my earlier book, *Pen and Ink Techniques*, pages 38 and 39.

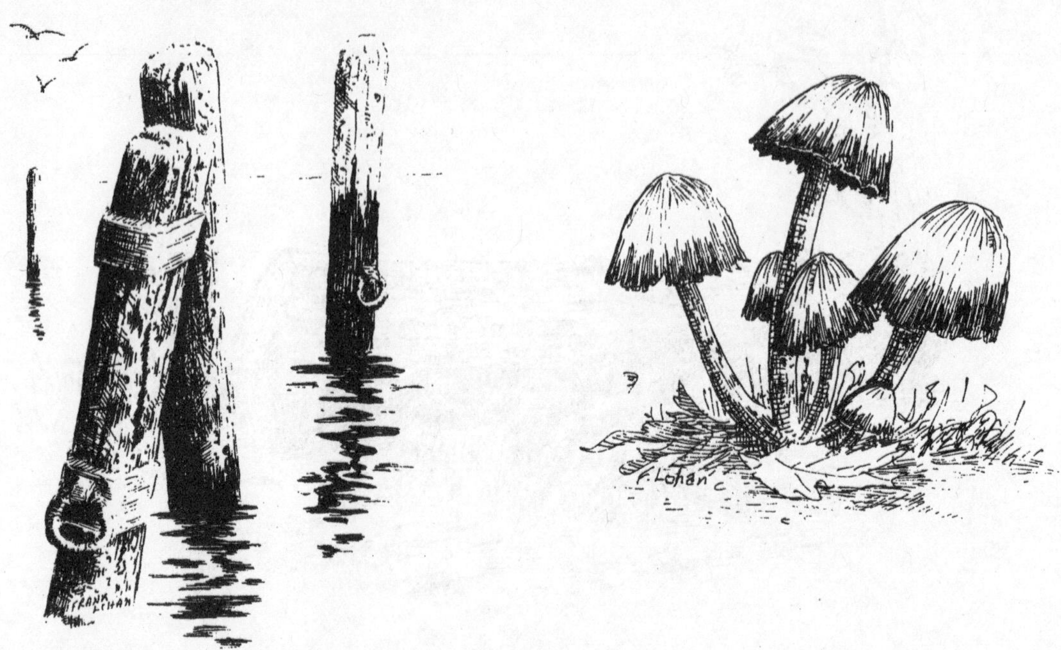

For these sketches, I first drew the main features of the wooden pilings in ink, then I crosshatched over them to complete the dark areas. The last thing I did was to put the little dots and marks over all the pilings to give them a pitted look.

The mushrooms are basically an outline sketch with the dark features built up by overlaying strokes in the same direction rather than using crosshatches (except for the stems).

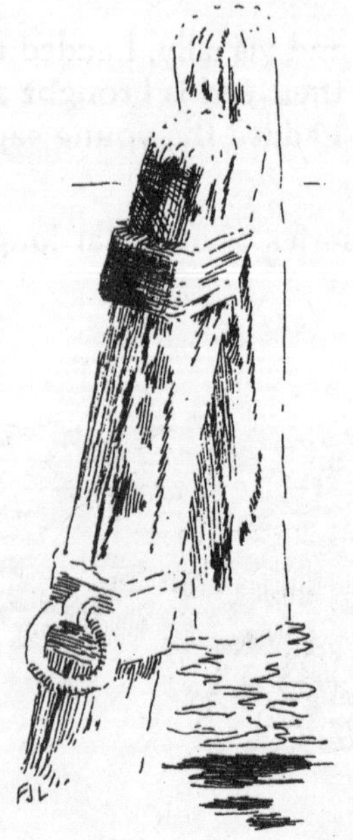

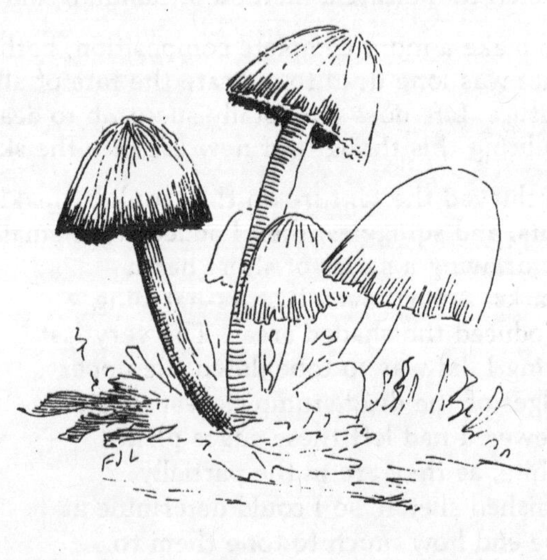

6: Landscape Subjects

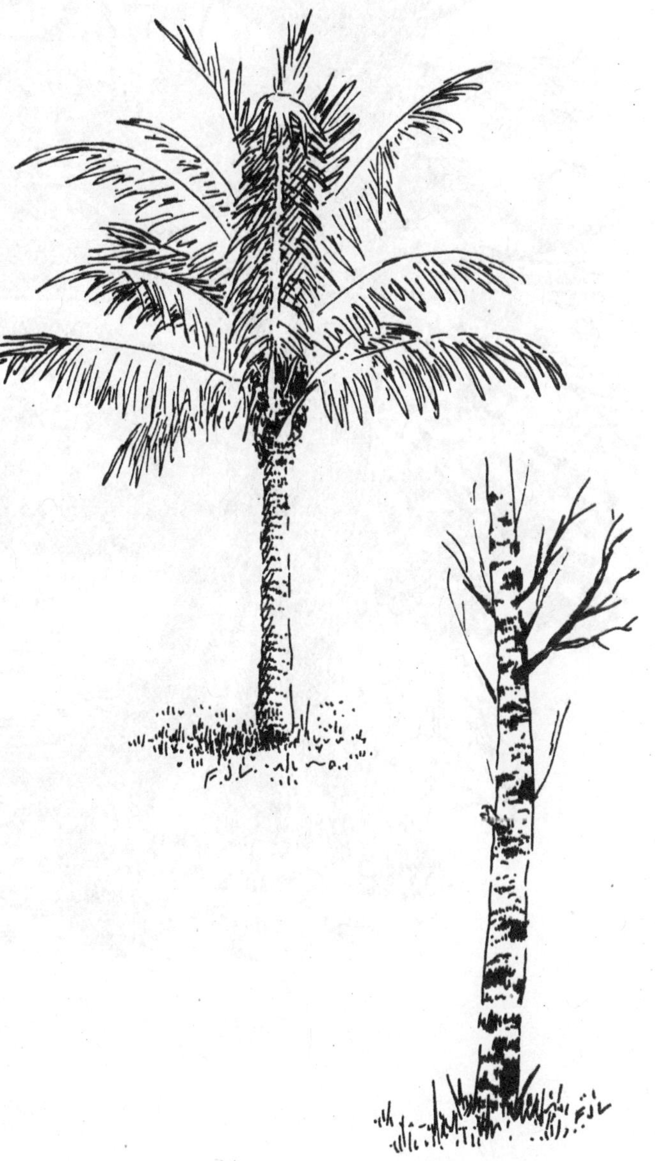

Trees, with all the various species, shapes, varieties, sizes, and variations of foliage, are one of the most variable elements of nature. This is to the artist's advantage. When drawing or painting trees, you have the widest latitude imaginable to fit this element to your compositional needs without losing realism.

A landscape sketch can have one or two tree forms as the center of interest and little or nothing else. Or it can have thirty-two visible tree forms plus numerous small shrubs. This latter is a tree count from the sketch *Sunny Clearing* (page 98) in this section, while the former describes the sketch *Birches* in Chapter 4. Each of these sketches is properly called a landscape.

The challenge of creating successful landscape sketches lies in realistic handling of foliage. I cannot say that such realistic handling *always* requires one to ignore individual leaves and concentrate on showing only the masses of leaves, although this is generally a good rule to follow. As an exception to this rule, see *Favorite Tree* (page 83) in Chapter 5. In this example only individual leaves are indicated, yet in this case it works. Still, I would not want to represent trees this way in general since it would get monotonous both to execute and to look at.

Although there are no hard and fast tabus in treating the matter of landscapes and landscape elements, I will describe in this chapter a few things I do that seem to be effective.

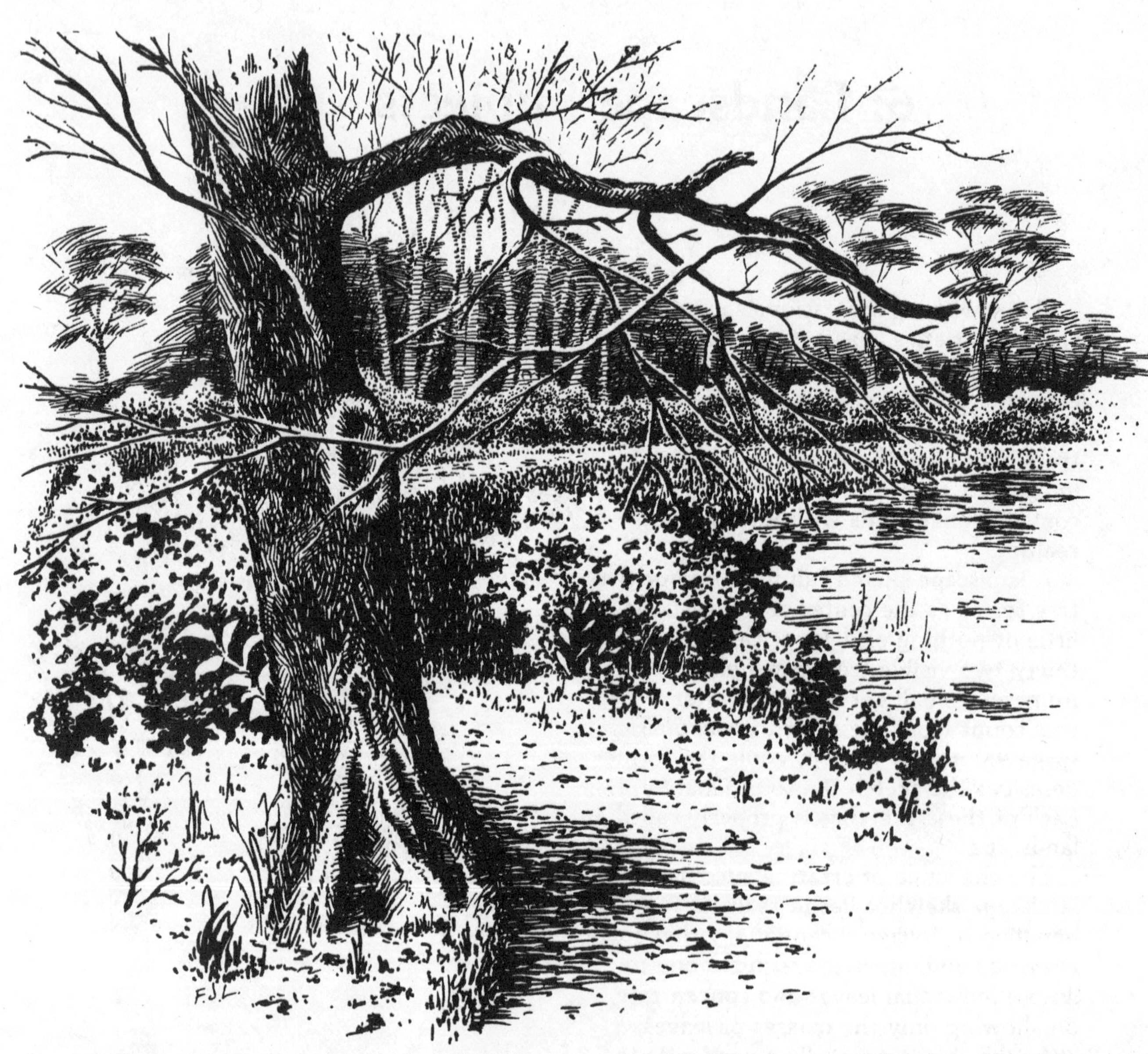

Around the Lake

This sketch of a path curving around a lake is based on a sketch by another artist in which a large country building was the main subject. To show my students yet another way to draw trees, I took one edge of that sketch and made the tree and foreground path a center of interest, adding some detail to the background.

Earlier, in Chapter 4, Subjects from Photographs, I used the sketch *High Country* to illustrate the alternation of light and dark values in creating successively receding layers of growth. You can see the same principle is applied here.

Auxiliary sketches A, B, and C indicate how I progressed from the initial pencil sketch and the first tone of the farthest trees (A) through development of the dark little tree trunks and the prominent trees (B) to completion of the shrubbery at the base of these trees (C).

In this instance the tree foliage is done totally with hatch marks and crosshatches to indicate the leaf masses. The shrubbery and lower growth at the base of this tree line is done primarily with stipple (dots), which are built up to a solid black at the bottom (C), against which the lighter grass is contrasted.

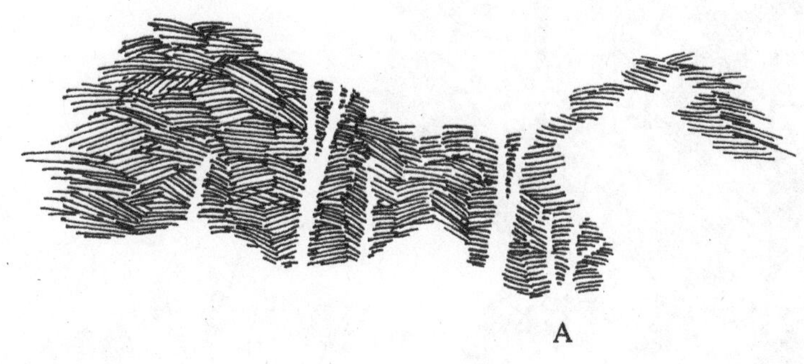

A

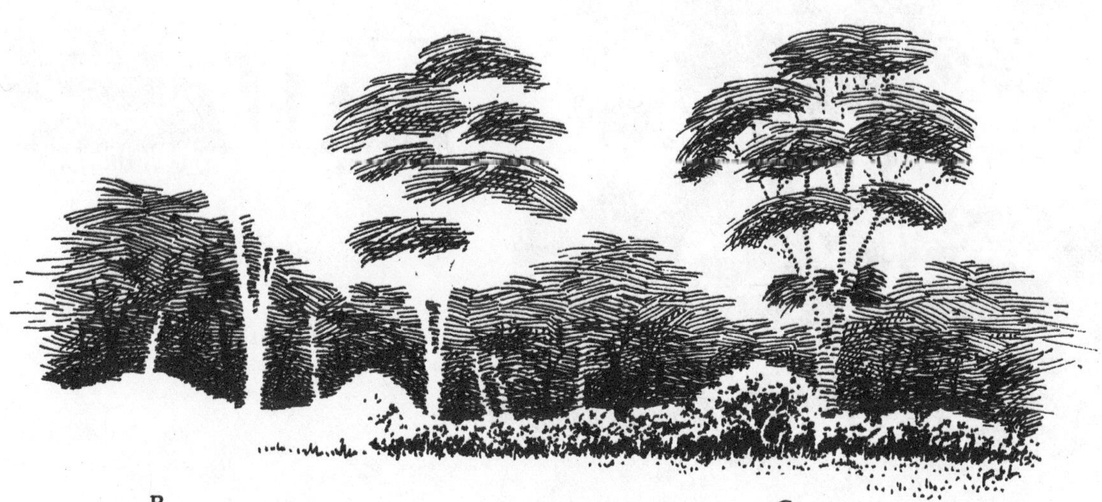

B

C

Foliage Step by Step

More often than not, my landscape sketches contain deciduous trees that I want to represent in a realistic manner. This takes some initial planning followed by a succession of steps that I have found produce the effect I want.

The illustrative sketch here contains two basic parts: the clump of three trees in the foreground and trees and shrubbery in the background. Taking the background first, the auxiliary sketch (A) shows how everything was carefully outlined in ink before the most distant trees and the dark area under the shrubs (B) were started. Next the dark area was completed (C), and then the farthest trees modulated a little in tone, the undergrowth shrubbery trunks hatched to tone them down a little and the shrubbery leaf indications added (D).

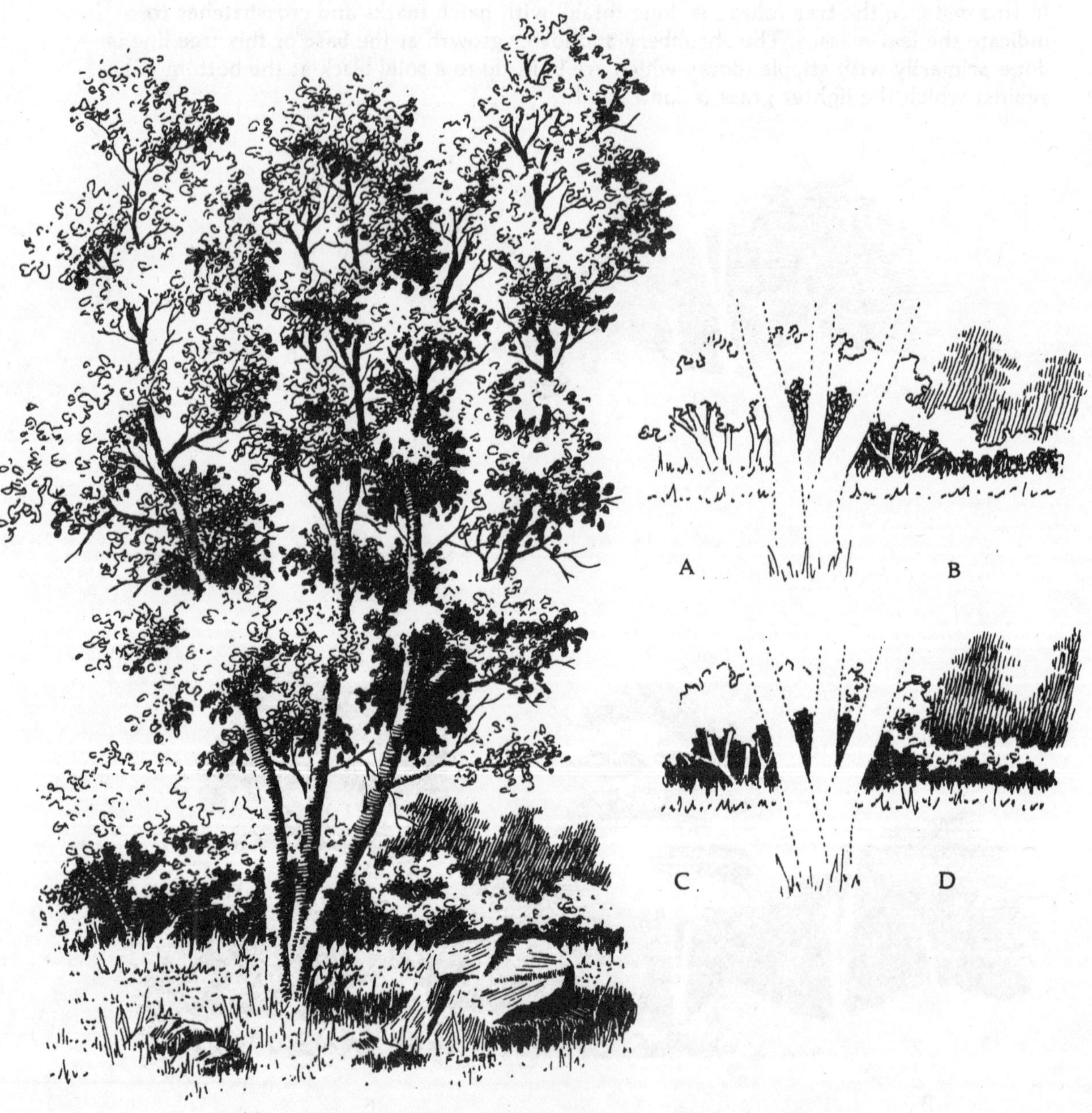

I follow six basic steps when sketching leafy foliage. First I make a tight pencil drawing outlining the light and dark leaf masses and the visible trunks and main branches (E). Then I outline these features in ink (F) and proceed to ink in the dark foliage (G). At this point, when the ink is dry, I erase all the pencil lines. Before bringing the dark foliage to its final value I darken the trunk and main branches, which will appear as dark silhouettes through the holes in foliage, and I show the shadow on the light trunks (H). Now I bring the dark foliage to its final value and add the little bits of additional dark tones (I). Finally, I touch up the dark sides of the trunks, add the small branches, and loosen up the foliage by showing some single leaves, both light and dark, just outside of the main leaf masses (J).

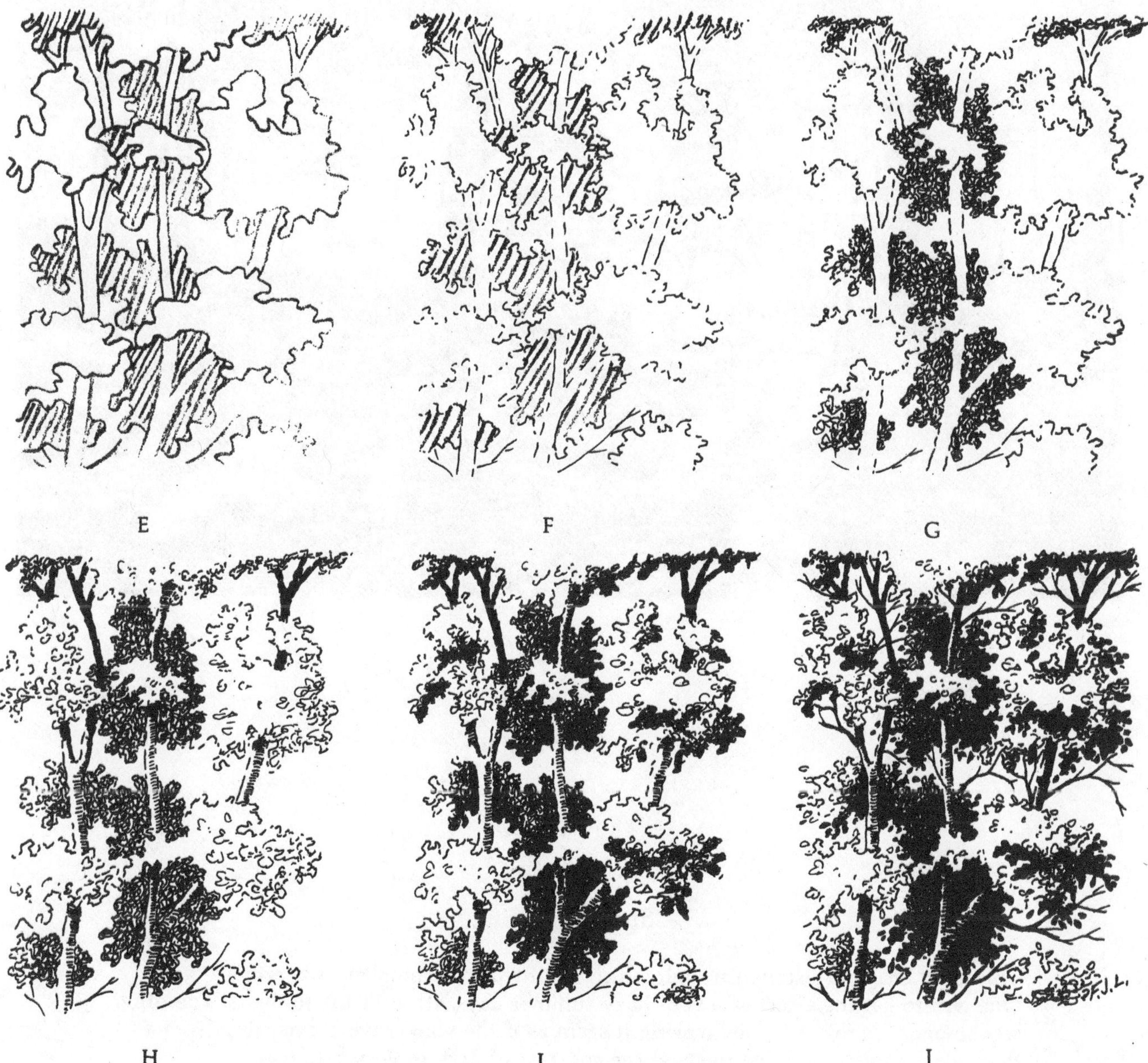

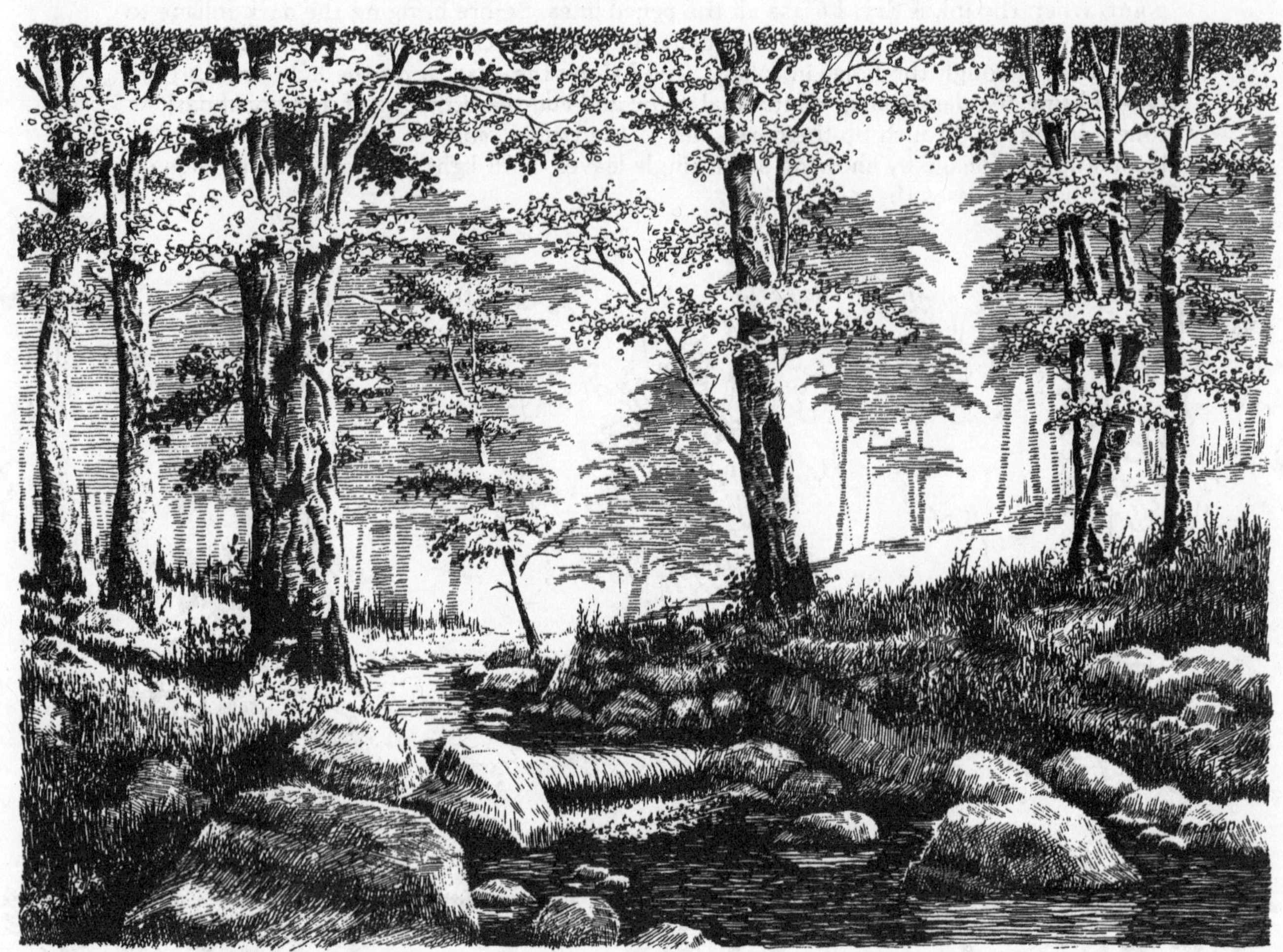

Sunny Clearing

This is an imaginary scene through which I wanted to accomplish two primary goals. One was to get the effect of a very hazy summer day with brilliant sunlight. The other was to enhance this effect by making it seem as if the viewer were emerging from a thick, dark forest. I wanted to show the contrast of dark to very bright.

Haze, like fog, tends to obliterate detail, making distant objects appear as flat monotones. The farthest trees were the first things I inked, as you can see in the detail sketch. Then I completed the foliage clumps and started on the tree trunks. These tree trunks are done in the style of Albrecht Durer (see Chapter 2), with relatively smooth but undulating bark. I next completed the water, then started the grassy areas in the foreground.

My first intention was to have the triangular piece of land to the right of the waterfall bathed in sunlight, with the dark shadowed strip behind it. However, this dominated, and the effect I wanted with the brilliantly sunny clearing toward the background was almost lost. I then put this triangular area back into the shade, leaving just the little patch of sunlight at the base of the nearest tree across the stream as bright relief for the foreground.

The distant, brightly lit clearing gave me an excellent opportunity to show undergrowth and weeds strongly silhouetted against it.

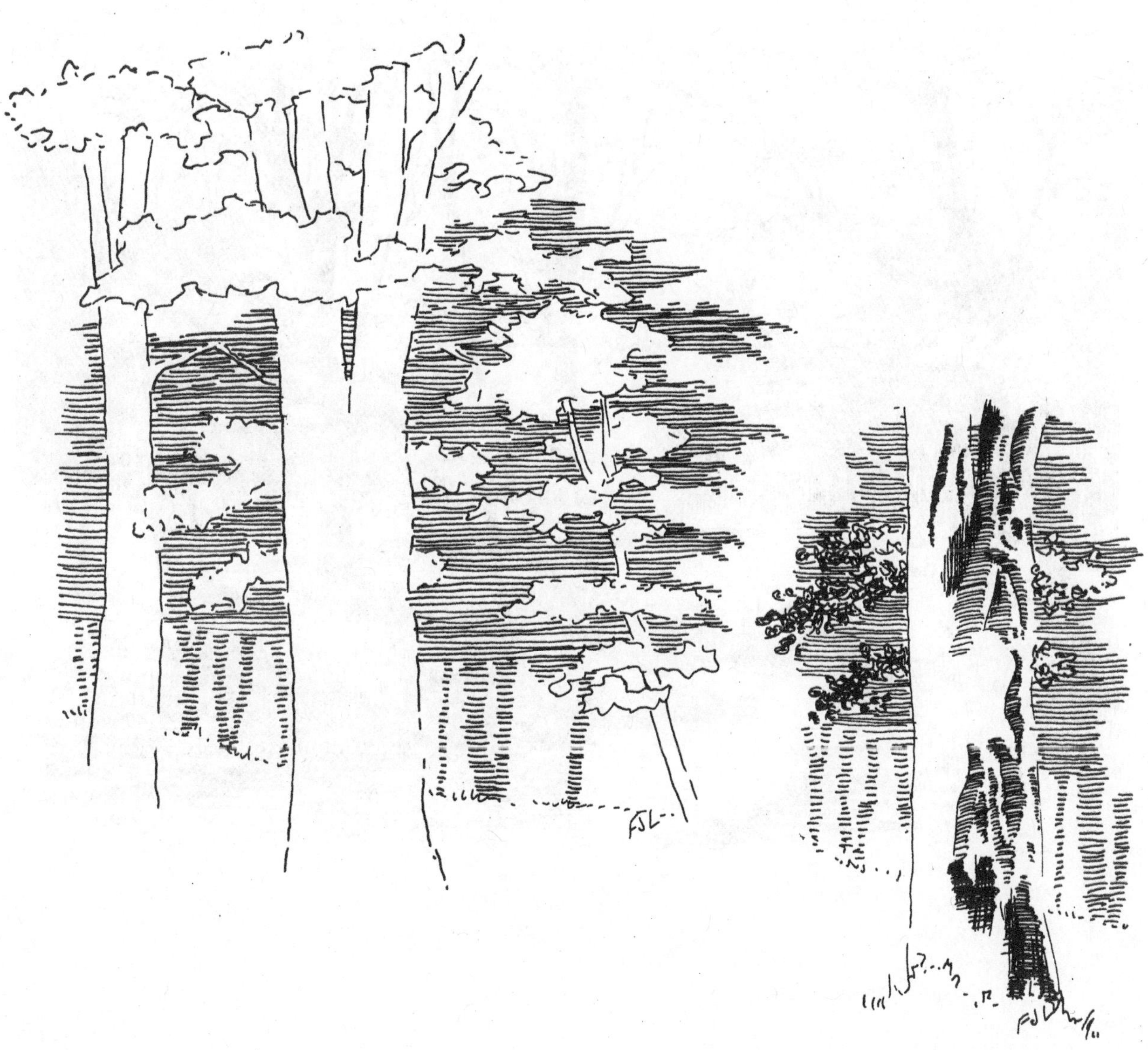

Brook

This forest scene differs in several ways from the sketch *Sunny Clearing* in this chapter (page 98). First, the haze illusion is not used—the background shows detail rather than creating a flat monotone. Second, the tree trunks are textured to represent the rough bark you would find on an oak, elm, or hickory rather than the smoother bark of a beech.

The sequence of steps I followed here was about the same as those described for *Sunny Clearing*: first, a tight pencil sketch, then inking of the background. I find doing the background first a good idea. It improves my judgment of just how dark and how light to make the trunks and leaf masses in the nearer trees.

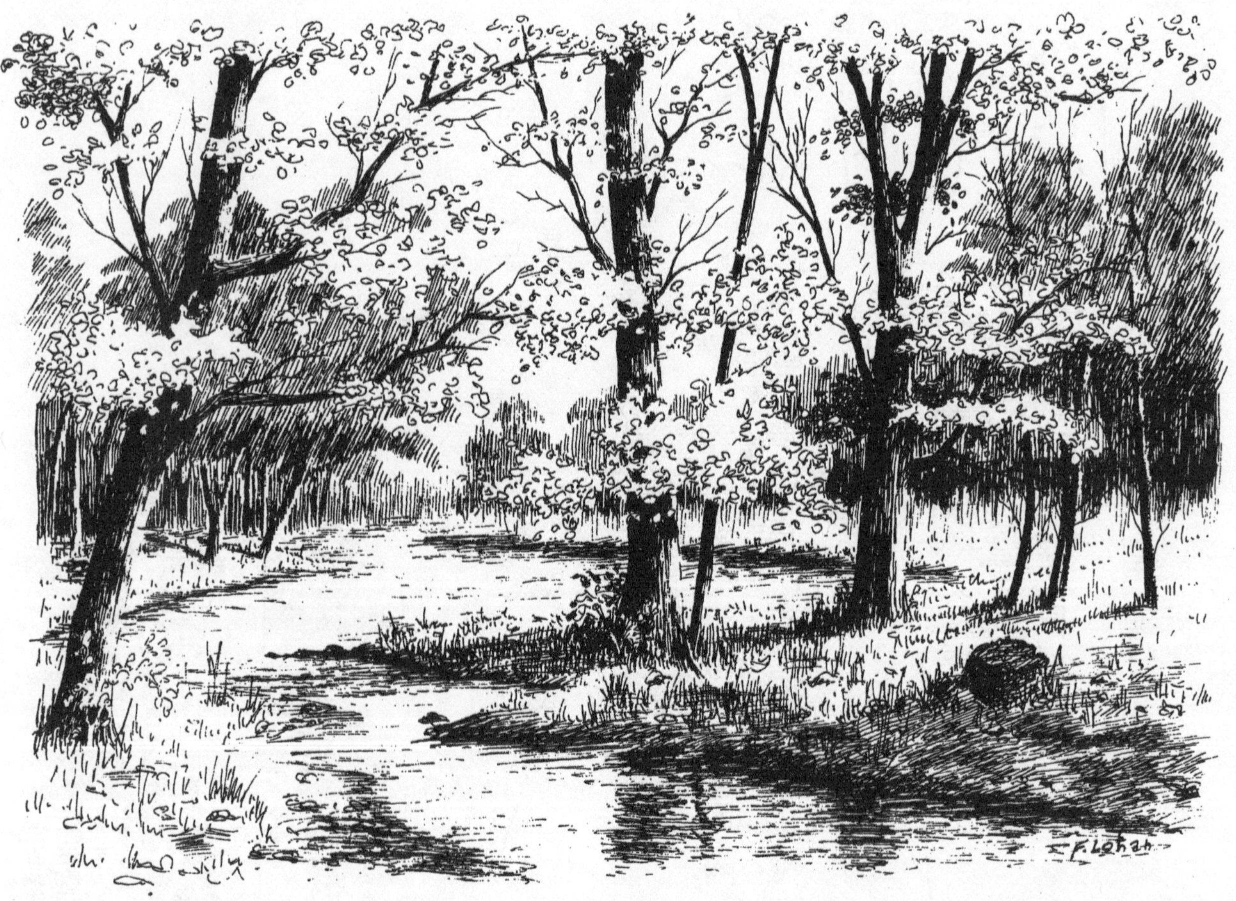

With and Without Foliage

To sketch realistic trees, you should first sketch a realistic structure of trunk and branches in pencil. You should then place the masses of foliage on this structure where they will do your composition the most good and in a natural-looking manner, depending on which branches come toward the viewer and which recede on the other side of the tree. You have considerable latitude with trees, since they lack the precise symmetry of faces and buildings.

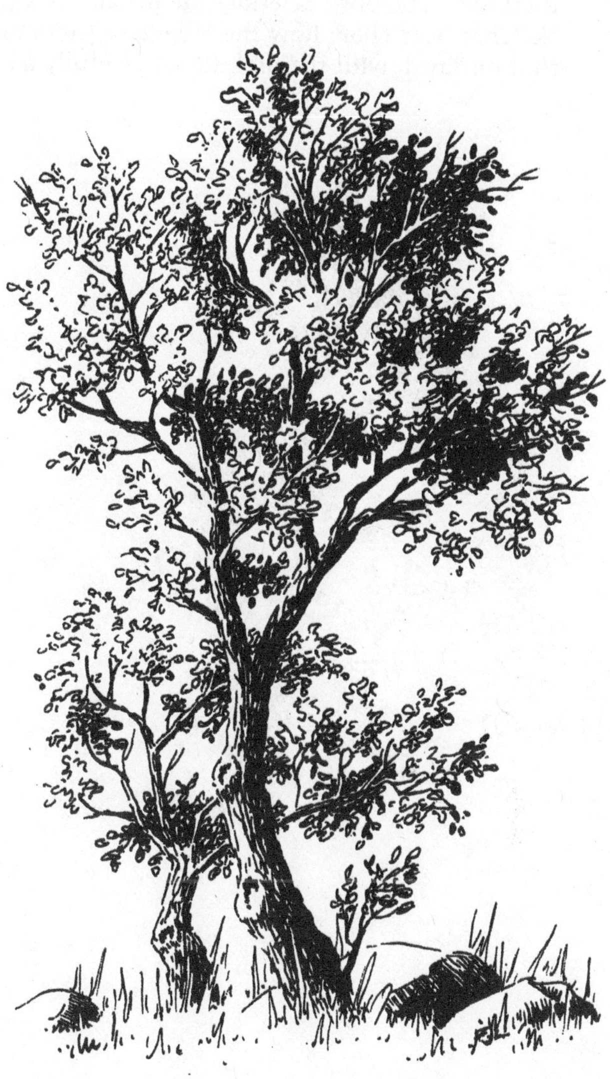

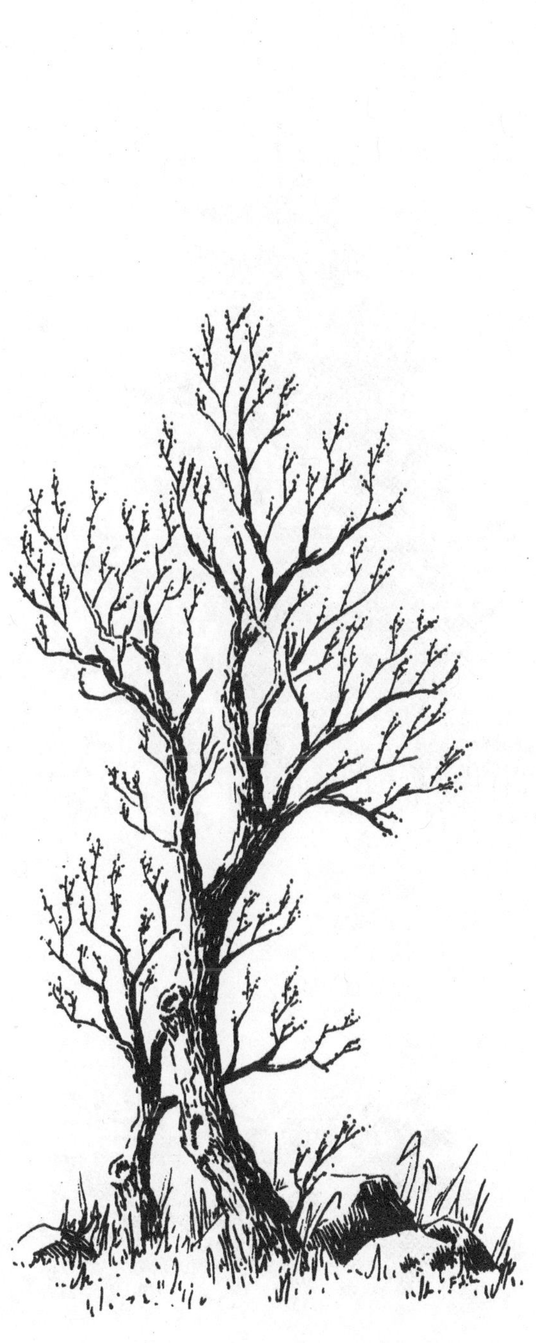

Evergreen Types

Evergreens are best depicted by a stroke that is totally different from the one that is appropriate for deciduous or tropical trees. The challenge is to suggest the needles by sketching clumps or by distributing them more or less uniformly, depending on the nature of the tree. Short choppy lines in the correct direction will do the job.

The closer the tree or shrub to the viewer, the more detail that must be shown and, therefore, the more carefully the pencil drawing must be executed. The two auxiliary sketches here show how the foliage in these cases, which I wanted to remain white, was first outlined, with the dark tones carefully added around this outline.

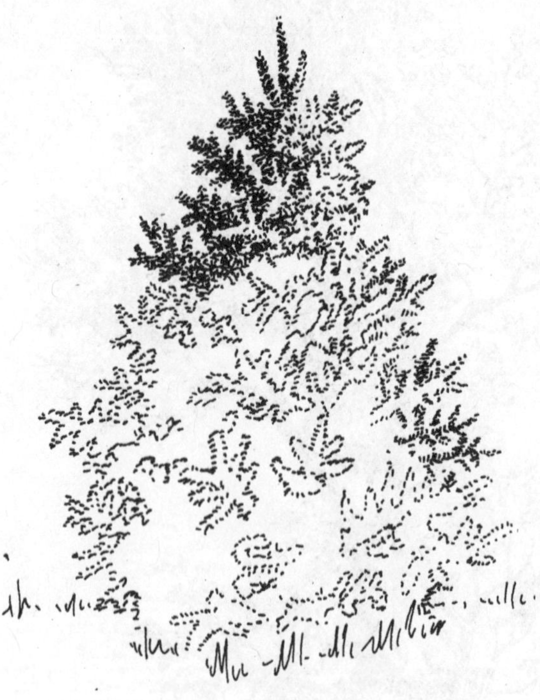

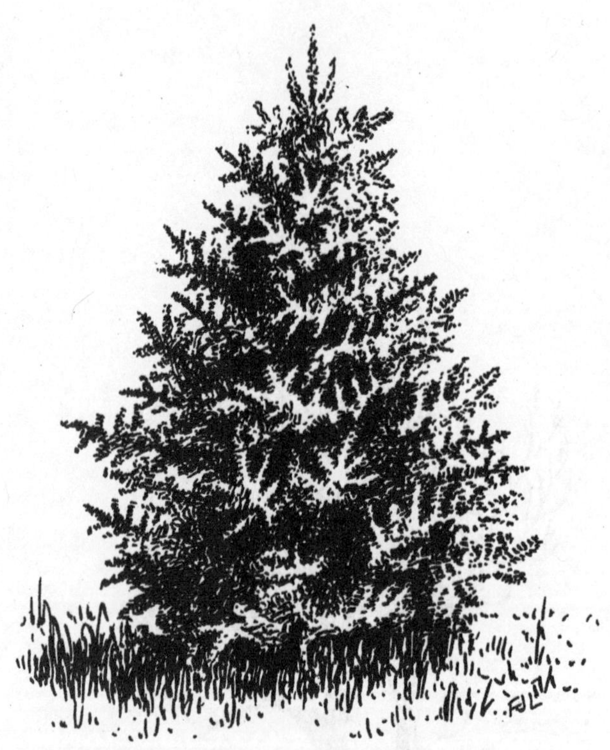

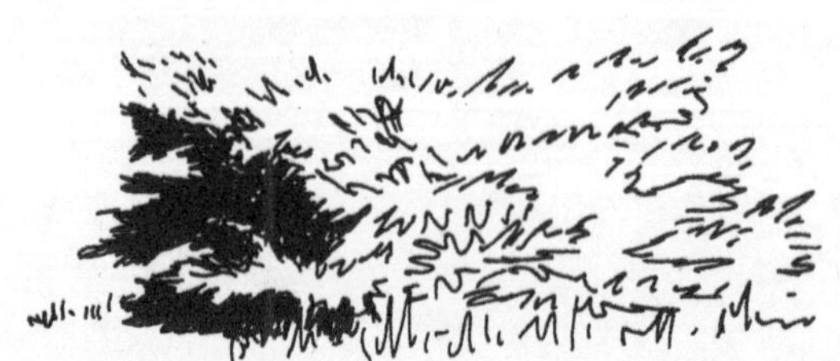

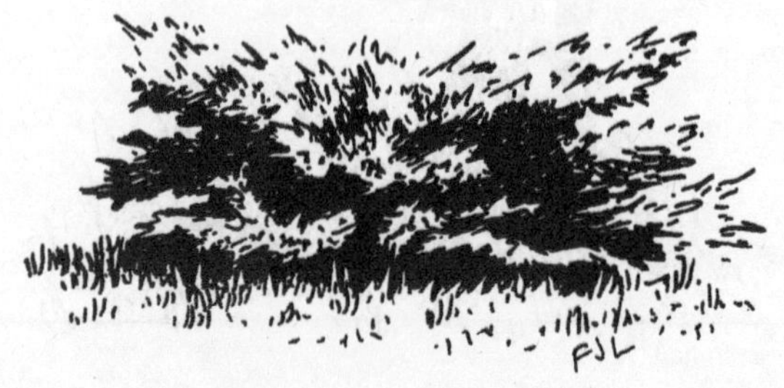

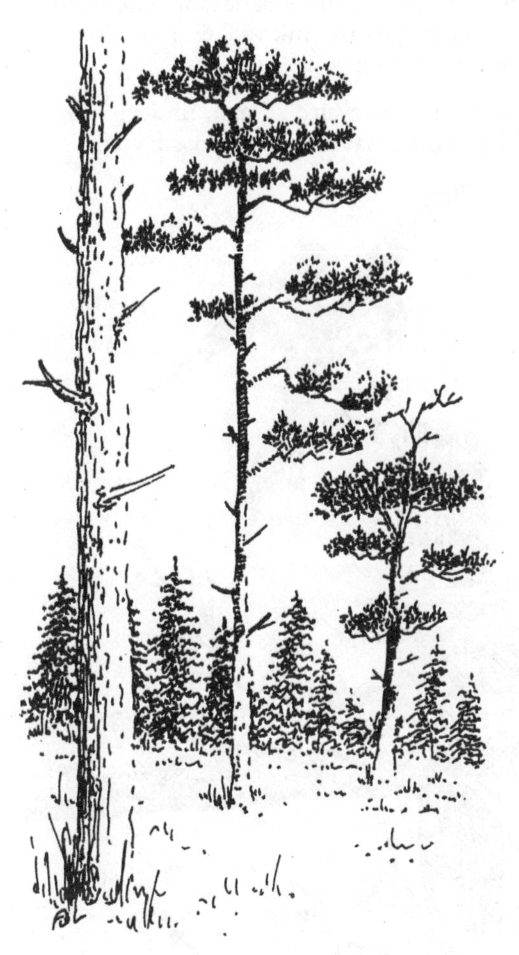

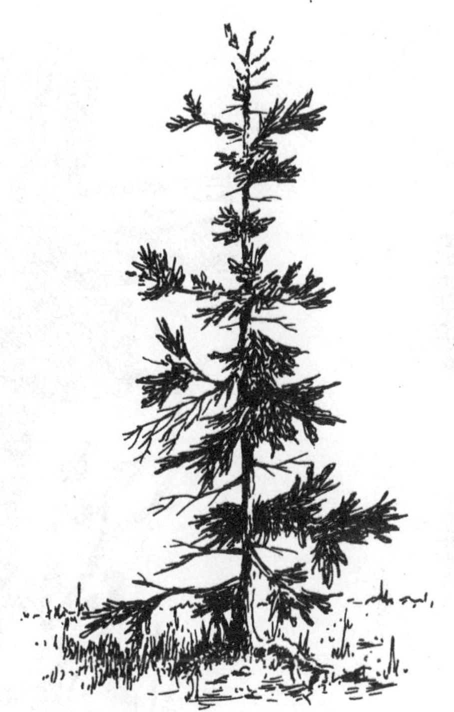

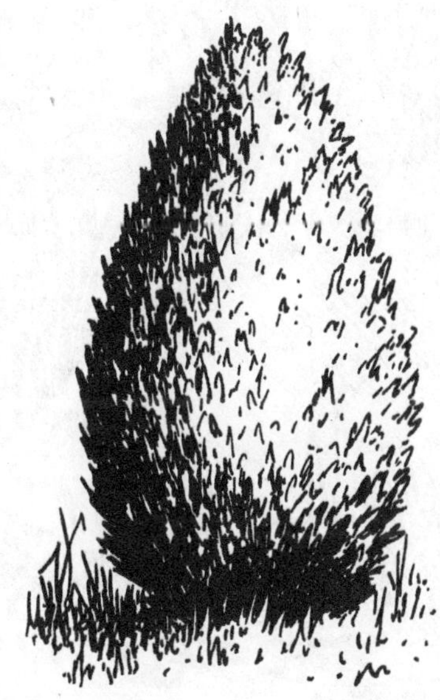

Bird and Fence Post

The original of this minilandscape, shown here in black and white, was an experiment I did with a new brown ink on scratchboard. I wanted to test the ink's behavior when the scratchboard tool cut through the solid dark areas. Sometimes the ink will chip off in flakes rather than allowing the scratchboard tool to cut fine lines in the ink.

In this case the ink worked very well. Finely incised lines in the bird's head, underparts, and wing tips contribute to the feathery feeling. This would have been impossible to achieve without the ability to scratch through the ink to obtain white marks on the black areas. The left side of the near fence post was also textured by scratching through the solid dark ink.

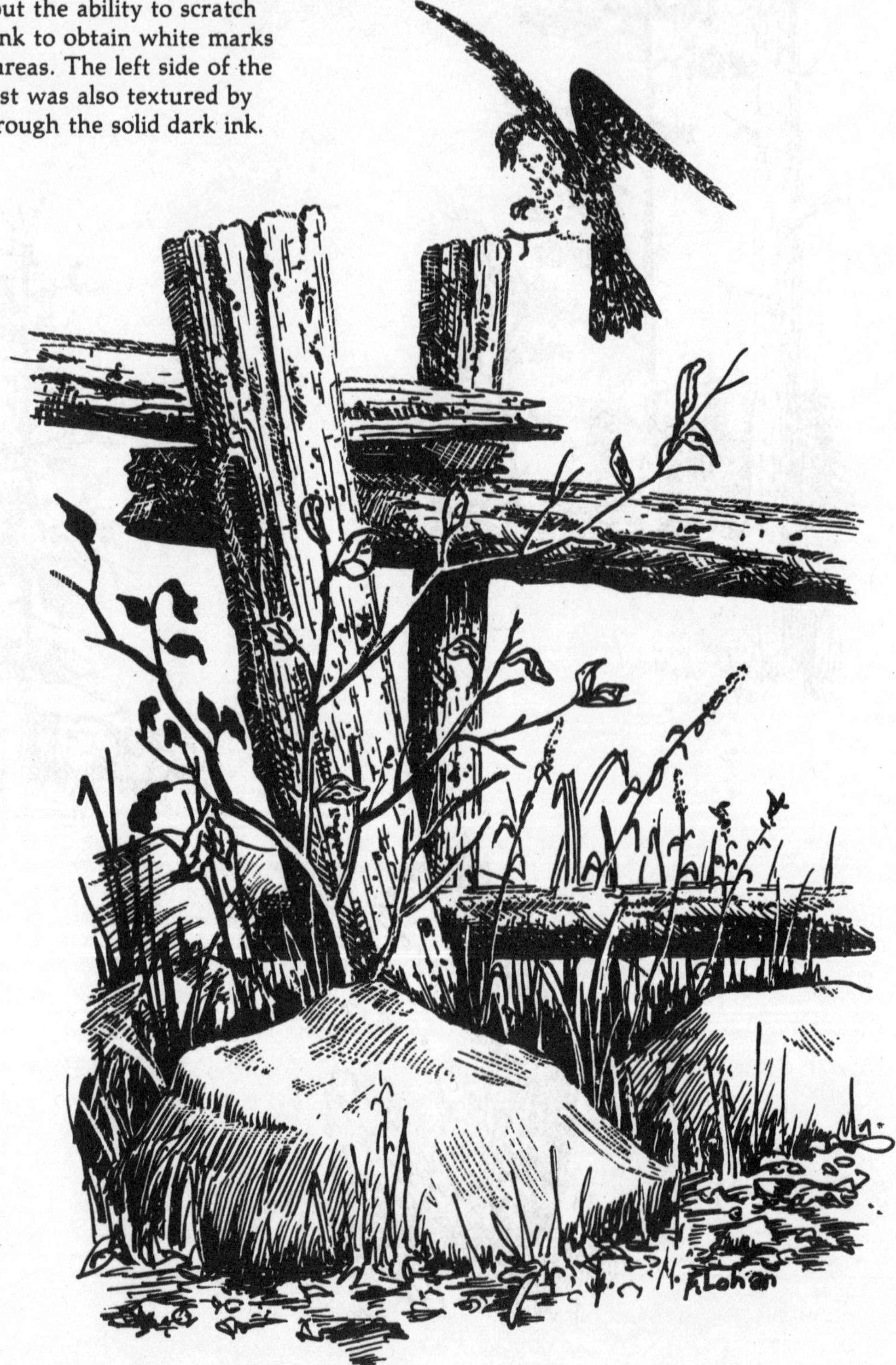

7: Your Point of Departure

From this point on it is all up to you. In this book I share with you some of the pen techniques that I find useful. It is my hope that you will also find them useful as points of departure for your own efforts. Many subjects in this book will serve well as practice pieces in *any* medium—ink, watercolor, oil, or acrylic—although my emphasis here has been on pen and ink.

As an artist, you belong to a select group of very highly self-motivated individuals. I hope that my thoughts give your motivation some additional directions for inquiry. I hope that you will now look for subject matter that was always there but which you may have overlooked.

What shall you sketch? I still don't know, but perhaps now you can answer that question more easily for yourself.

Bibliography

Borgman, Harry. *Drawing in Ink.* New York: Watson-Guptill, 1977.

Guptill, Arthur L. *Rendering in Pen and Ink.* New York: Watson-Guptill, 1976.

Lohan, Frank. *Pen and Ink Techniques.* Chicago: Contemporary Books, 1978.

Norling, Ernest. *Perspective Drawing.* Tustin, CA: Walter Foster Art Books.

Pitz, Henry C. *Ink Drawing Techniques.* New York: Watson-Guptill, 1957.

———. *How to Draw Trees.* New York: Watson-Guptill, 1972.

Sloane, Eric. *An Age of Barns.* New York: Funk & Wagnalls, 1967.

Note: Eric Sloane has written and illustrated a number of books on Americana. His pen sketches in any of them are worthy of study.

A CATALOG OF SELECTED

DOVER BOOKS

IN ALL FIELDS OF INTEREST

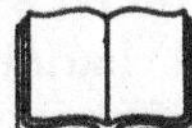

A CATALOG OF SELECTED DOVER BOOKS IN ALL FIELDS OF INTEREST

100 BEST-LOVED POEMS, Edited by Philip Smith. "The Passionate Shepherd to His Love," "Shall I compare thee to a summer's day?" "Death, be not proud," "The Raven," "The Road Not Taken," plus works by Blake, Wordsworth, Byron, Shelley, Keats, many others. 96pp. 5 3/16 x 8¼. 0-486-28553-7

100 SMALL HOUSES OF THE THIRTIES, Brown-Blodgett Company. Exterior photographs and floor plans for 100 charming structures. Illustrations of models accompanied by descriptions of interiors, color schemes, closet space, and other amenities. 200 illustrations. 112pp. 8⅜ x 11. 0-486-44131-8

1000 TURN-OF-THE-CENTURY HOUSES: With Illustrations and Floor Plans, Herbert C. Chivers. Reproduced from a rare edition, this showcase of homes ranges from cottages and bungalows to sprawling mansions. Each house is meticulously illustrated and accompanied by complete floor plans. 256pp. 9⅜ x 12¼. 0-486-45596-3

101 GREAT AMERICAN POEMS, Edited by The American Poetry & Literacy Project. Rich treasury of verse from the 19th and 20th centuries includes works by Edgar Allan Poe, Robert Frost, Walt Whitman, Langston Hughes, Emily Dickinson, T. S. Eliot, other notables. 96pp. 5 3/16 x 8¼. 0-486-40158-8

101 GREAT SAMURAI PRINTS, Utagawa Kuniyoshi. Kuniyoshi was a master of the warrior woodblock print — and these 18th-century illustrations represent the pinnacle of his craft. Full-color portraits of renowned Japanese samurais pulse with movement, passion, and remarkably fine detail. 112pp. 8⅜ x 11. 0-486-46523-3

ABC OF BALLET, Janet Grosser. Clearly worded, abundantly illustrated little guide defines basic ballet-related terms: arabesque, battement, pas de chat, relevé, sissonne, many others. Pronunciation guide included. Excellent primer. 48pp. 4 3/16 x 5¾. 0-486-40871-X

ACCESSORIES OF DRESS: An Illustrated Encyclopedia, Katherine Lester and Bess Viola Oerke. Illustrations of hats, veils, wigs, cravats, shawls, shoes, gloves, and other accessories enhance an engaging commentary that reveals the humor and charm of the many-sided story of accessorized apparel. 644 figures and 59 plates. 608pp. 6 ⅛ x 9¼. 0-486-43378-1

ADVENTURES OF HUCKLEBERRY FINN, Mark Twain. Join Huck and Jim as their boyhood adventures along the Mississippi River lead them into a world of excitement, danger, and self-discovery. Humorous narrative, lyrical descriptions of the Mississippi valley, and memorable characters. 224pp. 5 3/16 x 8¼. 0-486-28061-6

ALICE STARMORE'S BOOK OF FAIR ISLE KNITTING, Alice Starmore. A noted designer from the region of Scotland's Fair Isle explores the history and techniques of this distinctive, stranded-color knitting style and provides copious illustrated instructions for 14 original knitwear designs. 208pp. 8⅜ x 10⅞. 0-486-47218-3

ALICE'S ADVENTURES IN WONDERLAND, Lewis Carroll. Beloved classic about a little girl lost in a topsy-turvy land and her encounters with the White Rabbit, March Hare, Mad Hatter, Cheshire Cat, and other delightfully improbable characters. 42 illustrations by Sir John Tenniel. 96pp. 5³⁄₁₆ x 8¼. 0-486-27543-4

AMERICA'S LIGHTHOUSES: An Illustrated History, Francis Ross Holland. Profusely illustrated fact-filled survey of American lighthouses since 1716. Over 200 stations — East, Gulf, and West coasts, Great Lakes, Hawaii, Alaska, Puerto Rico, the Virgin Islands, and the Mississippi and St. Lawrence Rivers. 240pp. 8 x 10¾. 0-486-25576-X

AN ENCYCLOPEDIA OF THE VIOLIN, Alberto Bachmann. Translated by Frederick H. Martens. Introduction by Eugene Ysaye. First published in 1925, this renowned reference remains unsurpassed as a source of essential information, from construction and evolution to repertoire and technique. Includes a glossary and 73 illustrations. 496pp. 6⅛ x 9¼. 0-486-46618-3

ANIMALS: 1,419 Copyright-Free Illustrations of Mammals, Birds, Fish, Insects, etc., Selected by Jim Harter. Selected for its visual impact and ease of use, this outstanding collection of wood engravings presents over 1,000 species of animals in extremely lifelike poses. Includes mammals, birds, reptiles, amphibians, fish, insects, and other invertebrates. 284pp. 9 x 12. 0-486-23766-4

THE ANNALS, Tacitus. Translated by Alfred John Church and William Jackson Brodribb. This vital chronicle of Imperial Rome, written by the era's great historian, spans A.D. 14-68 and paints incisive psychological portraits of major figures, from Tiberius to Nero. 416pp. 5³⁄₁₆ x 8¼. 0-486-45236-0

ANTIGONE, Sophocles. Filled with passionate speeches and sensitive probing of moral and philosophical issues, this powerful and often-performed Greek drama reveals the grim fate that befalls the children of Oedipus. Footnotes. 64pp. 5³⁄₁₆ x 8 ¼. 0-486-27804-2

ART DECO DECORATIVE PATTERNS IN FULL COLOR, Christian Stoll. Reprinted from a rare 1910 portfolio, 160 sensuous and exotic images depict a breathtaking array of florals, geometrics, and abstracts — all elegant in their stark simplicity. 64pp. 8⅜ x 11. 0-486-44862-2

THE ARTHUR RACKHAM TREASURY: 86 Full-Color Illustrations, Arthur Rackham. Selected and Edited by Jeff A. Menges. A stunning treasury of 86 full-page plates span the famed English artist's career, from *Rip Van Winkle* (1905) to masterworks such as *Undine, A Midsummer Night's Dream,* and *Wind in the Willows* (1939). 96pp. 8⅜ x 11. 0-486-44685-9

THE AUTHENTIC GILBERT & SULLIVAN SONGBOOK, W. S. Gilbert and A. S. Sullivan. The most comprehensive collection available, this songbook includes selections from every one of Gilbert and Sullivan's light operas. Ninety-two numbers are presented uncut and unedited, and in their original keys. 410pp. 9 x 12. 0-486-23482-7

THE AWAKENING, Kate Chopin. First published in 1899, this controversial novel of a New Orleans wife's search for love outside a stifling marriage shocked readers. Today, it remains a first-rate narrative with superb characterization. New introductory Note. 128pp. 5³⁄₁₆ x 8¼. 0-486-27786-0

BASIC DRAWING, Louis Priscilla. Beginning with perspective, this commonsense manual progresses to the figure in movement, light and shade, anatomy, drapery, composition, trees and landscape, and outdoor sketching. Black-and-white illustrations throughout. 128pp. 8⅜ x 11. 0-486-45815-6

THE BATTLES THAT CHANGED HISTORY, Fletcher Pratt. Historian profiles 16 crucial conflicts, ancient to modern, that changed the course of Western civilization. Gripping accounts of battles led by Alexander the Great, Joan of Arc, Ulysses S. Grant, other commanders. 27 maps. 352pp. 5⅜ x 8½. 0-486-41129-X

BEETHOVEN'S LETTERS, Ludwig van Beethoven. Edited by Dr. A. C. Kalischer. Features 457 letters to fellow musicians, friends, greats, patrons, and literary men. Reveals musical thoughts, quirks of personality, insights, and daily events. Includes 15 plates. 410pp. 5⅜ x 8½. 0-486-22769-3

BERNICE BOBS HER HAIR AND OTHER STORIES, F. Scott Fitzgerald. This brilliant anthology includes 6 of Fitzgerald's most popular stories: "The Diamond as Big as the Ritz," the title tale, "The Offshore Pirate," "The Ice Palace," "The Jelly Bean," and "May Day." 176pp. 5⅜ x 8½. 0-486-47049-0

BESLER'S BOOK OF FLOWERS AND PLANTS: 73 Full-Color Plates from Hortus Eystettensis, 1613, Basilius Besler. Here is a selection of magnificent plates from the *Hortus Eystettensis,* which vividly illustrated and identified the plants, flowers, and trees that thrived in the legendary German garden at Eichstätt. 80pp. 8⅜ x 11. 0-486-46005-3

THE BOOK OF KELLS, Edited by Blanche Cirker. Painstakingly reproduced from a rare facsimile edition, this volume contains full-page decorations, portraits, illustrations, plus a sampling of textual leaves with exquisite calligraphy and ornamentation. 32 full-color illustrations. 32pp. 9⅜ x 12¼. 0-486-24345-1

THE BOOK OF THE CROSSBOW: With an Additional Section on Catapults and Other Siege Engines, Ralph Payne-Gallwey. Fascinating study traces history and use of crossbow as military and sporting weapon, from Middle Ages to modern times. Also covers related weapons: balistas, catapults, Turkish bows, more. Over 240 illustrations. 400pp. 7¼ x 10⅛. 0-486-28720-3

THE BUNGALOW BOOK: Floor Plans and Photos of 112 Houses, 1910, Henry L. Wilson. Here are 112 of the most popular and economic blueprints of the early 20th century — plus an illustration or photograph of each completed house. A wonderful time capsule that still offers a wealth of valuable insights. 160pp. 8⅜ x 11. 0-486-45104-6

THE CALL OF THE WILD, Jack London. A classic novel of adventure, drawn from London's own experiences as a Klondike adventurer, relating the story of a heroic dog caught in the brutal life of the Alaska Gold Rush. Note. 64pp. 5³⁄₁₆ x 8¼. 0-486-26472-6

CANDIDE, Voltaire. Edited by Francois-Marie Arouet. One of the world's great satires since its first publication in 1759. Witty, caustic skewering of romance, science, philosophy, religion, government — nearly all human ideals and institutions. 112pp. 5³⁄₁₆ x 8¼. 0-486-26689-3

CELEBRATED IN THEIR TIME: Photographic Portraits from the George Grantham Bain Collection, Edited by Amy Pastan. With an Introduction by Michael Carlebach. Remarkable portrait gallery features 112 rare images of Albert Einstein, Charlie Chaplin, the Wright Brothers, Henry Ford, and other luminaries from the worlds of politics, art, entertainment, and industry. 128pp. 8⅜ x 11. 0-486-46754-6

CHARIOTS FOR APOLLO: The NASA History of Manned Lunar Spacecraft to 1969, Courtney G. Brooks, James M. Grimwood, and Loyd S. Swenson, Jr. This illustrated history by a trio of experts is the definitive reference on the Apollo spacecraft and lunar modules. It traces the vehicles' design, development, and operation in space. More than 100 photographs and illustrations. 576pp. 6¾ x 9¼. 0-486-46756-2